The Village Schoolmaster

Two Daughters, Two Cultures

Elaine Mae Gunderson

Lori Christiansen

1st WORLD
PUBLISHING

THE VILLAGE SCHOOLMASTER

Two Daughters, Two Cultures

ELAINE MAE GUNDERSON
LORI CHRISTIANSEN

© Elaine Mae Gunderson 2010

Published by 1stWorld Publishing
P.O. Box 2211, Fairfield, Iowa 52556
tel: 641-209-5000 • fax: 866-440-5234
web: www.1stworldpublishing.com

First Edition

LCCN: 2010927030
SoftCover ISBN: 978-1-4218-9155-2
HardCover ISBN: 978-1-4218-9156-9
eBook ISBN: 978-1-4218-9157-6

To all the beautiful people of Shageluk,
from the past and in the present,
who have touched our lives so positively.
Truly we have found GOLD in Alaska.

TABLE OF CONTENT

Chapter 1
THE VILLAGE SCHOOLMASTER

Herman Ludvig Sakariasson Grimelandshaug Larsen

The stock market crashed in October of 1929. Conditions during the Depression were getting worse. The dust storms were terrible and the soil piled up like little hills across the prairie. Two months later, my parents – Herman Larsen, age 28, and Harriet Mae Hendrickson, age 19 – were married in the courthouse in Jamestown, North Dakota. Because economic conditions were so severe, my grandparents decided to send Dad, their son-in-law, back to the University of North Dakota in Grand Forks, North Dakota, to finish medical school. He had been alternating between teaching and going to school every other year for some time and was soon due to graduate. Mom went back to her parents' farm to help with chores until the baby came in the middle of the summer.

Mom was the youngest of seven children and had had an idyllic childhood growing up on the farm that her parents, Ed and Annette Hendrickson, homesteaded shortly after emigrating from Norway in the late 1800s. The farm was located 10 miles southwest of Mandan, North Dakota. Only once had she lived away from home. She went to high school in Mandan while living with her oldest sister Emma, who was 20 years older. Emma was married to a railroad engineer and had a nice little house not far from the high school.

Dad was the oldest of seven children and had less than an idyllic childhood. He was born in Forde, Norway, near Bergen, on March 5, 1901, to Henrik Larsen Sandal Jolster and Sophie Mosesdatter Grimelandshaug. Their farmstead was small and their house was one tiny room. Three years later his brother Sigard was born, and then another brother Martin arrived shortly thereafter. The children were expected to do the farm work with their mother as soon as they were old enough to hold a pitchfork. Their terrible-tempered father Henrik made cream cans, buckets, farm tools and repaired shoes in another small 8'x10' building. It was said he sometimes delivered his goods to the various farms when he thought the men were out farming so he could take advantage of the farmers' wives.

The first set of twins, Lina and Anna, then came into the family. Before the second set of twins, Alma and Hjalmer were born, Dad, at age 10, had to go live with his grandparents in Jolster because conditions were so crowded. There was no relief from the anger of his father because his grandmother also had a bad temper. He went to school and finished "reading for the minister" (catechism). At the age of 14 he left Norway with his cousin. They went to France and joined the French Army during World War I. They worked with a medical unit carrying wounded soldiers off the battlefield. When the military learned they were only 14 years old, they were sent home. Back in Norway, Dad worked as a porter on the Norwegian National Railroad, traveling between Bergen and Oslo. In the next few years he was able to earn enough money to pay for his passage to America. On August 18, 1919, he left his homeland.

When he went through Ellis Island, he was forced to change his name, Herman Ludvig Sakariasson Grimelandshaug, to something more easily pronounceable. He dropped the last two difficult names and used Larsen for his last name. He then boarded another ship for Duluth, Minnesota. From there he joined the U.S. military and was stationed at Fort Snelling in Minneapolis. For most of his stay in the army he was in the military hospital, as he had contracted a severe case of pneumonia. Nearing recovery he was given an honorable discharge.

After leaving the army he worked at a paper mill in International Falls, Minnesota, then found his way to Portland, Oregon, where he hauled cement for a bricklayer. At age 21 he moved to Fargo, North Dakota, where he found work and lodging with Mrs. Amerland on South 4th Street. Mr. Amerland was an invalid and Dad was hired to take care of him and to clean her house. He spoke highly of Mrs. Amerland; she was like a mother to him. During that time he went to Fargo Central High School, but because of his poor English language skills, he transferred to North Dakota Agricultural College, now called North Dakota State University, in Fargo, where Norwegian was commonly spoken by the professors. He continued his education until he earned his teaching degree.

His first teaching position was at Sweet Briar, a country school west of Mandan. He taught one year, then went to the University of North Dakota in Grand Forks to pursue a medical career. His last teaching position as a single man was at Huff, North Dakota, where he met Mae Hendrickson, a high school senior, at a Halloween party held on a farm near town. At the party they discovered their common love for music. She was an accomplished pianist and he played the violin expertly. Together they had a grand time entertaining. After Mom graduated she returned to her family farm. Herman and Harriet "Mae" wrote to each other often and managed to see each other on a few occasions.

Now in the spring of 1930, Dad was back at UND and Mom back in the windblown, dusty pastures herding sheep. When the sheep were done eating the grass down to the roots, she had to lead them to where there was more. She brought lunch to eat and a magazine to pass the time. Often the bottle lambs would tear the pages out of the magazine and the wind would blow them away. Because the top soil was blown off, it was a good time to hunt the exposed arrowheads on the ground. She also entertained herself by building stone pyramids on top of the large rocks in the pasture. The pyramids are there to this day. She herded sheep until it was time to give birth to their first child.

Their daughter Etola Jean Larsen was born on July 3, 1930.

In the graduation brochure given out by UND, Dad wrote his name in the class of 1931. With that his formal study of medicine ended. After he left school he returned to the education field and was able to get a superintendent's job. Mom, Dad and Etola lived in North Dakota for several more years, but his school debt was large and he was unable to support a family and repay his debt on his meager salary.

He then noticed a job opportunity in the paper to which he responded immediately.

The Alaska Native Service, a subsidiary of the US Department of the Interior, was looking for teachers. The ANS maintained many schools in remote native villages throughout the Territory. The children were taught English and the American way of life. In addition, the teacher was responsible to give first aid, assist the native people during epidemics, serve as postmaster, operate the radio where there was no other communication available, oversee the herding of reindeer if applicable, tag beaver skins and any other activity the government wanted the teacher to do. Husband-and-wife teams were preferred because of the isolation. The wife was usually hired as an assistant and was given two-thirds of the salary of the teacher, which would be a total of around $5,000 per year. He wanted both the challenge and the money.

Chapter 2
TO ALASKA

After completing and passing the required Civil Service Exam, Dad accepted the government teaching position offered by the Alaska Native Service. They packed their belongings in trunks and were soon bound for Shageluk, a small Athapascan Indian village in the interior of Alaska. Mom was unsure of this seemingly foreboding adventure, but she felt she had no choice. She had never been too far away from her family and friends or the prairies of rural Mandan, North Dakota. For Dad this was just another adventure. He was born and raised in Norway, and was already far away from home. This was a great opportunity to repay his debts and to satisfy his wandering spirit.

On July 28, 1938, my 37 year-old father, Herman Larsen, my 28 year-old mother, Mae Larsen, and my 8 year-old sister, Etola Jean Larsen, boarded the train in Mandan. They left a very sad and crying group of relatives and friends standing on the cobblestones of the train station. Etola didn't care for all the fuss; she was so excited that she started to write a letter home immediately, telling her grandparents, aunts, uncles and cousins on the home farm that she was having a grand time. She mailed the letter at the train station in Helena, Montana.

Herman, Etola, and Mae Larsen

They arrived in Seattle, Washington, on the morning of July 30, 1938. The Office of the Alaska Native Service had many forms and papers which had to be filled out and signed. The government doctor examined Dad twice. This made him a little nervous; he did not want some trifling health matter to stop his great opportunity. With all government requirements fulfilled, they toured Seattle for the remainder of the time. On Thursday, August 4, 1938, at 5:30 in the evening they were taken to the boat bound for Alaska, called "The North Star."

U.S.S. North Star

Mom described the journey in her diary. "We watched the skyline of Seattle fade away and we left the rest of the world behind. We crossed Queen Charlotte Sound during the night. This part of the trip takes only three hours. It is not protected from the ocean and can get quite rough at times. [Mom got seasick immediately.] The steward brought some toast for me and said it would stay down but the fish got that, too. I stayed in bed until they got to the Inside Passage. We have the best stateroom where Etola has a small bench to sleep on. The room is located next to the $100,000 engine room. It will be three days before we make a stop. We got acquainted with the crew. There are teachers, a nurse, and a doctor and his wife on board who are also being sent up to Alaska by the Bureau of Indian Affairs. We were given places at the table and are at first setting. Our meals are fit for a king. Etola is so excited because she has many young playmates. We spent most of our time out on the deck watching sea gulls and Canada's lofty mountains. There are many fishing boats along the way. The inside passage, which is the prettiest part of Alaska, is between mountains full of green spruce and high waterfalls.

Etola on the North Star

"We arrived at Ketchikan on Sunday, August 7, 1938, at about 10:30 a.m. Ketchikan has the largest fish cannery with mountains in the background. We visited all the curio shops. This evening we are in Metlakatla. Here people pay no taxes, have no light bills and no water bills. We went through the fish cannery where mostly Indian girls work. We watched the fish canning process from beginning to end. The girls were dressed in white garments and wore white hats. While we were touring the cannery we noticed that most of the women were celebrating some occasion and all were smoking cigars. The men did the heavy work such as piling the cans on steel carts and pushing them into big pressure cookers. The seagulls ate all the fish guts. It sure smelled fishy! Then we walked all around the village. Some little kids were spearing fish. Jack, the ship's third mate, was shooting fish from the boat. We left Metlakatla at 8 o'clock in the evening.

Salmon ready for Canning, Ketchikan

"In the morning a few of us stood on the deck in front of the boat. Boy! What a thrill. We passed the Bear Tooth Mountains and they sure looked like teeth. We met many fishing boats.

"The next day we saw forest fires on both sides of the passage. What a beautiful boat ride. The moonlight is breathtaking. We passed by Petersburg in the evening. It is such a neat little town. All the houses were painted white with green roofs. Captain Witlam sure tells funny stories. He says Petersburg is full of Norwegians, so they get tons of snoose (chewing tobacco) shipped in every year.

"The captain and Etola became such pals. He allowed her to come up to the room where the steering wheel was located. The nurse would take her down. Passengers were not allowed up there. When the nurse wasn't looking, he would sneak her up there again. The captain cut off a few of Etola's curls and put them in his billfold.

"We arrived at Juneau on August 10, 1938. It has lofty mountains and the largest gold mine in the world. We got further orders at the Federal Office, and then rode out to Mendenhall Glacier. It is two miles wide and twenty miles long. What a pretty sight. The glacier has a bluish tint at sunset. It thaws all the time and is rough like a group of mountains. I took pictures of it and Etola. It was 85 degrees above, in spite of all the ice and snow. We were told that some fellow tried to walk on it, but fell in a crevice and was never found. He has a cold grave.

Herman and Etola in Juneau

"It's Thursday and we have arrived in Haines, the only United States fort left in Alaska. It is a nice place. We often wished we could have been transferred here. Here we unloaded 150 barrels of oil and gas. The mountains are tall skyscrapers covered with snow. I looked all over the boat for Etola. She rode over to the town with the captain. Some of the soldiers are married to native girls. In the evening we came to Hoonah 'West Harbor'. We drank water from a tiny waterfall, had ice cream cones, and then sailed for Seward. The Gulf is so rough! I was seasick again.

Etola at Mendenhall Glacier

Haines, Alaska

"We came to Seward on Friday night. It is a nice place with high mountains and snow-covered peaks. The 'North Star' had to stay in Resurrection Bay to wait for the tide to come in, so we could get close to the docks. We stayed here waiting for some Eskimo teenagers to come from the school in Eklutna. They were going home. While waiting for them we tried to climb a mountain, but the mosquitoes and gnats chased us down. The kids played the jukebox often. The Hawaiian music was their favorite. We had supper, then went out to look at the town. It has a nice depot. There is a lot of drinking here! On Saturday, Herman, Etola and I went into a restaurant with some acquaintances from the boat. The men had beer, the kids had pop and I drank buttermilk. Then Etola and I went to Sunday school and church. One woman from the boat came to church with slacks on! Etola didn't want to stay for church, so she ran back to the 'North Star'. We had turkey and pumpkin pie for dinner. Etola sneaked into the kitchen at night and asked for another piece of pumpkin pie. She got it, too. Herman went out fishing with some of the crew. His face is all swollen from mosquito and no-see-um bites."

Dad refused to get up on the morning of August 15, 1938. He felt sick from the bites he had suffered the day before. Mom paid Johnnie, an Eskimo cook, 15 cents for the use of some liniment to put on Dad's face.

He remained in bed all day, but did have several visitors through his stateroom window.

The next day they walked around Seward, visiting stores, shops and restaurants. Back at the boat they worked on jigsaw puzzles with fellow travelers. On Wednesday they went out riding with the boss of the Jessie Lee Home, which was an orphanage housing 120 children. They drove around the mountains and saw some very nice homes. They purchased large gorgeous strawberries for $1.00 per gallon. At 5 o'clock in the evening the boat sailed on to Kodiak.

On August 18, 1938, mother wrote, "Kodiak is a dream. On our way here we saw huge whales. They are so big! The island is like a picture. The water near land is clear and one can see salmon swimming below. Kodiak has the largest bears. The nurse on our ship used to work here. When she asked the children what nationality they were they said they were half Eskimo and half sailor. The U.S. navy was here at times and left some of their remains. Unfortunately our stay in Kodiak lasted only 30 minutes.

"It is Friday, August 19, 1938. We are sailing to Akutan. We play a lot of checkers and cards. No one wants to sit by the doctor because he kicks. He swings his feet under the table. The sea is a little rough. Oh boy! We saw an active volcano slowly going up in smoke. Today is Saturday and we can't go to Akutan. We have met a storm. We are anchored out in the bay overnight. We are supposed to go through Umiak Pass but we have to take shelter between two small mountains because of the storm on the other side of the Aleutians. The wind is so strong it whistles and blows over the top of the boat. I caught a fish, but had to throw it back because it was so wormy. It is so foggy that the mountains look twice their size.

"We were able to make it to the Akutan station on Sunday morning. What a stink! After the storm we went out to look at the remains of a whale. The platform was so slippery with blood on it, it was hard to walk. The Eskimos make use of every part of the whale except the teeth. The mouth looks like a comb. The whale sucks his food. We also saw the gun or machine that catches the whale."

In the morning the boat left Akutan in the Aleutian Islands to cross the Bering Sea. Mom wrote, "Hello Bering Sea, you make me seasick. So

I'll lay me down with my door open and look at you. You are beautiful in the moonlight. Now I've had enough so I'll go to sleep. Now you rock me to sleep. Am I seasick? August 23rd is the same as yesterday. It is rough and adventurous. I prefer staying in bed with my door open. I watch the boat rock and read. Reading doesn't bother my seasickness at all. No one could stand outside or you would get a cold and salty bath. A teacher's kid, who was such a smarty pants, wouldn't stay in, so he stood out by the rail reading a book. Soon a big wave came and gave him a good soaking. That made us all laugh.

"That night it was rough and the second mate was at the wheel. The captain didn't get any sleep during the night because he was watching the compass by his bed. He didn't trust the second mate because he had been drinking. Maybe if we knew he had been drinking we would not have slept either.

"It is Wednesday and we are at St. Michael. It is great to see land again. The tide was out so we couldn't get close to shore. A barge came out and unloaded all our trunks and a year's supply of groceries. Then we were hoisted over to the barge, one family at a time. That was scary. All we had to hang on to were the ropes. We stayed at Captain Hoescher's. He is captain of the N.C.Co. He had an Eskimo for a housekeeper. The Eskimo children and a pack of shepherd dogs came to meet us. This used to be an army post. Herman bought 10 lbs. of butter from the "North Star" steward for $3.50. He knew it wouldn't keep so he so sold it to a fellow in St. Michael for $4.00.

"On Thursday we sat around and talked. I helped Captain Hoescher's Eskimo housekeeper do the cooking. The other women didn't give a hoot. The doctor's wife came into the kitchen and asked what we were making. I told her it was slop. She certainly had rubbed me the wrong way. In fact I didn't like her. She gets a lot of attention—especially from the men. She is Jewish and a Russian and is certainly not cut out to be in Alaska. She is always complaining about something. Her mouth goes all the time.

"Today is Friday, August 26, 1938. I don't get up very early in the morning just to make the days go faster. The doctor's wife is at it again. Herman bought three magazines, *Home Physician*, *Health Magazine* and *Beacon's Lights of Prophecy*. The latter claims there is a great controversy coming.

"It is Saturday. There is nothing to do but sleep and eat. Helma, Captain Hoescher's Eskimo cook, and I saw a few black whales playing and spouting in the sea. The Eskimos caught a fur seal and had a feast. Most of them have salmon hanging on lines or boards.

"On August 28 the 'Denali' anchors out about 5 miles. The doctor's wife is cheering. The next day the 'Denali' is still anchored out in the bay. The coast here looks like a graveyard. It has worn out boats and stern wheelers. There are no trees, so I will be happy to get inland. A tug boat is now taking us up the Yukon. The mouth of the river is 6 miles wide. Pushing a barge against the current is so slow. At 6 a.m. we left St. Michael on this dirty tug boat called the 'Misabe'. Now I have to cook again. It was the deck hand's job to cook, but he was busy and appreciated my help. We had a breakfast of white bread, butter, grapefruit and coffee. At 8:10 a.m. we passed by Stebbins, Alaska. Our pilot is a Russian Eskimo. Both he and the engineer look like they have T.B. Etola and I curled up in a quilt on the deck. Herman is having a little trouble with his heart and is taking Phenobarbital. It is now evening and we are stuck in the mud because the tide is low. One of the passengers is nuts. He thinks he can get the boat unstuck. He has T.B. and piles.

"It is August 30, 1938. We come to Kotlik, Alaska. Mrs. Pierce Starret is a teacher here. Her husband is a special assistant. He and a priest came out to meet us and to get the mail. Mr. and Mrs. Hirsch (teachers) and their daughter are on the 'Misabe'. Mrs. Hirsch is sitting in the pilot house suffering from seasickness. Now we are tied up 10 miles east of the mouth of the Yukon. We have to sleep with our clothes on."

On the Misabe

Dad wrote, "The wife is disgruntled and the kid is sick. We are taking turns sleeping. I have slept only four hours."

Mom's diary continues: "We are finally slowly pulling up the Yukon on Wednesday, August 31, 1938. At Hamilton, Alaska, all our freight was put on a house barge, which leaks like a sieve. One box of hams and bacon was left open. The salt, flour and sugar are all wet. Once in a while an Eskimo comes to bail the water out of the barge. In the morning we are at Fish Village, Alaska. The Yukon was so rough we had to stay the night."

Dad: "The dogs are howling and the sky is raining. We are still 76 miles from Pilot Station. Thursday morning the cook made awful greasy pancakes. The 'Misabe' is sheltered in a secluded bay. Mae has a stomachache. It's a Grand Old World!"

Mom: "After breakfast we walked around the village. The Catholics have a small church here. Some of the Eskimos have kayaks. There is much fish hanging all over. The Yukon is O.K. so now we have to go again."

Friday, September 2, 1938. Dad: "It is cold. It was so cold in the bunk with only one quilt. We left Fish Village, Alaska, and will soon be in Mountain Village. Mae made good pancakes for breakfast. No one helped her at all."

Mom: "We are now in Mountain Village. It was a relief to get rid of the husband and wife who will be teaching here. She never helped me with the cooking. The hospital doesn't look so bad from the outside. The doctor's wife says the inside is in need of repair. Herman talked with the doctor as the natives carried mail sacks to the postmaster."

Dad: "It is raining, foggy and blowing on this lovely Saturday. At two o'clock in the morning I bumped my head terrifically against the anchor head winch located above my head in the bunk. The food on the 'Misabe' is terrible. Our salt is wet, the flour is wet, and our boxes of books are wet. Captain Hoescher sent no provisions along to feed the bunch of us."

Mom: "We reached Pilot Station at 2:30 p.m. We got rid of the Hirsches. Their school leaks. The living room and kitchen were soaked. The school room is full of supplies. Everything is a mess. We left as soon as the Hirsches got their groceries off the barge. I made macaroni and tomatoes for supper. The barge is not so crowded now."

Sunday, September 4, 1938. Mom: "We came to Marshall, Alaska this morning at 7:30 a.m. The 'Nenana', our next boat, left yesterday at 4:00 p.m., so with permission from the Juneau office we have to stay in Marshall for two weeks. We are staying with Mr. Ray Hunter, a widower and the postmaster. He also had four other Eskimos living here."

Dad: "We slept on skins. I played violin for an old maid schoolteacher, Miss Hall. She has a wig and has been in Alaska for 30 years. Also in our company was Yellow-haired Pete Knudson, War Vet Billy Allman, Ray Hunter, of course, and his daughter Fortuna, who is Hirst's (in Juneau) private secretary. I paid N.C. Co. $107.10 for tickets and freight on the groceries. The check paid for the trip from St. Michael to Marshall, Alaska. Etola's ticket was $12.50, mine was $25.00 and Mae's was $25.00."

Labor Day, Monday, Sept. 5, 1938. Dad: "Mae was out of sorts, cranky and tired this morning, but she made a good breakfast of eggs, pancakes and coffee. Mae, Etola and I went to the neighboring village, Fortuna Ledge. There I examined a native woman, Mary. She felt better right away after I had been there. Then we went back to Marshall."

Mom: "The kids started school here today. I made bread and dough-nuts. We had deer steak for supper. Before we went to bed we ate squaw candy (dried smoked salmon strips). Mr. Hunter told interesting and funny stories about Alaska. We met Mr. Clifford Lellethun from Valley City, North Dakota."

Dad: "There was a Swedish funeral at the schoolhouse today (Tues-day) in Marshall, Alaska. Catholic Father Endall spoke in the school-house. He could not officiate as a Catholic priest, but as an American citizen. The coffin for the deceased, Christma, was made and carried by an Orthodox Greek Catholic native priest. Mae does all the cooking for the household. The housewife here is so lazy. All she talks about is her sickness. We didn't get to bed before late."

On Wednesday Dad went duck and goose hunting with eight other fellows from Marshall. With lots of liquor along, they left at 3:00 a.m. Archie, a native, ran the boat. They shot many ducks and geese down the river. All of them violated the law, including Dad, as there were no plugs in the guns. Most of the men were drunk the entire two days. One of them, George, almost passed out in the night. They tried to get some sleep but it was too cold. They arrived back at Marshall at 2:00 a.m. on Friday morning and slept most of the day. Still no plane or boat came to get the Larsens so they could complete their journey to Shageluk.

Dad filed and set saw teeth for part of Saturday. Then he sawed wood with Paul Hausler and Bruce Hunter. They met a fellow named Eric Johnson, who knew the great explorer Roald Amundson, who led the first exploration to reach the South Pole in 1911. Eric took care of Amundson's dogs when he had to go outside. Eric told about the time when Roald Amundson was almost killed by a polar bear and hardly recovered from the sustained injuries.

Sunday, September 11, 1938. Dad: "We are still at Fortuna Ledge. It is a quiet day. Mae and I talked about the future. Then we toured the jail. Mae played piano at Marshal Neeby's house. We had reindeer stew and salmon strips for lunch. It was elegant. Etola now has an Eskimo boyfriend, Vern Hunter. She is showing the boys how to do a backbend.

"Now it is Monday and there still is no airplane or boat to get us out of here. We stayed at Hunter's house all day.

"Tuesday is the General Territorial Election Day. The natives were told how to vote. The judges of the election were Bill Allman, Eric Johnson and Ray Hunter. No airplane and no boat came for us."

Wednesday, September 14, 1938. "We spent most of the day at Christ Betche's store. We heard the steamer "Nenana" was ten miles above Tanana, a town on the Yukon. The N.C.C. barge is standing at Marshall in the rain. Everything in it has become wet and moldy. We did nothing but loaf around on Thursday."

September 16, 1938, Friday. "We are still at Fortuna Ledge. A nurse, Miss Carlson, asked me to diagnose a case of scarlet fever for her. Agnes is a young girl age 25. She has rapid pulse, blue patches on her swollen legs and a fever of about 101 degrees. Her heart is good. She is subject to T.B. Her tongue is strawberry coated with red spots at the end. Miss Carlson and I then went to have a baked goose at Pete's house. I was nervous today.

"It is Saturday at Fortuna Ledge. Pete called us over for sourdough pancakes, bacon and eggs. A bunch of fellows were at Pete's drinking. They had a regular clean-up at Willow Creek, netting $23,000 worth of fish. Charlie Heckman and Doc LaRue are drunk, running up and down the Yukon in a motor boat. The steamer 'Nenana' was expected at Holy Cross. It is now at Nulato. We went to the N.C. Co. Barge and most of our supplies are spoiled."

Sunday, September 18, 1938. "I just visited with George Pilcher. He is a tall, erect fellow with a mustache, light complexion, gray hair and is 75 years young. He is a prospector and claims to have shot a man once. George is a Dakota-Ohio man. Then he told a story about Alex McKin-see, a humanitarian from Bismarck, North Dakota, who was a gold pro-moter among the Norwegians at Bismarck. Alex was made famous by Rex Beach, author of "The Spoiler", a story from Nome, Alaska. [Alex] later became a crook, receiving much from the gold mine. George Pilcher is a writer and a recorder of note. He has many diaries in his possession. He has written for the *Post*."

Monday, September 19, 1938. Mom: "I took pictures of Ray Hunter's house. Etola is dressed in a parka standing by a female Malamute named Gafeney. Axel Larson, a Swedish gold miner, played accordion and Etola danced. Herman played violin for a wedding dance at Fortuna Ledge. The U.S. Marshal got married. Erola, the nurse and I along with a bunch of Eskimos stood outside a big window and watched. Every time the guests danced by a table that had booze on it, they had a drink. A dentist and a trader had way too much alcohol and acted goofy. They went into the bedroom, took off their pants, and went back to the dance wearing only bright-colored shorts. The little schoolteacher kept her distance as she was afraid they would take off her wig. A gold miner stole the bride and took her up to his room for the rest of the night. This caused much excitement and the husband was unaware of what had happened. Some of the gold miners are drinkers, gamblers and really tough guys. The party lasted until

Etola with Gafeney

3:00 a.m. The 'Nenana' finally came as the party broke up. The lights were shining in our window, so we stayed up and watched."

Tuesday, September 20, 1938. "We left Marshall at 1:20 p.m. on the steamer 'Nenana'. It is a large flat-bottomed boat. The stern wheel is so large it looks like a small ferris wheel. Mr. Thompson, a horse buyer from Montana, is the chief waiter. He is a big red-complected fellow. Etola made a hit with the cook. He filled her pockets full of oranges. Herman wrote to Schwabacher Bros. in Seattle about our shortage of groceries."

Steamer Nenana

Wednesday, September 21, 1938. Dad: "We are now at Railroad City. Our arrival time was 9 a.m. I went to Nathan, the Alaskan Railroad agent, and paid $39.10 freight on our groceries and books. I was in a hurry to get back on the 'Nenana' for our last trip, so I did not get a receipt."

Mom: "We met a boat called the 'Idler' here. Mrs. Black and her daughter Adrian Peterson cook on the boat. The 'Idler' is neat and comfortable. Herman wheeled oil barrels for the owner George Black. Ray Jacobson is the engineer. We slept in the pilot house and froze. We are on our last leg of travel and will be in Shageluk tomorrow evening, Thursday, September 22, 1938."

The Idler at Railroad City

Chapter 3
SHAGELUK AND THE FIRST LETTER HOME

After traveling for 57 days, Herman, Mae and Etola finally arrived in Shageluk on September 22, 1938, at 9:30 p.m. The first thing they did was build fires and look over the house. It was very comfortable and complete. Mrs. Black and her daughter liked the building very much. Three Indians—Lee Howard, Joseph Hamilton and Arthur Fairbanks—helped carry the trunks and groceries from the boat to the school. The help cost $4.50. After unpacking until 3:00 a.m., it was time to try out the beds.

Shageluk School and Teacher's Living Quarters

On Friday they unpacked all the groceries and cleaned the house. Etola worked like a good sport. Dad was given information by Paul Keating on some of the characteristics of the natives. He reported that Mike Rope, Robert Painter and Peter Matthew were all very honest and trustworthy. Jack Woodford liked to work for the school, "Old Frances" was the medicine man, Blind Andrew liked to cut wood and the midwife in Shageluk was Mrs. John Woodford's mother, Cecilia.

Cunningham, Richards and John(Jack) Woodford

Brother Hess and Father Spills came up from Holy Cross on Saturday. They have quite a large mission school and church there with beautiful gardens, livestock and poultry. They brought a gift of many turnips and cabbages. In the evening Dad was called to deliver Mrs. Joseph Hamilton. Tassia Demientieff, an O.B. nurse from Holy Cross, was with him. At midnight Mrs. Hamilton gave birth to a big baby boy. Mr. and Mrs. Hamilton were so happy for Dad's help; they named their new son Herman Larsen Hamilton. Sunday and Monday were spent unpacking books, and checking and unpacking government supplies. Mom cleaned the dispensary, a very nice up-to-date clinic, swept the schoolroom, cooked, and put school books on the proper shelves in preparation for Tuesday, September 27, 1938, the first day of school.

Herman with Students in Shageluk

There were 14 students present when school opened the next morning: 13 Indian students and one white student. Their names and ages are as follows: Etola Larsen, 8; Raymond Dutchman, 13; Ida Dutchman, 14; Isabella Matthew, 14; Olivia Painter, 14; Woodrow Mailelle, 14; Martha Howard, 9; Hamilton Hamilton, 8; Johnny Dutchman, 5; Cecilia Hamilton, 11; Thomas Dutchman, 5; Hoover Howard, 8; Roxcenia Painter, 8; and Virginia Howard, 6. The children seemed very nice and eager to learn. During the first recess Dad went into the living quarters and ordered Mom to make Norwegian potato dumplings (Raspe Ball) for supper. This was his favorite food, but it took so much work to make. [The potatoes are peeled, ground by hand, flour and salt are added next. The ham and salt pork are cut up in little pieces and placed in the center of each dumpling. Each dumpling is carefully placed in a large kettle of boiling water and cooked slowly for close to an hour.] There was no school in the afternoon, so the Larsens unpacked all the school supplies and stored some upstairs. In the evening while Dad called on some sickly Indians, Mom cleaned out the bookcases in the schoolroom and finished cooking the dumplings. Dad returned home and repaired the indoor toilet. At supper he ate way too many Norwegian potato dumplings, as he always did.

Until the end of September, the folks were busy organizing their new home and schoolhouse. In the evening, Dad went out to visit those who were ill and those who came to his clinic with complaints of ill health. There was also a shop filled with government tools, which were loaned out frequently. Mom cleaned out the store room and hung up cabbages. She scraped all the mold off the hams and bacon. Then she checked the groceries and made note of the shortages. They missed not having butter the most. Mom washed the school windows and took down extra seats from the upstairs for more students. A new student, Adolph Hamilton, came to school and the Larsens were told that eventually there would be more coming. Dad hired Lee Howard to fix the chimney for $5.00. School was as usual; Hamilton and a pupil named Hoover had a fight ending with Hamilton crying, and Virginia and Hoover tore some plaster off the walls. Dad called them a couple of regular rascals and had to replaster the damage. Ice formed on the water on the night of September 29, so certainly late fall had arrived in the North Country.

On Sunday, October 2, 1938, Mom searched the storeroom, looking for the previous year's school reports and forms for vouchers. Then she drew and made artistic patterns for the first and second graders. In the meantime, Dad went for a walk in the village. He brought home a big kitten for Etola. In later years, Dad could not stand to have an animal in the house, so this was very much a surprise. She named the kitten "Pussy" and loved it for the rest of her life.

Dad called a 3:00 p.m. Monday meeting and invited the whole village to come. Many natives were present. After welcoming them they discussed cooperation, discipline, basket weaving, reindeer service, the proper attitude toward school, attitude toward medical work, getting wood for the winter, tagging fur for the game commission and tuberculosis. After the meeting, two older women went up to Mom and told her that Etola was a beautiful doll; Mom noticed they could not quit looking at her. Because she had such light blonde hair, many thought that she looked like an angel. She was also quickly learning the Athapascan Indian language, which impressed many of the villagers.

On Wednesday, Mom visited the Pius Savage home. Mrs. Savage wanted Mom to help her make baby clothes. Mom took Mrs. Savage back to the schoolhouse, where they cut up five yards of flannel. Mom showed her how to make baby diapers and how to crochet a baby cap.

John and Matilda Woodford came to the schoolhouse to store their potatoes in the basement. Mom gave Matilda a pair of canvas gloves, which
made her so happy.

It was a marvelous day with the sun shining. Dad opened the clinic
at 4:00 p.m. He treated two older ladies with boric acid for their eye trouble. Pius Savage's daughter was given zinc oxide for impetigo. Pius himself
had a bad cold, so Dad gave him psyllium seed. They then held a meeting
about the care of the reindeer herd at 8:00 p.m.

On October 7, 1938, Mom went berry picking with Mr. and Mrs.
Howard. She got one gallon of blueberries, three gallons of low bush cranberries and a terribly aching tired back. When she returned home, Dad
and Etola said they missed her so much and were so lonesome. The next
day Dad finally received a 50 lb. keg of butter from Holikachuk. The
charge was $1.50. Mom cleaned the house and the school room, checked
the books in the library, swept out the playroom and made more Norwegian potato dumplings for supper. Again Dad ate too much.

On October 9th the natives had a festival. Mom baked bread, buns,
and washed her hair. Dad went across the river to visit a T.B. patient and
a few others. Afterwards he wrote a long letter to Mom's sister, Emma.
Mom had gotten three letters written in August from her. Emma was
worried because she had not heard from them. Mom and Etola bothered
him fairly often as he wrote, but Dad didn't mind; he was happy to finally
be in Alaska. The letter follows:

October 9, 1938

Dear Emma,

Here we are in Shageluk and today is Sunday, Potlatch day, an Indian
holiday. But first let's reminisce a little. I just finished reading your letters,
starting with the oldest down to the most recent. They were very good!

Mae just came in from the dining room looking over my shoulders.
(She is afraid I will say something she doesn't like). Where shall I begin?
Well, your wonderings, imaginations, consternations and anticipations
have been sufficiently aroused to accept a nonsense letter from me, too.
I have lost track of the number of letters Mae has written, so don't feel
bad if I repeat a few things. Here comes Etola (Tootsie), who wants to see
how it is going. You see, I sit in the kitchen and write. It's so nice in here.

Etola has a baby tooth that is bothering her. She took it along from home. She was sitting here in the kitchen whispering to her mama, "Don't tell Daddy about my tooth, will you Mama?" "Oh, no." But I heard it and you see I have my dispensary full of elevators, Novocain, and extractors. There is where the trouble lies. There is where the peeking comes in. She doesn't mention the tooth anymore, rest assured.

But back to one of your letters, written on the 23rd of September. At that time we were approaching St. Michael. We arrived there the next day about noon. When you wrote the above letter we were out on the Bering Sea. Oh boy! Some sea! Mae and Etola were a little sick. Not much though... they stayed in bed mostly. I managed to have some things sent up to them. Some I carried myself from the ship's kitchen. Fine people on board! I wasn't seasick, but that fishing trip at Seward sure was crazy. Plenty of fish, good trout, but plenty of gnats, no-see-ums and mosquitoes. My, they were tough. It was a hot day, too, and they put me to bed for a couple of days. Outside of that I never lost a meal. On board was a family from Nebraska, one from California, one from New Mexico and we, the North Dakota family. Perhaps Mae has told you about this before.

At St. Michael we got acquainted with the doctor's wife at Mountain Village, up our way. You see, she could not stand Alaska. Did not want to stand it. Made no effort to get along. She could tell the weirdest tales about the hardships and so on, but we were already educated from the boat to fanciful stories—really good ones. Those kind that have an emphatic last sentence for a hair-raiser. Etola (Tootsie) just came in from the dining room with her tooth in her hand. Now she is standing here talking a blue streak. I guess Mae got a streak to write, too. You'll be reading letters for two weeks. I hear Etola trying to say the letter "S" with a lisp. Some girl, eh? She sure seemed to make a hit with Captain Witlam on the "North Star"—more so than the rest. He invited her upstairs to the cabin every so often.

Back to St. Michael and the doctor's wife. She was from Detroit, Michigan. City bred, you see, and for her nothing was good enough. A Mrs. Starret, teacher of Chenaliak up our way, up the Yukon from St. Michael, got together with us to argue about delivering babies. To say I laughed is putting it mildly. We all laughed. This Mrs. Starrett said teachers as representatives of the (educated?) group had to deliver babies, and often they were called upon to perform this undesirable duty. But the doctor's wife insisted this was a duty that should be left to the doctor. I could hear then, knowing nothing myself about Alaskan conditions, that she knew nothing about the country. Even after a year's stay.

At St. Michael we plodded on for four days. I made the acquaintance of a young assistant, a fine young Hawaiian, whose wife was a teacher at Stebbins. From him I gathered much sound information. Mind you, he came in one evening from Stebbins when it was pretty stormy in a small boat, with a kicker and two natives. It is peculiar how they can handle those small boats. Brave sailors, out in all kinds of weather! St. Michael, an old government army post, is a very windy place. It blew every day for four days. We were scheduled to leave up the river in a large boat, but it so happened that we were sent off in a small boat, 'Misabe', up the river. And what a boat! Mae perhaps told you how we were laid up in a side creek, protected from the wind, for two days and two nights. What a life. "Life on the Misabe" will be my next book. We slept in our clothes for a whole week. The help, consisting of two men, machinist and pilot, were tubercular. Mae did much of the cooking. A family going to Pilot Station from Nebraska, did nothing but complain. Perhaps rightly so, but it didn't help matters any. It was the only time on the whole trip it fell my lot to swear. One night Mae and I were sleeping together. About two o'clock in the morning the winch head was connecting with my head. Oh boy, did that hurt. You see, the bunks were so close to the ceiling one could not turn around. I had to sneeze. Tootsie Etola: pleads, "Daddy, don't scare me like that." Some girl, eh? She is in the sitting room with Mae, standing on her head. You see, it's Sunday night. Mae has baked a lot of nice bread right in front of my eyes. I am hungry. She has been working on a Sunday and we are supposed to be proper church people.

Finally after a week's stay on 'Misabe the Great', we got to the famous city of Marshall or Fortuna Ledge, but first of all we unloaded Hirsh and his stuff at Pilot Station. Not much of a school building in that place. But they were glad to get there nevertheless.

At Marshall we had to stay for two weeks. More correct, 16 days. They were eventful days, too. I was invited out duck and goose hunting with no license. But that matters not. The U.S. Commissioner there took the plugs out of his gun. If he could commit a crime against the game laws I was told to pay no attention either. I never shot so many ducks and geese in my life. We shot from sand bars. Everything was shot while flying. Six or seven of us went. One trader, one dentist, one Standard Oil supervisor or manager, one owner of a gold mine, the U.S. Commissioner, a native and the teacher at Shageluk. We must have shot 100 birds, three of us hunting. We stayed for two days, and then went back to Marshall.

The government nurse is Alma Carlson, whose brother is a doctor at

Warren, Minn., county seat of Marshall County, near Oslo, Minn. She is nice. I was out on medical work among the Eskimos with Miss Holly, the territorial teacher, and Miss Carlson. I said our stay at Marshall was eventful. The U.S. Marshall got married and the night of the wedding, I played for the wedding dance. Miss Holly, the schoolteacher, was there too, and what a party. Mae and Tootsie went to bed. It was a drinking party and the good wife I have did not come into the dance. She says to tell you she peeked through the window. Yes, we finally saw the government boat 'Nenana'. (But now the wife came and had to get a kiss. She is making me a sandwich for that. I know how to handle her). Off on the 'Nenana' Tuesday the 20th of Sept. and what a parting! Everybody (it was in the afternoon) was drunk. I mean all on land. They were dancing and hooting like wolves. We waved the best we knew how. Excuse me, I must have my food. I am undernourished at 210 lbs. The slice of bread was good. Now I will begin writing again. (Back to the 'Nenana'.) Now I have to write properly. (The wife is standing here, you see.) I should say right here that today I did not feel just right. It must have been something I ate late last night or yesterday noon. Mae is teaching the little Indians today the 18th of October.

We got into Railroad City the next day, Sept. 21, early in the morning, about 10:00 a.m. We didn't get to see Holy Cross. We were lucky though. Even if we didn't get any butter and a few things like that which were lost in shipment it will be sent later, whenever that will be. We got onto a private Innoko boat called the 'Idler' at Railroad City. This boat belongs to a famous name of George Black. The steamer 'Nenana' made its last trip for the season. Perhaps I mentioned that before. Everybody was in a hurry to get to the outside (Seattle). So no time could be wasted you see. Still it was or is a fine boat, very fine indeed. Really a splendid boat! I am sure it will be on that one we will go when we go outside. Or else we'll fly. There is much flying in this country. Almost everybody flies. It has the reputation of being the safest way to travel in this country.

The 'Idler' did not go that same day to Shageluk. It is a day's run from Railroad City or about 10 hours. Fine trip, though. I helped Mr. Black, the owner, load 100 barrels of oil that day at Railroad City. It was the first real work I had done since I left North Dakota. But I used to wheel with truck wheels in the Old Country, many hundred years back. So that was the kind of a wheel I used then. It was good for me. It gave me a good appetite. Back to Mr. Black. By descent he is half Dane and half Swede. Not such a bad combination. Did I tell you we had two barges along with us to the Famous City? We did, and they were loaded with all kinds of things clear up to 100 tons. There were gold derricks used for getting the gold out of the ground. They were big and clumsy. Anyway we got going the next morning, Thursday, Sept. 22, at 9:00 a.m. We made no stops. The people on the 'Idler', beside Mr. Black, were Mrs. Peterson, their daughter and Mrs. Black, a good old-fashioned German. I guess she said she is a little mixed. Mrs. Black's husband has the mail contract up the Yukon to White Horse from the city of Nenana, and a crew of six men. Most of them were a little "cracked" in the head. So they aren't all in the best of shape intellectually in this country, either. And now the ribbon on my typewriter is haywire. I wonder if I can get this letter ready by the first of November. Let's hope so. As I said we had a nice trip. What sort of surprised me was that the big government building at Railroad City, the only building there, was deserted this trip on the 'Nenana'. It was all locked up for the winter. Mr. Nathan, the agent, went this time on the big steamer. I believe Mae got a picture of the boat so you can see what it looks like. This old timer had his wife along with him. That seemed to help him considerably. I don't know what these fellows do in this country without their good wives. Perhaps some of them aren't so hot. They have to go some to beat mine. She is picking up new things every day. By the time we get back to North Dakota, she will be hard to beat. Anyway, we got to Shageluk in the evening of Sept. 22—10 p.m. to be correct. We could see the schoolhouse from way down the Innoko River as Mr. Black turned the spotlight over the adjoining country. Tootsie got so excited that I had to tie her to the bed post with a rope. She was, I believe, going to jump over board to get to see her new home. Funny kid. I don't believe the rest of us were that crazy. She talks about her grandma every day, but she doesn't seem to be homesick. There is one consolation. When we get tired and want to go home, we go, that is all. Then we will travel the same 5,000 miles we came. I hope we don't have to go for three years. We have a lot of things to accomplish first.

The natives were all there in a body to see who these white people were. We could hear their jabber in their own peculiar ways saying, "Hope they are good to us and give us lots of things." Mae and Etola got off first. Mae grabbed one of the natives and made him get the key for the schoolhouse. I was surprised she would do it. She is brave now, I tell you. She can even stay alone in the house while I am out in the reindeer camp. Mae and Etola built a fine fire while I was at the boat settling with Mr. Black for hauling the Royal Family and their subsistence to port. The next move was to get the groceries off the boat to the schoolhouse. The only mishap was a sack of cabbages falling in the river. But that has to be perfectly all right in this country where everybody does the complaining and nobody says anything.

Three of the natives helped me take the goods, groceries and things, to the schoolhouse for which service they charged me one dollar an hour. They worked one hour and a half. I worked with them--three of them. No, now this darn typewriter is haywire. I am going to requisition a good typewriter for next year. That is all there is to it. We can't get along without good tools for working. Those buggers charged me a lot, but we have to pay it I guess. We won't spend much on shows, I reckon. Not many show houses in Shageluk. About the only show is taking the ringside seat around the dogs to watch them jump and hear them howl. That is something, I assure you. Lots of people would get a kick out of hearing those everlasting malamutes go good. I was sick today. Etola thought I was starving, so she made me some white cracker sandwiches and brought them into bed for me.

How about this Christmas Season? I am thinking about some gifts for everybody, but I'll be darned if I know how to get them out of here. No packages or parcel post in the wintertime. I hope I am wrong. The only dollars we have spent so far are [sic] for our fares and groceries. Of course we didn't have enough to pay for all that, but the government is supposed to pay us back, or reimburse us, is a better word. They will, too, when they get around to it. It always takes time to get things from Washington up here.

Mae just let out the kids, and I believe she is happy as a result of it. The natives are going to have a dance here this coming Saturday. Mae is so enamored with one of these silly boys that I believe I will be without a wife when I get back home. No, as long as Tootsie is around you can believe Mama will listen up.

October 18 and the wood is all hauled in for the evening. Etola fetched water this evening. I split the wood. Etola carried it. Poor Tootsie. I helped her with the water though. Not only that, but we had clinic today—a couple of T.B. cases. After that I had to issue some supplies to destitutes in exchange for work done for the school. Now Tootsie is wondering why everybody looks at her. I guess I'll never finish this letter. Tootsie was here wondering when I am going to get done. I have in my letter that Mae went to bed, but she is very much alive now. Two weeks ago she actually did go to bed while I was writing. She got tired looking at all the talk. Today is, of course, a different day, though. I even heard that our stuff that we were short has showed up at Marshall, Alaska. This information was passed on over the radio.

Mrs. Black and her daughter got off the boat and visited the building. The only remark they made was, "Wish we could live here, too." Well, I don't blame them, for the building is fine. We worked until three o'clock that Friday morning in order to get things lined up. Most of our stuff was in pretty good condition, except the sheets and some other things that were a little moldy. A few papers were also rather tattered and torn. Well anyway, on that Friday, I guess it was not on the 13th either, we worked like good fellows. On Saturday we had company. Father Spills, a Catholic priest from Holy Cross, came up to see us. He really was not coming perhaps to see us so much as to have church in the school on Sunday. He visited with Mae a little. I guess they had a nice visit. You see, this was my fatal night. I had to deliver a woman. Of all things. I hadn't even gotten acquainted with my dispensary. I was there from seven in the evening until about after ten in the evening. I then examined her and found she wouldn't be ready before about eleven or twelve midnight. I went home and went to bed. I had no more gotten into bed, or so I thought, before there was a knock at the door. I had slept for about two hours – all tired out. I went back and delivered a baby boy. I don't know how heavy he was because there was no apparent scale around.

No, now here comes a crazy guy who was trying to cut off his own neck. It was an awful cut. It was the brother of the wife to the storekeeper here. He's not a native. No, now I don't know if I feel better or worse. If I didn't eat so much raspeboller [potato dumplings] that I am ready to burst. And Tootsie, can you believe, she ate 10 big raspeboller, at least. I think she takes after Mae.

By the way, I was talking about Holy Cross. This town is located about fifty miles down the river from here. It is a large Catholic mission. They have everything under the sun—cows, pigs, sheep, goats—everything. They can raise the best garden stuff. Father Spills gave us some kohlrabi, the biggest I have ever seen. They raise, I guess, anything and everything there is to raise. He also gave us one big cabbage weighing 20 pounds and 16 ounces (21 lbs.) That's a lot, I would say. About four to a 100 lb. sack. As I said, Father Spills had a nurse with him who helped me on that first baby case in this country. Her name was Tassia Demientieff. A little Russian, I believe. But the worst part of the whole case was that the baby came before we got there. And her mother was there as a sort of help. She was not very clean, and as a result, the woman got puerperal fever on top of a weak heart. I had quite a time, I am sure, but we have a pretty good dispensary. That sure helps.

There is another person at the door. Another woman is to have a baby. I must grab my bag and run. Perhaps these people will be as appreciative as the other people who named the baby after me. You see, they lost one child two years ago at the Mountain Village Hospital, where a trained physician was in charge. They sure think I am some doctor. There are six more women due in a short time. Mae is showing them how to make baby clothes. But, we have a fine home. The best ever, I assure you. Everything is perfect. We have the best equipped manual training shop in Alaska, I believe. There is everything. 16 miles away are trees and a sawmill (Holikachuk). So we can actually make things. We have a fine government blacksmith shop with all kinds of tools.

I talked about butter a short time back. When we left the boat George Black gave us four lbs. of butter. And this morning there was a whole keg of butter on the front door step, 50 lbs. in brine. Mae often says, "What have we done to deserve anything as good as this?" The building is heated by two furnaces, kitchen stove and parlor stove. We have a well-equipped school with a class room and a large gymnasium. That sure helps the discipline problem. Besides, it is often used for native dances. The natives do work around here for a certain amount of remuneration, groceries mostly in exchange for labor. People down the river laughed at me when I was talking about furnaces, especially the teachers at Pilot Station. But every word is true. It is an up-to-date school plant only a few years old. The people here are very friendly. Today is Sunday. They came after me in a motor boat from across the river. I had to attend their grave ceremony. Afterwards, their potlatch. I had a meeting in the schoolhouse the other day and all the natives were here. "No teacher had talked like that." It didn't take much to satisfy them.

Lots of things have happened since last Sunday night. Then I wrote 'til 12 midnight, decided to go to bed and start Monday again. Here it is almost Sunday again. No, not that bad, but it really is Thursday the 13th of October. Tootsie just said it will take Auntie a whole day to read this letter. I hope so.

Just think of it. We are living in Alaska now. Mail doesn't travel every day. We just got your mail but we had no chance of sending out mail. Therefore we are so busy getting all our reports ready in case, as promised. A fellow from Holy Cross, 50 miles down the river, should arrive for the mail. We are the busiest people on earth, I guess. We haven't had time to get either restless or lonesome, neither sad nor glad. We are at equilibrium, so to say. Still, we are continually busy. No chance for story writing. No chance for even decent thinking. To attend to personal necessities is often hard.

How is it going with Mama? Glad she got a big Swede to work. Hope she is happy. Wish I could reach her with my nice big fresh salmon that I got tonight. It so happened today is clinical day. One part of our population lives five miles down across the river. A man came to get me on a sick call down that way. The mother and father of a 30 year-old lady whom I delivered liked me so well that they gave me a nice big salmon. Tomorrow is Friday, fish day. Mae is preparing it and boy, will it taste satisfying.

Tomorrow also I go out to look at the reindeer. By law I am reindeer superintendent. Tootsie was just mimicking a girl, the daughter of a teacher at Pilot Station, who has a strong southern drawl. Tootsie also was entertaining a fellow named Robert Painter by showing him her family pictures, explaining to him in his native language just what they all meant. I guess she had out the whole family anthology. He nodded complacently from time to time punctuating his sentences by eh, hee, and teeh hee. Once in a while "yankola, rolla, kutchlo"—meaning "very interesting, I like'm fine." "Kottilla, mudsello"—meaning "girl like angel, sweet and white." You see folks, Mae had asked one of the girls what they called boat. The answer was swift-guts, whatever that means. Both my girls are talking things I don't quite understand. I believe at times they are learning native. Just so they don't forget their white heritage.

Mae has to teach tomorrow while I go way out into the mountains to reindeer camp. She also has to speak to the native women about basket making and selling, how to plan their winter supply of baskets for early spring delivery. Mae is sitting here looking wise. She is sending you a sketch of our house. Tootsie is funny. She adds to the blue print a couple of toilets used by the school children while in school. When it's nice the family royal uses them. "It's a nice copy of a toilet," Tootsie says. She wonders what Auntie will think of my letter. Etola is worried already. It's now 9 o'clock in the evening. The family is now arguing how the steamer 'Nenana' traveled, how the big machinery worked, the steam, how it exerted itself to make things move. At times they are wondering if Daddy saw this and that, what the girls saw. Daddy had to tend to medical work on the way up, so perhaps he lost out on some things. But there weren't many things either of us lost out on. People to talk to, cowboys, prospectors, tramps; they are not called tramps in this country. In fact it may surprise you to know that Alaska has no such things as tramps or relief. Everybody is willing to work and everybody gets paid good wages. There is plenty of work in Alaska. The pay on the average is about 7 or 8 dollars per day. Not bad, eh?

Now the wife is out cooking us some coffee. Tootsie is taking down the menu. I guess it's all right, whatever they make. It is a strange family I have. Now they are standing in back of the stove to warm themselves. I was thinking they should get me something to eat, but that probably won't happen. They are naughty too, the rascals. Now they are standing here reading what I am writing. The mobsters.

Tell me, Emma, if there are any complaints about the money. That is, is the bank complaining? The bank in Seattle may pay out all our accrued bills first, leaving the rest to wait. How about it? We want to do the right thing with everybody. The fact remains we all feel good. In spite of all my work my nerves are perfect. The pulse is slow compared to what it has been. Certainly I don't believe I have high blood pressure anymore. I know things will be paid eventually, most of it this year. We are trying very hard to make good. If we don't it won't be our fault, I am sure.

It is so quiet here you can sleep like a rock. Only sound here is that of howling dogs (wolf species) about five in the afternoon. Otherwise we are all happy. No complaints to make. The kids are all nice. The parents tell me to give them a licking if they don't behave. Tomorrow I won't get my nice salmon before I come home from the reindeer corral. A regular Norway of its own. There is one thing true. When we get out of debt, if we get tired of Alaska, we can make a living in the States. Especially when we have a few dollars saved. Whether I practice law or medicine, I shall make a living, a good one too. What a difference it makes in a person's life to have few worries. Here comes the coffee on a tray served cafeteria style. Gee, that coffee was good. Mae is going now after a sandwich. She spurts, "I wonder who would get me a sandwich if I asked for it?" All I have to do is remind her about the sea and ocean trip, that's all.

I hope we shall like Alaska ever so good until our debts are paid. Mae is now fixing up things for me to take along on my trip to the reindeer. I shall go to look over the herd. She is sending coffee, milk, a kettle for cooking coffee in the open air, three or four oranges, then some sandwiches. We shall take two good rifles along. One for me, one for the other fellow. The country is wonderful, hunting is good. But tonight it was cold in the boat coming back up the Innoko River from the Lower Village. Of course it was in an open boat. I had on my blue old suit, Comming suit, heavy underwear, thin shirt open at the neck, my ordinary shoes, gloves and W.P.A. cap, and it's the thirteenth of October. Not bad for this country.

Mae was out taking a picture of the schoolhouse while school was in session. The sun was out in all its glory. If the picture is as nice as what you have already returned, it will be fine. We sure enjoy those pictures. Tootsie is looking at them now. Never is she too tired to look at them. For next year we shall buy much Alaskan stuff—like king salmon, smoked king salmon strips put in oil—best on the market. Our vegetables we shall receive from Holy Cross, what we can't raise ourselves. We are going to raise a big garden ourselves. That way we can save much. We are saving enough to have no financial worry in case we have to go outside. We can always get outside if necessary. Planes always go in the winter time. It takes only five hours to get places where boats run all year.

Glad to see and hear that you are all happy. Four weeks is indeed a long time to wait for a letter, but now before it freezes up here (around the 15th of November) mail doesn't travel very often. Once every six weeks. We always try to get our letters off on first mail. I understand airplanes will be here this year for the first time, twice monthly. That will be lovely. Before dogs they tell me mail got around twice yearly. We just have to take things as they come. Next year the government is going to put in radio. That will be fine. We need one. The Juneau office gets impatient once in a while for hearing so slowly and late from this country. But reports go out as fast as we can get them out. Peculiar, even people who live here don't realize how slow the mail is.

Lots of love from us all, Herman and family.

P.S. I must go to Holikachuk tomorrow to give medical care to the natives.

Chapter 4
GETTING SETTLED

Dad intended to get up early on October 20th to go to Holikachuk to see the sick, but the alarm didn't go off. Mom: "Herman's temper flew like fury. It sounded like he was in Hell for a few minutes. Still the alarm wouldn't go off. Poor Herman. I was called a dumbbell and still the alarm didn't go off." Dad finally left for Holikachuk with Willy Newman in his boat to administer medicine to the whole village. The day started out badly and Dad's lack of luck continued. He lost Willy's wash basin in the river and had to pay 75 cents for a replacement. Mom taught school both Thursday and Friday.

On Friday afternoon, Mom and Etola went visiting in the village and stopped to play with the pet bear. In the Athabascan culture, a father would often bring a bear cub home for his child. The little cubs are usually caught in the late spring or summer. The bear is tied to a stake near the house. At this age, they become friendly and playful. When freeze-up comes, a four-foot hole is dug on the river bank, lined with grass, and the bear happily hibernates in the hole for the winter. A bear cub may be a pet for two summers, and then is set free because of its size. If the bear becomes a menace to the village it is killed. The meat is never eaten because it had been a pet. (Cornelius Osgood , "Ingalik Social Culture," pg. 259.) Etola played with the pet bear often. When it started to play roughly, it was indeed taken out to the woods.

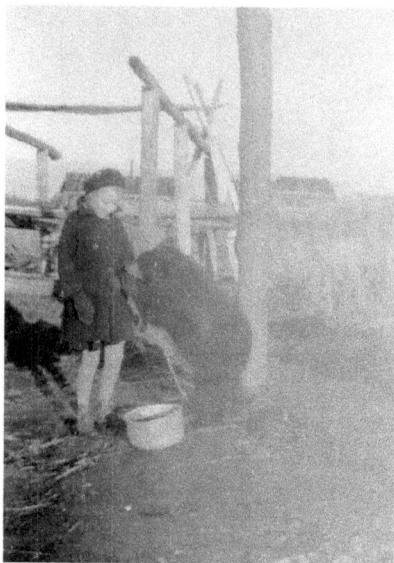

Etola and the Pet Bear

Late in October, the Larsens hosted a Halloween party in the schoolhouse. The children and the unmarried people of the village were invited. All came wearing masks. Dad dressed up as a ghost and went upstairs. Everyone went up in the dark to shake hands with the "ghost" and was so scared. The guests enjoyed the party and were given candy and suckers. The party broke up early at 9:30 p.m. when Dad had to go on a medical call. Nikoli Hunter's lungs were hemorrhaging.

There was a lake by the schoolhouse where the natives enjoyed ice skating. By October 29, the ice was already two inches thick. Mom, Dad and Etola often went out in the evening to skate. Dad: "The ice is wonderful and the air is penetrating in this country." One Saturday evening the moon was so beautiful they hated to go into the house. Mom and Etola made sandwiches and coffee while Dad had to check the government tools. The shed was filled with tools and supplies, which were loaned to the natives. Returning back to the house, Dad stepped in a pile of dog feces and dragged it into the house. Mother never showed anger even when it was appropriate. So after she scrubbed the floor, they had lunch and began working on the constantly required government reports until wee hours of the morning.

Dad had a fine medical dispensary. Matilda Woodford assisted in keeping it clean. He tried to hold a few clinical days each week, but the villagers knocked on his door many times each day. The knocking itself made him very nervous, because in his childhood years in Norway he was told that the Devil would come knocking on the door to take him away if he misbehaved.

Shageluk Lake behind Schoolhouse

There were many cases of tuberculosis in the village. Dad made a tonic for this using iron, quinine, elixir and strychnine phosphate or he gave the patient a bottle of Brown's Mixture. One could follow the path taken by someone with T.B. because there was blood (from the victim's lungs) splattered in the snow along the way. When Mom had guests for coffee, she would boil the cups for a long time to make sure they were germ-free.

Cod liver oil was dispensed to everyone as a preventive measure. Rheumatism was treated with camphorated oil. Patients with gall bladder problems were told to drink olive oil. Constipation was treated with C.C. pills or Epsom salts. One older gentleman was having a terrible time with his bowels. Dad gave him a good dose of Epsom salts. Mom saw the fellow going back and forth to the outhouse and heard him saying, "Oh shit, that teacher gonna kill me."

Zinc oxide was the salve of choice for sores and boils. One young man came to ask Mom for help. He had a very large painful boil on his neck. She uncovered the bandage to look at it. It was covered with a feather. When asked why he had a feather on it, he said his mother had placed it there so it would fly away.

Most of the medical problems, tooth problems and injuries were treated in the medical dispensary, but baby deliveries were done in the homes. At 6:45 a.m., November 15th, Pius Savage knocked at the door. Mrs. Savage, age 22, had started labor at about 1:00 a.m. When Dad arrived, the patient was standing on her knees over a pillowed stool in the corner. Her mother was with her and could not speak a word of English. There was no light and no towels. At 8:00 a.m. she had a baby girl. Her mother wanted to pull the placenta, but Dad somehow made her understand that she could not do so. The baby's eyes were treated with silver nitrate; then he left for a full day of teaching.

When Dad himself became ill he would follow the advice of Bernarr Macfadden (Editor-in-Chief of the eight-volume "Encyclopedia of Health" published in 1933). He stopped eating at the first sign of an illness and went on a fast. He then drank quarts of water with lemon juice and had an occasional glass of tomato and lemon juice mixed. In addition he walked 5-7 miles each day. Once the illness left he would break the fast with a glass of milk, later hot milk toast, then resume normal eating. He believed the body could heal itself more quickly without having to digest solid food. [As a child I believed it was a good way to get weak and starve.]

The Athabascan people in Shageluk were very superstitious. Mom: "There was an eclipse of the sun one day which scared the natives. No one was allowed to go out without a coat over his head. The kids were in school at the time and we got a fantastic look at the eclipse through smoked glass. The young people didn't believe in their elders' superstitions but had to obey the customs in order to keep the peace. When a girl entered womanhood, she had to stand in the corner and never cross the river or the Devil would stick up his horns at her. A second grade boy wanted me to correct his math papers. I told him I would if he cut his long and dirty fingernails. He claimed he could not because his grandmother said he would not be able to catch anything to eat. He thought about it and finally cut his fingernails." Mother then gave him a good grade on his math. Dad always claimed it was difficult to get the natives to clean themselves.

Mom: "Expectant mothers were not allowed to make things for the baby before it was born. When I saw they were pregnant I would ask the missionary in Anvik to bring a bundle of baby things, store the bundle away, then deliver the gift when the baby came. The new mother would ask where I got the clothing and I would admit that I had had them for a long time. The clothing was received with welcome even though it was against their superstitious thinking. The Indians felt that if one planned for a baby before it was born it would surely die."

Every morning, Mom or Dad fired up the two furnaces in the schoolhouse. The logs were cut to four-foot lengths and were quite heavy. They employed someone to cut wood every day. The first person who won the government contract was a blind man named Andrew Feetcar. He was called Blind Andrew by everyone. He cut wood with a large saw on a chopping block and was paid in money or groceries and supplies. He first asked for a pound of black tea ($1.00) and a pound of sugar (50 cents). Mother went over to his house one day to get a list of supplies he needed and was surprised that he had a very clean house in spite of his blindness. On cold days, Blind Andrew sawed for only two hours. Other days he placed a log on the chopping block and simply left, but he generally worked very hard and the Larsens were well supplied with wood.

There was much gift giving and trading in Shageluk. Mom and Etola were given many gifts because they were gentle and so friendly. They were learning even more of the Indian language, especially Etola. At the beginning of November, Matilda Woodford gave Mother a very large Indian basket she had made. Sometimes the trading was neither fair nor equitable. The government supply of prunes was full of worms. Dad gave 20 ½ pounds of prunes to Mrs. Lee Howard and a few pounds to Matilda Woodford. Matilda loved to make her family's favorite prune pie. In exchange for the prunes Mrs. Howard gave the folks a beautiful pair of beaver mittens.

Large Spruceroot Basket

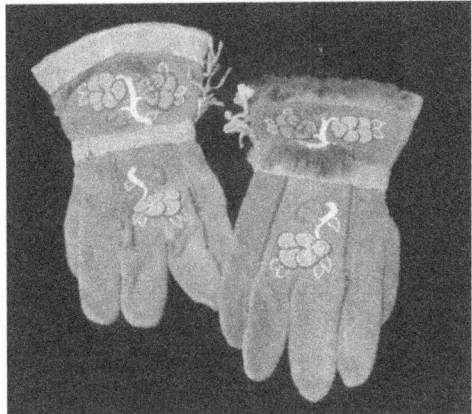

Beaded Beaver Mittens

The mail came only when planes were able to fly or someone was able to get the mail by dog team. Mom and Dad wrote letters to their parents and friends often. By the time the mail came it was not unheard of to have written four or five letters to the same family. Dad was constantly working on government reports, preparing invoices for reimbursement, ordering supplies, sending copies of hunting permits to Juneau and filling out orders to Sears and Roebuck for the natives. On Nov. 5th Mom wrote, "Our mail plane had to turn back to Anchorage to put skis on. Etola often prays for the mail to come." Nov. 24th, Thanksgiving Day, Mom's diary entry said, "The long-sought airplane came. Whoopee! I got three letters from Emma and one from Mama. Etola received letters from her cousin and three pen pals. Dad received much mail. We haven't had mail since the 1st of October."

Star Airways

Along with Father Spills and Brother Hess, who came from Holy Cross representing the Catholic Church, there was an Episcopalian priest named Rev. Henry Chapman and his assistant, Gabriel Walker, who came from Anvik to hold services and give communion. They traveled in winter with Gachidle Workman who had nine beautiful dogs. Rev. Chapman generally stayed with Mom and Dad for two days. He visited the people in Lower Village (about a mile from Shageluk), then returned for supper.

Mother always fixed a wonderful supper of reindeer roast, potatoes, vegetables and apple pie when he came. After supper he held services in the school. Mother played hymns on the piano for him. At one time she noted, "A drunk woman took Holy Communion. Oh, my!" Church services were well attended by the Shageluk Indians, but most still adhered to their own religious practices in their ceremonial building called the Kashim, where they held many dances, feasts and funerals.

Dad and Mom were responsible for many duties in the village. Their school teaching duties were divided. Mom generally taught art, music and sewing and Dad taught the rest of the subjects, including manual training in the shop. The students enjoyed school when Mother taught because she was so lenient. Dad, on the other hand, was very much a disciplinarian and often lost his temper when things didn't go just right. By December the schoolhouse and the living quarters had water running down the walls and the windows. Dad made the students wipe up the water and clean the flies out of the windows. The worst problem in school was head lice. Etola became infested with lice. Mother was told to apply kerosene to her head. This cured the problem, but Mom felt so bad because Etola's scalp was covered with blisters.

By the end of 1938, the Larsens were quite settled in Shageluk. This way of life was a perfect fit. In spite of all the work, this job was much appreciated and the pay was good. They began celebrating a quiet Christmas Day by sleeping until 10:00 a.m. Mom gave Dad a large loaf of nut bread and Etola a moose skin bookmark. Dad gave Etola mittens and gloves and Mom received three yards of cloth and a pair of moccasins. The total for Christmas presents was only $5.50. The gifts from the family in the lower 48 and Norway did not arrive until January 26th of the following year because the mail did not come.

Chapter 5
THE FIRST FULL YEAR

January 1, 1939. Mom: "Happy New Year! All is quiet here, but from what I hear the natives had too much hooch. We didn't get up before 10:30 a.m. We lay in bed reading the newspapers (*The Mandan Daily Pioneer*), which Emma sent. Then I got up and made toast and coffee and washed up two days' supply of dirty dishes. One must start the new year right, you know."

As the mail plane was expected, they worked on government reports. Mom and Etola focused on the reindeer inventory as Dad prepared other required documents. They stayed up the entire night preparing and typing. The mail plane did not come.

Mom: "We felt sort of tough losing a night's sleep so we tried to have a nap, but there were too many knocking at our door." Blind Andrew announced that he was not going to work because it was a holiday. Pius Savage burned his eye with cigarette ashes saying the wind blew them into his eye. Eli Wilson cut a deep gash in his thumb while cutting meat for his supper. Mom: "He is 24 years old and a nice looking Indian boy. He lives alone. He says Herman is a good doctor."

Eli Wilson in Doorway
of his Home

School resumed on Tuesday, January 3. Mom washed clothes but did not finish because she had to thaw more snow. She was able to finish the washing and ironing the next day, along with baking bread, then went out visiting in the village. She went to John and Matilda Woodford's home. They had a pet cock robin with clipped wings so it couldn't fly onto the stove. Matilda was thawing fish. Her daughter Agnes had pierced ears and was wearing earrings made of beads. Then she went to the Kashim where the villagers were preparing for their native "Doll Dance."

The Doll Ceremony is a very serious ceremony held once a year after the snow has fallen. The Kashim is decorated with one large hoop made by tying six-foot lengths of split spruce poles together. The hoop is painted with rings every three feet and bunches of ptarmigan feathers are fastened between the rings. This is suspended from the corners of the ceiling. The ceremonial table is set up at the right side of the entrance of the Kashim. In the meantime, someone goes out to the woods to find the dolls, which have been wrapped and stored on a spruce branch. There is one male doll and one female doll each about one foot in height. The dolls heads are carved from spruce and are painted red. The bodies are made of grass or caribou hair and dressed in proper Indian attire. The male doll holds a small drum and drumsticks. The female doll holds nothing. After supper on the first ceremonial day, the dolls are unwrapped to see what the future holds for the natives of the village. If there are fish scales under the body of the male doll the fishing will be good or if an animal hair is present the hunting will be good. Blood on the male doll's parka foretells of a death in the village. If there are scratches on his face it means there will be sickness or if charcoal is found under his body there will be war. If there are dried berries on the female doll there will be plenty of fruit in the upcoming season.

The dolls are then tied to a stand and the feasting, ceremonial songs, dancing and beating of drums begin and continue for the next three days.

Women can listen but cannot take part in the festivities. A string is tied to the arm of the male doll that is holding the drumstick. Someone pulls the string during the night to make the doll's drum beat. The doll makes medicine to keep the people healthy and to increase the food supply for the people.

On the fourth night the medicine man talks to the dolls. He shakes a parka in front of them. Once the dolls start to speak in a low whistle, the medicine man puts out the lamp on the table near them and starts to interpret. He tells about the upcoming fishing season, etc. Finally the male doll quits talking and says, "No more!" The ceremony ends, but the male doll beats his drum throughout the last night. The next morning the dolls are rewrapped and taken back to the branches of a spruce tree. No one is allowed to look at them and if one happens to look at them his eyes may go bad. Then the hoop is broken down and discarded along with the ceremonial table and stands. The Doll Dance ends with a big feast. The food is brought and consumed by both men and women (Cornelius Osgood, "Ingalik Social Culture," Yale University Press, 1958, pp.135 - 137). This Doll Ceremony ended on Monday, January 9. The students were not in school for the first half of the day, therefore they were kept until 4 o'clock in the afternoon all week to make up for lost time.

For the remainder of the week, the students learned how to produce a school newspaper which was to be distributed throughout the village. At times, Dad would scold them for being awkward and backward, but in spite of the reprimands, the paper entitled Klagakjitna Honnik (school newspaper), Volume I, dated January 13, 1939, was hot off the ditto machine by the end of the week. The students involved were: Raymond Dutchman, editor; Grace Benjamin, assistant editor; Ida Dutchman, rewriteman; Isabelle Matthew, first cartoonist; Etola Larsen, second car-toonist; Olivia Painter, business manager; Hamil Hamilton, reporter from first grade; Adolph Hamilton, reporter from second grade; Mary Work-man, reporter from third grade; Etola Larsen, reporter from fourth grade; and Olivia Painter, reporter from seventh grade.

Shageluk School Newspaper

The paper reported:

SCHOOL NEEDS MODERNIZING

What could be better than running water in the school? We children would like to see a pump put into the basement on top of the cement foundation. The teacher is willing to cooperate if we can get someone to test for water. Then we can send to Juneau for pump.

School room this summer needs fixing. When the weather gets warmer, water leaks through the ceiling in many different places.

ALL EUROPE IN TENSION

Hitler, in a sworn statement, is taking the world in his own hands. The Fuhrer was very emphatic as he spoke to about 45 million people. The people cheered him as he mounted his schwartzen steed. Many howled and shouted, "Long live the Fuhrer!" A tremendous enthusiasm arose among the soldiers, who themselves did not fight in the last war. "We shall fight to the finish," Hitler says in no uncertain terms. Much unrest prevails in Europe according to the Associated Press Wires. The President of the United States is trying hard to prevent another war. He, in substance, says from his Hyde Park home, "We must be friends." The same message was called to the Fuhrer in Germany. Zshechoslovakia [sic] is much alarmed over the situation and is moving troops to the border. "Germany has no right to interfere with our people," says the Zshecho-slovakian [sic] foreign minister. "We must protect our people."

VILLAGE RECREATION

The church on the other side of Blind Andrew has been secured from Rev. Henry Chapman. The school children and Mrs. Larsen are going to fix it up for a community recreation hall. Maybe we can, in time, build up a library.

ETHEL KEATING DIES

News came to Shageluk early Tuesday morning that Ethel Keating, daughter of Paul Keating, passed away at the Holy Cross Mission. Death was caused by a sore throat. Her sudden death is very saddening to her many friends.

WARNING!

All who have a sore throat or who feel the least bit of soreness in your throat gargle with salt water two or three times a day and take a good lax-ative. See your doctor if necessary.

On the weekend, Pius Savage and Lee Howard helped Dad put up ice. Pius hauled it on his dogsled and piled it in the school ice house. They managed to haul 2 ¼ tons, but had 3 ¾ tons to finish. Dad was extremely tired afterward, so Mom soothed him with his favorite supper of Norwegian potato dumplings and they all went to bed early.

The remainder of January was very cold with temperatures hovering between 20-40 degrees below zero. They hauled ice, wood and snow daily. The people came often for medical treatment of one form or other. Dad taught school with Mother taking his place when necessary. By January 26th, Mom's 29th birthday, the mail plane came. Mom: "I was teaching school when the mail plane came. Etola was so excited she could not sit still in the classroom. I made a cake and then we opened the Christmas packages from 'home.' Etola was so happy she cried. Then Willy and Genevieve Newman came over and had coffee with us. At night we wrote letters before the plane came back to pick up the mail."

At the end of February the weather became more tolerable at 25 degrees above. A visitor came from Holikachuk named John Deacon. The people of Holikachuk wanted to start a school and he had received a letter from Juneau regarding the request. Dad and John went to Holikachuk to discuss the "new school" with the people. Mom: "Got up at 7:30 a.m. Cleaned out the school chimney before I could start a fire. While I was teaching the water dripped terribly in the schoolroom and playroom. The floor was covered with pots, pans, pails and buckets. I had the kids seated in all directions so they wouldn't get wet. The little kids tried to catch the water to drink when I wasn't looking.

"Herman came back from Holikachuk all tired out and had a big crowd of people with him. The Indians there speak English so well and are very nice. We held a dance in the schoolhouse. Herman and I played country music, the Indians' favorite. They danced in their moccasins, which made the floor so shiny. Clara Pike stayed over night here. For a thank you gift she gave me a beautiful beaded picture frame."

Beaded Picture Frame

Dad celebrated his 38th birthday on Sunday, March 5th. Dad: "Gertie Rope was here with a fish for my birthday present. Her husband Mike wanted me to pay 25 cents for it. Gertie also asked me if a 1936 fur license was good for 1939. The good wife fixed the fish and did a marvelous job in its preparation. I heard on the news that Hitler died from poisoning and an Italian Cardinal was elected Pope."

By the middle of March, Dad went around the village notifying the people to send their children to school. Many had been absent for no reason at all. At this time he also called for bids on the government wood contract and spent many hours in helping the villagers figure out the same. Willy Newman won the bids. He was to provide 35 cords of wood for $220.00 for the next heating season.

Alma Carlson, the government nurse, came to Shageluk and stayed at the school. Dad found her to be very intelligent and helpful. She outlined the type of work that ought to be done in the village. Billy Painter aroused them at 5:20 a.m. on Saturday, March 18. Dad appreciated that Miss Carlson went to deliver the baby boy who came at 10:15 a.m. Later Miss Carlson and Dad exchanged views on nutrition. She discussed that eating needle fish, bones and all, is responsible for the perfect teeth of the natives at Hooper Bay. Expeditions from the States had been there to investigate.

Another visitor from Pilot Station, named Dr. King, came at the end of March. She was a school supervisor of some kind who went from village to village assessing the performance of the schoolteachers. She and Dad worked on a new proposal. The children were not to do more than 335 minutes of school work per day. She suggested he was to teach by playing games and each recess was to last 25 minutes. She held a meeting with the women of the village expressing the importance of school attendance. Dr. King suggested changing many of the textbooks presently in use and even analyzed the use of center mounted curtains hanging on the windows. Dad had to order new ones.

Spring birds returned to the North Country by the middle of April. The snow melted quickly, making conditions terribly sloppy. Mother taught school often while Dad worked on a story for the Alaska Sportsman magazine called "Fishing on the Kenai." Etola was busy carrying and sawing wood for Willy Newman. Roxcenia Painter sat on a stump nearby playing the accordion for Etola while she sawed. Dad mailed his story on April 20th with bush pilot Dan Victor. Mom: "Dan says this is his last trip. Oh my! Now we won't get mail before June."

With few days remaining in April, amidst snow, freezing, and thawing, Mom started a garden in the greenhouse. Father Spills from Holy Cross sent planted cabbage seedlings, turnips and tomato plants. Adolph Hamilton made garden boxes where she planted the vegetables. Etola worked with her, planting flower seeds. Many of the villagers had already left for their fish camps, giving Mom a bit more spare time. Only 12 students remained in school. On April 28, Dad walked to Holikachuk for medical work. John Woodford came late in the afternoon announcing the arrival of a new baby boy. Mother went immediately to the Woodford home. Mom: "When I got there everything was on the floor. I cut and tied the cord and put the baby on the table. His feet were like ice. I cleaned him and covered him up good. There were no clothes for the baby." Then she went to take a picture of a 15-dog team in the village. Upon returning home, Woodford came again saying that Matilda's mother, Cecilia, was being too rough with the baby and nearly tore the bandage off its navel. Mom went back to see if everything was alright. She felt the baby would be O.K., but worried that Matilda's milk would be bad because she chewed so much tobacco.

In Holikachuk, Dad treated a few T.B. cases with Brown's Mixture, examined a child's tonsils and visited with Clara Pike. She relayed the story of her mother's death. She was the daughter of the Indian chief. The University of Pennsylvania sent a group to Holikachuk in 1935. While the group was there, the mother was found tied loosely with ropes with a gun at her side. She was foaming at the mouth and getting cold from the feet and up. After she passed away they held a potlatch (Indian burial ceremony). She was taken into the Kashim through the door. Each person in attendance danced and danced to chase the devil away. Her body was taken out through the window. She was buried in a silk-lined coffin with her knitting bag, fish and pots of food.

After treating the ill and visiting, Dad walked back to Shageluk from Holikachuk. At seven miles, Willy and Maurice Newman caught up with him. Dad: "We took off to the river. We were on high banks, but it was a fine road. We stopped at Lee Howard's fish camp for a cup of tea. Lee was across the river cutting wood. There were many moose tracks and muskrat houses. Back at Shageluk we saw many geese. We walked 20 miles. When I got home I fixed up a radio and a broadcaster."

By Monday, May 1, only seven children remained in the village. All others went to fish camp with their parents. School was dismissed until fall. Dad purchased a large Remington shotgun, powder and shots from Frank Walker in Holikachuk. Now he had time to try some hunting because there were ducks and geese flying all over. Mother washed and repainted the kitchen. Etola played house with her friends Roxcenia Painter and Virginia Howard on the front porch or they played out in the cache where food is stored in the winter. The ice on the Nenana River broke up at 1:26 p.m. on April 30. Summer had truly begun.

Mom and Etola took long walks on the river bank, viewing the country in a season they had not seen before. They saw large cranes and seagulls playing on the river. The seagulls cried like babies. The woods were full of songbirds, including robins, blackbirds and grosbeaks; the birdhouses were full. The buds were popping on the birch trees. The Innoko River had water along the edge. Ducks were playing in the open space in the lake below the schoolhouse. The sun, which appeared to be bright red, did not set until 10:30 in the evening and was up before 4:00 a.m. The Larsens survived the first winter quite nicely. Now it was beautiful and so much warmer…a time in which to hunt, fish, gather, stock, repair and clean, in preparation for the next school session and the next blast of winter.

Dad went hunting with Mike Rope on May 14 and shot two ducks. Nikoli Hunter gave them a big goose that he had shot. The Larsens had not had fresh game in their home since January. Mother roasted the ducks and goose. The goose was so fat and delicious. Along with fresh game, they received four cases of eggs—which had been missing from their plates for a long time—in the mail.

There was again much activity on the river. The men repaired their boats and canoes. Others were trapping cranes on the sand bar. Old Grandma Cecilia, Matilda's mother, got into a great argument with the other women regarding her crane-trapping rights on the sand bar. Nikoli Hunter was excited. He caught a crane in his trap, but when he went to get the crane only one foot was left. Dad explained to him that more than likely a fox had taken it.

The rain came down pretty hard on Sunday, May 21, and so did the mosquitoes and the no-see-ums (gnats). The following weekend the ice ran off the river and all went fishing with large dip nets. Mom, Dad and Etola stayed out by the river until 1:00 a.m. catching fish, then returned at 6:00 a.m. to dip net for more. They cleaned and salted 60 fish. The villagers were catching fish as much was hanging out on racks to dry all around the village.

On June 1, Mom, Dad and Etola were up at 6:00 a.m. to tag beaver. They tagged for six hours, and then Mom and Etola went with Billy and Bella Painter to Holikachuk. Mom: "We got there at 6 p.m. I tagged beaver steady after supper and kept on until 1:00 a.m. I was so tired I nearly wrote my name as Mrs. Beaver. We were supposed to go back to Shageluk in an open boat, but were lucky to catch a ride in a larger enclosed boat owned by two fur buyers from Fairbanks. Etola steered the boat half the way home. We had coffee, oranges, apples and cookies. It was a beautiful ride. We arrived home at 2:00 a.m. and scared Herman."

Mae Larsen Holding Whitefish

The "Nancy Belle" came on June 5th with stacks of mail and much government freight. Dad wheeled freight for three hours and spent two hours unpacking. Along with the freight came a new rug, which Mother had ordered for the living room. Dad had a very sore back from hauling freight but left for Holikachuk with the game warden and the game commissioner to inspect the beaver-tagging books. Etola helped Mom put the new rug down, which added so much life to the living room.

Herman and Etola Dipnetting on the Innoko River

Amelia Fairbanks Drying Dog Salmon

When Dad was in Holikachuk, an elderly woman gave him a kitten for Etola. Jonas Fairbanks brought the kitten back to Shageluk for her. It was so small they had to feed it with a bottle. Many of the children came to see the little feline. Etola loved her new little pet and was allowed to keep it in the house. Etola often played with her kitten by rolling marbles on the floor. Mom: "Herman at times would forget to read and just watched the kitten play."

With much fishing, gardening, fixing, tagging, and repairing, June soon turned to July. The third of July was Etola's 9th birthday. Mom baked a birthday cake and they had coffee and cake late in the afternoon. Etola received a storybook in which Dad wrote a poem. She loved to read and was overjoyed.

On the Fourth of July, Dad went on the "Sea Wolf" to Holy Cross. To begin the celebration, Father Spills gave him two glasses of good wine. Later they shot off a number of fireworks. The next morning after a breakfast of sourdough pancakes and prunes, they went out to the fish wheels on the Yukon to gather salmon. Dad: "The Sisters and the girls at the mission are able to cut up 1,024 fish every day. This is one day's catch. Our freight arrived on the 'Nenana'. We loaded our boat all night and got one hour of sleep. I paid my personal freight charge of $90.89 and we left for Shageluk, arriving at 1:00 p.m.

Fish Wheel on the Innoko River

Then I wheeled up the government supplies and our own. While I was gone Mae washed and painted the entire medical dispensary."

They checked all the groceries. Etola was thrilled when 24 pounds of popcorn came in the shipment. She popped a bowl of corn and all thought it was so tasty. Mom and Etola brought some corn to Matilda. They also gave her daughter Celene a dress that Etola had outgrown. Etola gave Matilda's mother, Cecilia, some beads for fixing her favorite moose mittens.

With all the purchased groceries stored, it was now time to gather food from Mother Nature's supply. The salmon berries were ripe in the middle of July. Mom and Etola went with Arthur and Amelia Fairbanks and Old Cecilia to the mountains. Mom: "The trip was beautiful—in and out of the hills, by rivers and along lakes. Everything was bright green. Cecilia had a hunting knife on her belt for protection—she was afraid of wolves. When we returned, Herman caught a king salmon. I took a picture of it."

On July 28, Mom remembered that one year had gone by since they left home. She was weeding the garden, noting that the carrots were a little slow but the rest of the vegetables were growing fine, when she got a visitor. Mom: "Today Lee Howard came over with a freshly butchered porcupine and asked if I wanted meat. I said, 'No, thank you.' Then he informed me that if a dog gets quills in its mouth, it is fed porcupine liver and the quills let loose."

Herman Holding a King Salmon

Most of August was spent doing repairs to the schoolhouse and grounds. Dad cut the tall grass with a scythe and then went to a large hill to get sand to permanently fix the government chimneys. During the last school year the chimneys had often fallen over in the wind and as he was starting fires, the schoolhouse filled with smoke. He had to run for water to put out the fire, crawl up to the roof to set the chimneys upright, then start over again. After the chimneys were mortared in place, they cleaned the stove pipes, put asbestos in both rooms between the pipes and the walls, renailed the roof, cleaned the closets, and poured gas and kerosene into smaller containers from the large barrels. With all of this done, the Larsens had a few days to relax before school started. Dad listened to war news at Willy Newman's. On September 3, President Roosevelt gave a speech for peace.

School resumed on Wednesday, September 6. Dad walked around the village to see where the students were, because there were only six attending. He discovered it was good berry-picking weather and the students were in the woods helping their parents with this necessary task. He held a meeting ten days later and stressed the following points:

1. All should attend meetings regularly.

2. Medical work will be done between 3:30 and 4:30 p.m. daily.

3. Will loan tools from 4:30 - 5:30 p.m. daily.

4. Students will attend school on a regular basis.

5. All will help cut a path to Lower Village.

6. Blind Andrew must cut wood for the schoolhouse daily.

All people attending the meeting agreed to cooperate.

The garden was harvested and stored by the end of September. From the Holy Cross Mission they bought three 100-pound sacks of potatoes, one dozen rutabagas and one dozen cauliflowers for $17.20. Willy Newman brought the remainder of their groceries, weighing 739 pounds, which had been transferred to his boat from the steamer 'Nenana' at Holy Cross. All of this was stored upstairs in the schoolhouse. The groceries arrived in good condition except for five rotten grapefruit.

Rev. Chapman and the game warden arrived in Shageluk on Thursday, September 28. Rev. Chapman wanted Dad to go moose hunting. Dad purchased five boxes of cartridges at the store for $5.00 and off they went. Dad: "It's raining hard on our way to Anvik. There Jimmy Walker gave us a piece of moose steak. Chapman's boat was tied up to the warden's boat because Chapman ran onto a bar at Piamiute Slough. We arrived at Railroad City about 8:30 p.m. We slept on Mr. Lattin's floor and used his kitchen for cooking our fine moose steak.

"I guided the game warden across the Yukon River. Rev. Chapman and I proceeded up the river. We had lunch on the Kasruski River and saw very little game. It was a terribly cold day. I froze so that I shivered by the time we got to Anvik. Mrs. Chapman received me at the door. They have a lovely 6 ½ year-old daughter named Laura. She is very bright. I went to church on Sunday with the Chapman family. He gave a nice sermon and we spent the rest of the day visiting.

"Monday we went out hunting again. The motor was troublesome and it stopped dead. The contact points were badly worn. We took it apart upriver and floated back. I filed the points straight and it worked. But at 3:00 p.m. it was too late to go back up river. The water and weather were very cold. Then we hit shallow water and broke part of the propeller. We took it apart on the sand bank and got it back together again. Then we turned around and went home. We saw nothing—not even tracks. Charlie Wulf took me back to Shageluk in an enclosed boat. We arrived home on Wednesday, October 4, at 3:00 a.m."

The first snow of the season came on October 8. It was below freezing on the second floor of the schoolhouse. All the freight was moved to the basement. By October 12th, the lake below the schoolhouse had four inches of ice and was strong enough for skating.

October 16, 1939. Dad: "We had news of the war this evening. This is the first time in the history of the world that the Germans are dropping bombs on British soil. Minnie Jack from Lower Village died Monday at 12 midnight. Tomorrow we shall have our annual picnic in the woods.

"The girls were not interested in helping with the fire nor making coffee or tea. I went out hunting. The kids got so scared at the likeness of a wolf that they climbed tall trees. Yes, the boys climbed with their skates on. We walked home again. Most of them were so scared they would not go out again.

"The war in Europe includes much ground fighting. I serve as an interpreter of war news for the natives. We also heard the great novelist Zane Grey died of heart trouble at age 64.

"In school we are having many contests and games. The kids like their lessons when they are in the form of games. We give out gold and silver stars for the winners of each competition. We even play volley ball. The students show much interest. Mae is showing them how to make beautiful Halloween posters.

"We had a big Halloween party. The posters were hung all around the schoolhouse. I was dressed up like the Devil. Everyone was afraid of me, even the elders of the village. We played many games such as ring numbers, sack race, bowling and blind man's bluff. We partied until 2 o'clock in the morning. Everyone had a grand time."

In November night school began. The students had to make up for days missed in the fall during berry picking and hunting and in the spring when many left early for fish camp. They taught sewing, basket making, sawing and played more games. Dad also had many natives, often 15 at a time, coming to school in the evening to have him interpret the news they heard of the ongoing war. Many came in spite of the disagreeably cold weather.

By November 14 there was an outbreak of measles in Anvik and in Holy Cross. In Shageluk the people, one by one, were afflicted with a bad intestinal flu. Dad administered medicine to all and by the end of November he was sick in bed. Dad: "I'm suffering from acute indigestion. Mae is teaching and the kids are misbehaving powerfully. She tends to me with a soft heart. I've been in bed for four days with agonizing pains. The mind is befuddled, the head aches, the eyes are sore and my whole body is in an uproar." By December 3, he improved and was again called out into the village to administer medication to others who had the flu. On December 14, Willy Newman asked Dad to handle the mail because his daughter Aggie had died. The next day the radio reported that it was Douglas Fairbanks' funeral. He was 56 years old. Only actors were admitted in to the Hollywood Chapel. Thousands of others attended outside on the chapel grounds.

In school, the children made Christmas decorations. The Christmas program was held on December 22. The kids spoke their pieces nicely. One of the villagers reported that the program was no good, but she attended in a total state of drunkenness, laughing as she complained. All who came received presents such as earrings, candy, oatmeal or beans.

By Christmas, Mom was ill, but she was able to make a fine dinner of roast moose, potatoes with the skins on, gravy, bread, butter, apple pie, ice cream, pears and coffee.

They sang songs, read from the Bible and opened a few gifts. Most of their Christmas gifts were still in the mail somewhere.

They tried to hold school between Christmas and New Year to make up for lost hours, but had to close because, according to Dad, "...intestinal flu is raging all over the country. Louis Deacon came from Holikachuk to get me. His wife is very ill. The trip was nice but cold. I stayed in the sled all the way. I spent the night at Frank Walker's place. Mrs. Deacon did not want an examination. Instead, I examined a young woman ill with T.B., hemorrhage and pending childbirth. The baby was normally located, but the mother was too weak to give birth.

"Now I had no way to get home. The store owner offered me either his three skinny dogs or his snowshoes. I left Holikachuk at 3:00 p.m. on the worst road imaginable, going through the trail on snowshoes with 255 pounds of supplies. I got here at 10:15 p.m. after a most trying trip. My feet were sore and the whole body was bad. I bought four flashlight batteries and used the flashlight all the way. That helped me. Otherwise

I went through the trail every so often. When I got here I was stiff all over."

Snowshoes and Sled

On the last day of 1939, Dad wrote, "Three people came to ask us to hold a dance, one came to buy chickens and I had to examine a baby who vomits all the time. It is snowing hard."

Chapter 6
1940

N ew Years Day, Monday. Dad: "The natives came this morning to ask for a dance. They want to use Rev. Chapman's church. We told them we have nothing to do with giving permission to do so. Tonight without permission all the natives are dancing and celebrating in Chapman's church!"

School began again after the holidays. Night school was also held to make up for lost hours. Dad taught for a day and a half when a young man named Walter came to get him to help deliver his first child. Dad: "I was there with four old witches, ladies. She was not ready yet to deliver so I slept on the table. The women slept on the floor in prone position. We all slept with our clothes on. I went home at 2:30 a.m. and slept until 8:30 a.m. After breakfast of coffee and pancakes I went back. This time there were eight old men and five old women in the place. All were going to work on young Violet. The men were coming and going, smoking and talking. The women were jabbering in their own language. [When a woman gives birth in the village, ropes are hung from the ceiling over the bed. The woman is in a squatting position and hangs on to the ropes to stabilize her.] Violet discarded the ropes and was seated on the floor the old fashioned way. The medicine man and the other bucks were starting to blow and make whistling noises while the women were holding Violet and bearing down, pushing on her abdomen with terrific force. The patient was howling. The men began to sing and dance.... such terror. Being outnumbered, I withdrew from the case at that point, promising to return if needed.

"The young husband called me back at 11:15 a.m. Mae taught for me. When I got there, only four old women remained. All the men had gone. I assured Violet, who by now was extremely nervous; that everything would be O.K. Nature must take her course. At 1:15 p.m. I sent for Mae and dismissed school. Violet needed someone calm and gentle. At the time of delivery, 4:15 p.m., all the old women hollered like nobody's business. Violet delivered her first, a girl, without a tear in the birth canal."

A week later, Dad heard that Violet was feeding her baby canned milk without mixing it with water. She and her mother were supplementing the baby's diet by giving it flour mixed with water. Rev. Chapman came down from Anvik at the end of January. Violet had her baby baptized. Dad was the godfather.

Along with other official duties, Mom was asked by the Juneau Office to take the census of Shageluk and other surrounding villages. She went to every home to read the questionnaire, hoping to get the appropriate response. She often complained that the job was difficult because of the language barrier. The natives also did not want anyone to know what they owned and how many children they had; it was nobody's business. Dad responded by saying, "It appears that some of these people do not want to strictly adhere to the truth."

While Mom was taking the census, Dad held meetings in connection with the Indian Reorganization Act. Dad: "Our second meeting was held February 13, at 4:00 p.m. We met for two hours. Eighteen people were present. I explained the by-laws of the act. All are in favor of setting up a proper government, so as to be able to borrow money to build their own store, a cooperative. All present wanted to have a police department." This was decided because it was difficult to depend on the U.S. Marshal to come to settle matters as he had so much territory to cover, often being hundreds of miles away. At present, the village had a male miscreant who was threatening to kill some of the women. Under the present system it was the duty of the village schoolmaster alone to settle disputes, domestic violence, divorce, theft, drunkenness, and cheating on game laws.

The Juneau Office was not only an entity for government business, it also engaged in the buying and selling of artifacts. Many of the village women made beautiful spruce root baskets. The Larsens often went around the village gathering the beautiful works of art. Dad and the basket makers agreed on a dollar amount and he kept meticulous notes as to the maker and the price. Together he and Mom carefully boxed large quantities of baskets, insured each box, and then sent them to the Juneau Office. They paid $4.00 for a large basket, $3.00 for the medium size and $2.00 for small baskets, trays and wall pockets. As soon as all were aware that the package was sent, it wasn't long before each person would come to the schoolhouse asking, "Where is my money? Haven't you gotten my check yet?" Finally when the checks arrived from Juneau, Dad went around the village disbursing the funds. The extra money was well received by each participant.

Spruceroot Tray

The mail arrived on March 20. The Larsens finally received their Christmas presents from the relatives in the United States. Mother would have expressed greater joy but she was suffering with a terrible toothache,

Spruceroot Hanging Basket

lying down often because the pain was severe. Dad was unwilling to work on the family's teeth in case he would make an error, so she made plans to go to Anvik to the person most capable in dentistry. Eli said he would make two trips for ten dollars. Mike said he would go for less. On March 27, Mom and Etola made the trip with Eli. There Rev. Chapman pulled Mom's tooth. Mike went to get them five days later. They arrived back at 10:00 p.m. For some reason, the trip made Etola very nervous. The following day Eli and Mike came to settle the dispute as to who was going to get what amount out of the ten dollars. Dad paid Eli $7.50 and Mike $2.50. Dad felt sorry for Mike and later gave him baking powder, peas, beans and figs.

Mom was quite ill in the latter half of October and all of November. She was very weak and had terrible pains at the pit of her stomach. Her temperature was high. Dad helped by doing the kitchen chores because she could do nothing. For the duration of her illness, she was given only juices to drink, especially grape juice, and water. At the end of November, she had a painful miscarriage with the placenta presenting itself first. With this ordeal over, she was back to work within a few days as if it had only been a bad dream.

During the year, Dad was preoccupied with the news of the war. His entire family was still in Norway. Excerpts from his diary show his worry:

January 24. "Heard Norse, Swedes and Finns are holding their own against the Russians."

February 18. "The English are lambasting the Norwegians for sea interference."

February 26. "The Russians shot down 19 Finnish airplanes."

April 10. "Germany walked into Norway last night. There is big fighting in Norway. The biggest battle in history was fought outside Bergen."

April 11. "I don't know what will happen if Germany doesn't give up..."

April 12. "Germany has moved to Oslo. Norway is trying to get them out. The English and the French are assisting.

April 21. "I stayed in bed a long time. I am spending a melancholy time. I'm sad as can be over Europe's war. I hope England and France win to save Norway."

April 22. "We have bad war news. There is great fighting in Norway."

April 30. "It looks as if all of Norway is being taken by the Germans. The English and French troops are trapped in the mountains."

May 1. "Germany is just bombing the poor Norwegians around Andalsnes and Namsos. A Red Cross nurse said it was awful how the Germans bombed the poor people. There were so many wounded that many had to take refuge in graveyards behind gravestones."

May 2. "I'm feeling so bum today. I'm studying but am so worried about Norway. It is rumored that the King of Norway has gone to Stockholm or London."

May 5. "The news was no good. The Germans just throw bombs all over trying to kill all of those attending church in Norway. King Haakon is still with his people ready to fight until the end."

May 9. "Hitler invaded Holland by parachutists jumping out of planes."

May 13." Holland has been cut in two. There is severe fighting in Belgium. England has a new fighting plane (The Super Marine Spit-Fire), the secret of which cannot be let out."

May 16. "The Germans were stopped in Belgium by the English and the French."

May 23. "I went to Holy Cross; Father Spills and Brother Hess are sympathetic of the Germans."

By November 27, Dad received a letter from his family in Norway, which was dated July 12, 1940. On December 12th he wrote, "I am sick in bed, ill at heart."

Chapter 7
1941

January 1, 1941, 1:00 a.m. Etola: "Happy New Year! We just had coffee and lefse. Now we are going to bed."

January 1, 1941, 7:00 a.m. "A bunch of people came over here this morning to wish us a Happy New Year. Gertie got bit by a dog. Mamma put iodine on it."

School started the following Monday, and Etola was anxious to start. She got the giggles in the classroom because Hamil tried to find New York in South Africa. There were not many students present that day. Many of the people had been drinking in Lower Village. When the parents stayed up half the night so did the children. The other students who were missing had been dancing all night in the Kashim. In the afternoon Dad treated a young man for bruises on his face. He was hit hard by his old father for carrying whiskey into the Kashim.

Violet came to get Dad. Her father-in-law Walter was very ill from drinking poisoned beer. He had been ill for three weeks before Dad was called to help. Walter was treated for three days before he died from uremic edema. He possibly also had tuberculosis. Dad gave Walter one of his old suits and suspenders for burial. He was also dressed in a cap, stockings, mittens, parka and moccasins—a full winter outfit. Etola noticed that people kept stuffing food into Walter's mouth so that he would have plenty to eat on his journey to the great beyond. Walter was buried four days after his passing. Many people came from Anvik and Holikachuk.

Dad: "Germany is breaking through the fog over England. This is the second year of war. The Italians have been driven back by the Greeks. Russia is buying much cotton and oil and is selling it to Germany." By January 22, the thought of war hit even closer. Dad received Soldier Registration Blanks in the mail. He sent word around the village that boys in a particular age group had to come to register for the army. Eight young men came. It was difficult to tell how old each one was because birth records were not readily available.

Friday, January 24, 1941. Etola: "Everybody has the flu in Holy Cross, Anvik and Holikachuk. We are getting it here too." One Sunday, Reverend Chapman and Gabriel held services. It was Mom's birthday, so all attending had coffee and cake after church. On Monday the flu started in Shageluk so Dad gave each of the kids a physic [laxative] and sent them home.

Monday, January 27, 1941. Dad: "I visited everyone in the village and gave out cc pills and aspirins. I worked for ten hours."

Tuesday, January 28, 1941. "I covered both Upper and Lower Village. Old Francis is pretty sick. Hunters and Old Rope and Martina are very ill. Shay at Lower Village is pretty sick and is spitting blood. Woodfords, Hunters and Old Francis have no wood. Maurice and I had to go back to Lower Village by dog team. We tipped over four times."

Wednesday, January 29, 1941. "Everybody has the flu. The natives are pounding on the walls and blowing for all they are worth to get rid of the evil spirits. I am on the go 14 hours a day. Mae and Etola are also ill with headaches, bone aches, and muscle aches." Etola: "Mamma and I don't feel very good. Our eyes hurt when we try to read so we have to go to sleep."

Sunday, February 2, 1941. Dad: "I am sick in bed with the flu. It is thirty degrees below and Old Francis has no wood today." Etola: "Mamma's eyes were worse. Even so she got up and worked. I got up too, but I didn't feel so good towards evening."

Monday, February 3, 1941. Etola: "There is no school today either. Martha, Hoover and Roxcenia came to school when we were in bed, but I told them there will be no school until tomorrow so we are sure they are all well."

Tuesday, February 4, 1941. Etola: "At last we had school."

Wednesday, February 7, 1941. Dad: "It is dripping terribly in the schoolhouse. It is wet all over. The flu is still raging. George died from the flu and so did two of Andrew's kids."

February 8, 1941. "I don't feel good. I'm very nervous because of lack of sleep."

By the end of February the flu had made its rounds and the village was back to the normal routine.

March 5, 1941 – *"Sweet Forty."* Dad allowed all the little kids in the school to spank him. They held a birthday party in the afternoon. Dad went for a long walk in the woods. He ended up in the Indian graveyard. It was considered disrespectful to disturb the final resting place of the ancestors, but because he was from a different culture, he looked inside the grave houses built over the deceased noting the contents. He walked back home to report his findings to the family. He saw rusty guns, beads, pans, bows and arrows, weasel skins, snow shoes, accordions and bowls, which, at burial, had contained food. This news piqued Etola's curiosity. Now she, too, felt she could go exploring in the graveyards. At the end of March she took part of a skull out of a small grave, thinking it was part of a bowl. The natives warned, "If anyone looks at the skull he will become very ill." (March 24, 1941)

Death in the village was frequent and mostly related to tuberculosis, which afflicted the young and the old.

Wednesday, April 2, 1941. Mom: "Old Francis died. Now there is no more medicine man." Dad: "Violet's baby apparently has a slight paralysis. Her bowels are very hard and inactive.

Sunday, April 13, 1941. "Violet's baby is pretty ill. They gave her too much candy. Her mouth is very white."

April 14, 1941. "Violet's baby died this morning at 5:00 a.m. She had tuberculosis and was fed the wrong food. They fed her too much while she was ill."

April 23, 1941. "No school—all to fish camp."

Mom realized for a month that she was pregnant again. She and Dad agreed that it would be best for her and Etola to return to Mandan, North Dakota, for the birth of the baby. With the recent memory of the last miscarriage and the thought of seeing her family, she readily packed her bags. Dad also felt it was best for the children to be born in the United States so that we did not have to apply for US citizenship, as he did, at a later date. Mom and Etola left by plane for the outside on Friday, April 25, at 12:30 p.m. There were many villagers at the plane to say goodbye.

Dad was on his own for the next seven months. He visited often around the village but certainly felt his closest friends were Matilda and her husband, John Woodford. He cooked for himself as best he knew how. His favorite meal was two sandwiches made of cheese, sausage, garlic and onions. Each time he ate this, he became awfully sick. "I shook like a leaf." Then he decided to work hard, eat only one meal per day and drink a lot of juice and lemon water. With this routine he felt better. Perhaps his nervousness was more attributable to not having Mom and Etola there. The news of the war was not helpful to his state of mind.

Thursday, May 1, 1941. "Russia is on the verge of war. Turkey leans toward the Axis. The U.S. is closer to war."

Saturday, May 3, 1941. "The old cat is trying to catch birds. I guess I shall have to shoot her. She's always cranky. I sure did work today – cleaned the whole house, had all the clothing out, shook them and brushed them, washed the floors, cleaned the toilets, cleaned the washroom from one end to the other, cleaned all barrels and filled them full of ice. I didn't eat all day long and felt very peppy. I carried in heavy ice chunks and fed the two cats. I dusted and aired everything. Then I heated water, took a bath and ate a full bowl of tomatoes."

Monday, May 12, 1941. "I am beginning to feel better. Matilda caught some fish for the pussies. Matilda's girls Celene and Agnes came over and helped to take all the eyes off the potatoes in the cellar for which I gave them candy."

Wednesday, May 14, 1941. "Went down to Woodford's. Matilda is catching fish. Woodford told me about Devil's Lake, which is down by Charles Lehman's place. He told me of the many kinds of animals in the lake. No one dares go into that lake right by Bonezela Slough or a little below Swiftwater. He told me about Peter Matthews and the fact that he saw the Devil and a little man dressed in caribou clothes over on the big mountains. The man said nothing but disappeared when spoken to. His father was a medicine man and told about many wars. The victors of the wars ate many human eyes and became great runners and jumpers. There were people who had been starving for fish for 600 days and then died. Some ate each other. These people are very superstitious."

May 17th is Norwegian Independence Day. Dad: "I wonder if anyone in Norway is celebrating? I guess not."

He listened to the war news, which claimed the US was getting closer to war. He was nervous. The days seemed long and he had not done any personal study since Mom and Etola left. The ice was off the river, so he and Lee prepared to go muskrat hunting. Before they left, Dad packed and insured five sacks of fur for Leo, 13 beaver and $1,500 worth of muskrats, then fed two fish to the cats.

May 21, 1941. Dad: "We rowed 16 miles from Shageluk, past Eli's fish camp, where he left his dog to starve. We went ashore and gave the dog one muskrat. We caught no more rats today. There are many ducks, which the natives are shooting just for sport. We spent a very cold night at Eli's camp. Lee shot three muskrats in the lake nearby. I found a very long pole and fished them out of the water. Lee wanted to stay overnight again at Eli's fish camp, but I wanted to go home. We brought Eli's dog with us back to Shageluk and arrived at 2:30 a.m. On the way, the dog ate another muskrat. I asked Eli why he left his dog at the camp to starve. He said the dog ran after a moose and he couldn't catch him, but promised to take care of it from now on."

May 27, 1941. Dad: "Roosevelt is perhaps plunging the country into war. The 'British Hood' was in place to torpedo the German ship, the 'Bismarck'. Instead it was bombed by the Americans, with a plane made in Danish waters."

Wednesday, June 4, 1941. Dad: "The 'Sea Wolf' came at 12:10 a.m. 15 cords of the government birch wood came. I packed a big box of baskets and insured them for $50.00, collected and helped make out game reports, and tagged game for Matilda. She is to be left in charge of feeding the pussies and loaning government tools. The boat left at 7:30 p.m."

Thursday, June 5, 1941. "I slept for three hours on the bunk and feel fine. We arrived at Holy Cross at 9:30 a.m. I visited and collected white tags for the game commissioner. Frank Walker held a dance Friday night. I danced a little, but played my violin most of the night. Mass was held on Saturday morning. I went but was very sleepy."

On Monday, Father Spills and Brother Laird worked on Dad's newly purchased used boat. Dad: "I borrowed some tools, bought a case of gas and some oil, and away I went to Shageluk at 12:30 a.m. I sailed all night and got home at 9:30 in the morning. The boat was pretty good. All the natives were out looking when I came in. The 'Sea Wolf' came in at 5:30 p.m. and unloaded all my freight by the schoolhouse. I carried all of it into the school and most everything arrived safely.

Friday, June 13, 1941. "I was watering the garden when Joseph came by. He wants to buy my boat for $260.00."

Sunday, June 15, 1941. "I'm going to Holikachuk. My boat is too small for the engine. The engine runs pretty good, but it took five gallons of gas and eight hours to get there."

Monday, June 16, 1941. "I'm having much trouble with the engine. I got home in five hours at 5:00 a.m., went to bed at 7:00 a.m. and got up at 1:00 p.m. When I got down to the boat my engine was burned up. I don't know what happened. Perhaps the canvas caught on fire. Lee is going to rebuild it for $35.00. It was a poorly built boat in the first place."

June 19, 1941. "Yesterday Matilda was here helping me wash clothes. I put up a rope and helped her all through the washing. Today she is here folding clothes. I gave her $3.50 worth of goods, twenty pounds of flour, nine cans of milk and five cans of soup. Woodford was here for medicine for TB. I know I have ulcers of the stomach. Woodford had a bowl of my beef-vegetable soup and a glass of milk. I was careful to wash his dishes in very hot water and Clorox. Lee is fixing my boat. He came to get two more boards, a half gallon of paint and oakum for caulking. I went to see how he was doing and got eaten up by mosquitoes.

June 21, 1941. Dad: "Today is the longest day of the year. I worked on annual government reports until 12:30 in the morning. I helped Mike make out an order for stuff from Sears & Roebuck. Elizabeth was here ironing. I gave her one dollar. Roxcenia was here to see how Elizabeth was doing. Elizabeth was never here alone at any time, so the girls in the village have nothing to talk about. The whole tribe of Indians was here today."

June 24, 1941. "I am doing no personal study. I try to get plenty of sleep at night but am unable. I painted my boat engine, and then Matilda came over for a beer that I found on the sidewalk close to the school. Lee is not such a bad boat builder. The girls around the village are still talking. I went over to Matilda to give her a beer that I found by the boat landing. Somebody is leaving the booze all over. I painted the boat until 9:30 in the evening, then went over to visit Woodford."

At the end of June, Dad and Lee launched the boat. The propeller was too large and was changed to a smaller one. The boat itself leaked like a sieve. They pulled it out of the water, recaulked the seams with oakum and repainted it. They launched it again when the paint dried. Dad spent the first two weeks of July pumping water out of the boat on a daily basis. He was so frustrated with it, claiming that no one in the whole village knew a thing about boats. He let the boat repairs go by the wayside for a while because there was a matter of greater concern needing his attention.

Edward Matthews

Saturday, July 19, 1941. "I treated Edward for insomnia."

July 21, 1941. "Now Edward has gone completely crazy. Eli and Riley went over to Holy Cross with a letter for Father Menager. He is to broadcast for the US Marshal to come. I'm getting no sleep because I have to see Edward all the time."

July 24, 1941. "I have had no sleep. Edward jumped into the river and almost drowned. He tore his shirt off and fought me when I came. I had to apply artificial respiration and worked on him all night. I made handcuffs out of leather and he tried to pull himself loose. He is manged. It's raining and this whole village is berserk. There is no plane coming with help. Fairbanks is full of dirty politicians. They are crooked boys – all of them. Reverend Chapman came. I am very tired, but made supper for him, then went back on duty with Edward until 1:30 a.m."

July 25, 1941. "I fixed breakfast for Reverend Chapman. He held a church service in the school with very few attending while I was on duty with Edward. He is gradually getting unmanageable. I paid Ralph fifty cents to take me to Holy Cross to see if help was coming. We left at 2:15 p.m. The boat almost swamped twice through the terrible storm and heavy rain. We arrived at Railroad City at 10:15 p.m. and went to Lattin's. He was already in bed but got up to cook some coffee for us. We slept on the floor."

July 26, 1941. "The storm is still raging. We had a hard time getting across the Yukon. At the Holy Cross Mission, Father Spills got on the radio at 2:30, 3:00, and 4:00 p.m. We cannot seem to get a message through the Signal Corps at Flat or Anchorage. The Marshal arrived by boat late in the evening. We left Holy Cross at 10:45 p.m. It is still somewhat stormy."

Sunday, July 27, 1941. "We arrived back to Shageluk at 8:15 a.m. and went directly to Edward. He was almost passed out. By examination, his heart is weak. He is seriously ill—respiration 40, temperature 104 and pulse 148. We are taking Edward by boat up the Innoko River. The weather is fair and the boat is going good. I requested to go along to take care of the patient and as a government witness. We left Shageluk at 10:45 a.m. At 7:40 p.m. we are at Thompson Slough, close to the mouth of Yukon. I signed a complaint for Edward's commitment."

July 28, 1941. "We are en route up the Yukon. It seems that Edward has improved somewhat since we got him. I am giving him salt water and he is sleeping a little. At 8:00 p.m., two miles from Kaltag, Edward died from tubercular meninges."

July 29, 1941. "We arrived at Nulato at 3:30 a.m. Some of Edward's relatives are here. They feel so sorry about his departure. We are all making arrangements for Edward's burial."

July 31, 1941. "Father Beau officiated for Edward's funeral. It was very nice. He was buried three feet into the ground. I made out a death certificate and signed it 'Herman L. Larsen, M.D.' "

While at Nulato, Dad decided not to return to Shageluk. He needed to get away from the village for a while. He boarded the 'Steamer Nenana' on August 6 at 10:00 a.m. and arrived in Fairbanks after six days of travel on the Yukon. There he went to the dentist to have a big molar pulled and all his teeth cleaned and x-rayed for $5.00. He and a friend, Father Mac, walked to the airfield and back. Dad visited the Army base noting "all the girls are crazy about army officers." He toured the Goldstream Mining Company, and then went to the doctor for a check-up. The doctor felt he was all right to spend another season in the bush. Fairbanks was impressive and beautiful with a nice university and much potential for farming in the outlying area. After an enjoyable break, Dad returned to Shageluk on August 23.

On August 27, he went to Holikachuk on official business to get the wood purchase orders fixed. He had trouble with his boat motor; it didn't seem to get gas. On his way back the motor stopped right out of Shageluk. He couldn't restart it and rowed the rest of the way home.

School started on Tuesday, September 2. The war news reported, "USA is giving stern warning to Japan to keep its hands off the Pacific."

September 11, 1941. "President Roosevelt made it clear that any German ships will be shot down without warning if they show no restraint."

September 12, 1941. "I taught all day, then went to Lower Village on medical calls—heart trouble, drinking, boils and rheumatism. My engine blew up completely running back from Lower Village. I had to leave it half way. Paul came up from Holy Cross and towed my boat back. The kids broke off the oar locks. I shall not use it anymore. Now Lee wants to buy my boat for fifty dollars."

Dad did not enjoy being alone so long and often wished that Mom would return. He felt nervous and was often ill. November 17, he received one of Mom's letters written in the summer. The news in her letter was very destructive. Dad wrote, "This year has been the worst in my personal history. It has cost me more money, damaged my studying and set me back thirty years. My married life is a complete failure. Then the kid Etola had to fill up on candies and white sugar until diabetes got her. Some life!" The next day he wrote that Matilda had been with several different men throughout the summer.

By Thanksgiving, November 20, Dad heard that his family would arrive in Anchorage on November 23. The mail plane came on November 24. Dad: "A Mr. Herbert Hilscher, Editor of *Alaskan Life*, stepped off the plane for a while. He is a very nice and interesting fellow. He told me about a man in Seward who drenched a fire with kerosene only to have it explode and burn down half the town. The army had to put up emergency camps to feed the women and children. Hilscher has written articles for the *Saturday Evening Post*. He claims five *Post* stories make a writer. Hilscher has also been in China. He knows George Marshall of *Collier's* magazine. He is writing a story for *Collier's* called 'Money on Ice'. This is a story about building an air field at Bethel, Alaska with Coolidge, Hoover and other presidents. The Eskimos are getting $50.00-$60.00 per week for helping in the construction of this field and have no idea what to do with all this money."

Dad watched for the plane daily. Finally on Sunday, November 30, a bush pilot, Morgan Davies, came with the family. Etola brought many gifts to give to the natives who came to greet them. In Mom's arms was the newest member of the family. Dad was presented with a baby girl named Yvonne. She was born in Mandan, North Dakota, on October 16 at 6:25 p.m. Etola was so thrilled to have a little sister. Dad thought she was cute.

With the family back together, Dad's life returned to normal, except for the news of the war and the presence of a new illness in the village.

December 8, 1941. Dad: "I examined all the kids and found two cases of scarletina. School will be closed for one week to see if an epidemic can be avoided. The US declared war on Japan at 1:30 p.m. It was a unanimous decision in both houses except that one Montana congressman, who had voted against the 1917 war, voted 'No' with tears in his eyes.[Jeanette Rankin, a Montana congresswoman who supported the cause of peace throughout her life, was the only member of Congress to oppose the declaration of war on Japan.] Charles Lindbergh declared that he is now 100% American, no matter how much he disagreed with the government up to this time. Japan attacked the US and its possessions, Hawaii and then the Philippines without warning."

December 18, 1941. "Russia is advancing on all fronts. England bombed heavily north of France. [The coast island of Martinique was taken over by the USA.] The Japanese are losing on all fronts."

Wednesday, December 24, 1941. Dad: "We had a lot of visitors all day, then had our own Christmas program. It was nice. I got a diary from Mae and a book of short stories from my darling Etola. Earlier today one of the men made a remark to Etola, 'Why don't you get your own dogs so we don't have to haul you around all the time?' Pretty nice, eh? After treating their sickness and being up with them half the night—sometimes all night—these are some damn people! Why Uncle Sam should try to educate these people is more than I can see."

Wednesday, December 31, 1941. "There is heavy fighting this last day of 1941. Winston Churchill is in Washington. All of the natives in the village are preparing for some pagan dance."

Chapter 8
1942

Thursday, January 1, 1942. Dad: "War! War! War! Our beloved country is at war. President Roosevelt and Winston Churchill are in church together in Washington praying for world peace. Manila has fallen to the Japs."

Throughout the remainder of January the natives held a dance at the Kashim that was to last for five weeks. Dad was intolerant of the ceremonial dance because it interfered with the cooperation of the students in school. Everyone was supposed to stay up all night in the Kashim. The students, having lost so much sleep, were not receptive to learning. Regarding this issue he wrote, "I despise teaching." He was critical of the Director of Education in Washington and critical of the entire idea of having an Alaskan Native Service. Later he seemed to explain the true reason for his criticism, "I am teaching, but I feel terribly rotten. The good wife is doing her best, but sometimes she doesn't get after Etola to help. However, they don't understand what it means to be sick. My nerves are awful. I can't stand anything."

During the second week of the dance, Father Spills came from Holy Cross. He tried to hold church services but very few attended. He spoke against the celebration in the Kashim, saying it was the Devil's way of fooling people. His message fell on deaf ears.

When the dance ended in the Kashim, most of the villagers became ill with the flu. School attendance had been poor during the last five-week period, but now it was worse. Dad felt the illness spread quickly because the people did not know how to keep clean. By Friday, February 13, another ceremony was held in the Kashim. This time it was the mask dance. This dance is performed to increase the number of animals that are of economic importance to the natives. It is also important because the people thoroughly enjoy it and a feast is held where people can bring gifts to obtain privilege and prestige. (Cornelius Osgood, "Ingalik Social Culture," Yale University Press, 1958, p.81)

In spite of the terrible snow storm, many people came from other villages. The natives thought it was the greatest dance ever held in Shageluk. The mask dance ended by early Tuesday morning. Then most everyone became ill with bad colds.

Saturday, February 21, 1942. "The Star plane came for the army boys. Only Eli had to go from Shageluk. All the men saw him off while the women were standing at a distance. The Japs are going strong."

Sunday, March 1, 1942. "The mail came and I got a raise in salary. It is a very nice day. Eli came back on the plane, because he did not pass his physical for the army. He has heart trouble."

Tuesday, March 3, 1942. "I am teaching. Some of the kids are out trapping, but things in school are going pretty good. The weather is nice, but the news in the village is bad. Matilda had baby twins, but one died. It is said they are light. Woodford is part Russian.

Thursday, March 5, 1942. "It is my birthday. We are having a party in school for the kids with cake for everyone."

Sunday, March 8, 1942. "I took a bath and studied. It is a beautiful day. I went to visit Matilda. The baby looks real Indian. Some said it was white. Gossip."

The spring of 1942 was much the same as the previous year. School attendance increased as the weather moderated. Dad was quite pleased that the children were learning at a more rapid pace. Etola loved school and was very helpful with her little sister, Yvonne. As an art project, she beaded flowers to sew onto Yvonne's tiny moccasins. Mom tagged many beaver again along with her other household duties. Dad listened to the war news as often as possible. The American-Japanese war did not effect his psyche as much as when there was fighting on or near his home territory. By April 30 many of the students were at fish camp so school ended on a snowy day.

Dorothy and Helena Workman, Etola and Yvonne Larsen

Yvonne wearing mocassins made by Dora Workman, Etola beaded them

Sunday, May 3, 1942. "It is a quiet day. Martha and Lillian came over to play with Etola. They had fun wrestling. We made certain both girls had plenty to eat before they left this evening at 11:30 p.m."

May 13, 1942. "The ice on the Innoko is still intact but is beginning to move. It looks like a late spring, but the birds are already singing. Many people are building swallow houses."

May 19, 1942. "The river is

coming up high. The Yukon ice is still running with a few drift logs coming down. The Germans are fighting desperately at Karkov and Rostov in the Donets River Basin. The Japanese ships are cruising in New Guinea and the Royal Air Force is hammering France."

With the mosquitoes out in full force, gardening resumed in the village. Dad went around preaching to everyone to increase their food supply by diligently hoeing weeds and keeping the gardens watered. There was no shortage of seeds or seedlings, which were given out freely by the Holy Cross Mission.

By June 19, it was 80 degrees in the shade. Dad put screen windows on the schoolhouse to take advantage of the cool night air. He carried out the toilets, chopped wood and battled with the mosquitoes. In the larger battle he heard, "The Germans are fighting hard but so are the American bombers. The Japs settled on the Aleutian Islands but cannot be driven out because of dense fog. Tobruk fell, Alexandria is in great danger, Sevastopol is falling and Clara is drunk."

July 8, 1942. "Mom is again very ill. She has her same old trouble. Etola is helping by making breakfast and cleaning the house. She is tough and good."

July 9, 1942. "Mae is pretty sick. She vomits all the time. Her liver is not good, so I put her on a fast. She has lost many pounds."

July 13, 1942. "Mae is still very ill. Etola is still helping with the household chores."

July 14, 1942. "Mae is seriously ill. She is still fasting and vomiting nothing but yellow stuff. Many people have heard of her illness and are coming to see us."

July 16, 1942. "Mae did not sleep comfortably. She is so ill in spite of fasting for 15 days."

July 17, 1942. "I am trying hard to get a plane for Mae, but the plane does not come. My whole time is devoted to Mae and the mail. The people seem to be quite concerned. Woodford says he is praying."

July 18, 1942. "There is still no plane. Mae, Etola and Yvonne are already packed up for the trip outside. I am attending to Mae at all times. She has lost thirty pounds, is now 70 pounds and is nothing but a skeleton."

July 19, 1942." No plane comes. Mae is seriously ill. I sent Roland to Holy Cross with a telegram to get a plane. He returned. There is no change in Mae as of yet."

July 20, 1942. "Mae is a little better today. There are some signs of improvement."

July 21, 1942. "Today Mae was able to drink a part of a glass of milk. She has lost so much sleep."

July 22, 1942. "Etola is doing all the cooking. I worked out in the garden. Mae is better."

July 24, 1942. "I got up and made breakfast. I tended to Mae. She is still pretty sick, but it looks like she is over the hardest part."

July 25, 1942. "Ralph was here from down river. He got Etola out of bed and away from baby Yvonne at 4:00 o'clock in the morning. When Etola came home I gave her an awful licking."

Sunday, July 26, 1942. "It looks like rain. The weeds are growing sky high. Mae is somewhat better. A miscarriage has set in. She possibly also has some T.B. The natives were quite concerned."

July 28, 1942." Mae is much better, but now there are rumors of measles around the country. It is the dreaded kind from which many die."

Dad was indeed on the run for the next month treating all afflicted with measles. Those who had been fishing in other areas returned home and brought the disease with them. Parker lost his wife and baby. Flora died. Dad encouraged the people to be careful, but the measles spread quickly and furiously. He borrowed a boat and went to fish camps, fur camps, Anvik and Holikachuk treating the ill. The measles were raging. The Larsen family was somehow spared from the disease but many others, young and old, died. At the end of August, Dad was summoned to treat Matilda's mother.

August 24, 1942. Dad: "It is raining and raining. At 1:45 this morning I was awakened to attend to Old Gramma Cecilia. She is very ill and has been agitated all night. I rubbed her down with Vick's and gave her a potassium bromide pill to settle her nervousness. She eats and chews tobacco in spite of orders to the contrary."

Three days later Old Cecilia died from pleuritis and old age complications. Her body was taken in through the door of the Kashim and after

Mildred Workman, Ida, Raymond and Rolland Dutchman at Flora's Grave

the appropriate burial ceremony was removed through the window. A dead body cannot go back where it came from because this would disturb the spirit's journey to its final home. She was buried at 9:00 a.m.

For the past few weeks Matilda's husband had been spitting quite a bit of blood related to his tuberculosis. Dad was again called on Saturday, September 5, 1942. "I was on duty with Woodford until 2:00 a.m. He is very ill. I came home and went to bed at 3 in the morning. I went back to see him at 11:00 a.m. I worked on his heart with a hot cloth. He died at 1:30 Sunday morning. I gave Matilda a shirt and new pants for Woodford to wear for the funeral. I also gave her lumber to build a coffin."

Dad was sad when Woodford passed away. They had been friends. Woodford sawed many cords of wood for the schoolhouse. He was a very skilled craftsman and had made a beautiful high chair for Yvonne. Now Matilda, the only adult remaining in her household, had to work harder to feed her children. She not only cleaned the medical dispensary but took her husband's place sawing and hauling wood for the schoolhouse.

It was berry picking season when school began, so of course many of the students were missing. Etola picked berries with the natives on the weekend so that she would not miss school. Yvonne crawled around the classroom while Mom assumed the teaching duties. Dad had to make several boat trips to Holy Cross to haul shipments of groceries and government supplies.

Wednesday, October 14, 1942. Dad: "I have been teaching all day long. Jonas and I are getting ready to go to Holikachuk to hunt moose. We are off. We got a little way up the river and Mae's gun fell in. It is lost."

Jonas and Young Victor Rock and Cleo Fairbanks

October 16, 1942. "The last two nights have been terrible. Last night we went through thick ice the entire way to get home. The boat got all cut up and leaked badly. When I got home I went straight to bed and stayed there all day to get warm. It was horridly cold. The trip was terrible."

Monday, November 2, 1942. "Yvonne is starting to walk. There are mumps all over the village. Mae has the mumps. There is no school today because no one came. Etola is out visiting in the village. The river is trying to freeze, but the constant thawing is breaking it open again."

On November 20, Etola got the mumps along with most of the people in Lower Village. The next day Dad heard there had been a few cases of diphtheria in Holy Cross. The natives came to express their fear of all these strange diseases.

Thursday, November 26, 1942. "It is Thanksgiving Day. It is nice and clear and only 8 degrees below zero. There is no mail plane. We had delicious fish, buns, baked potatoes, pie and coffee for dinner. Yvonne ate plenty. She is so cute. Friday Etola and I went out hunting. We saw ptarmigan, mink and weasel tracks. Etola is boiling her traps. We went to the river to put up the American flag for the airplane."

November 28, 1942. "Etola and I went out to set traps for mink in the afternoon. Then we went visiting in the village to see how everyone is getting along. The plane never comes. We don't know what is wrong."

The mail plane did not come until December 20. Dad thought that Shageluk had been forgotten.

Dad borrowed Michael's dog sled to get a tree for the Christmas program. With the tree in the sled, the dogs took off for home. They went too fast, so many of the branches tore off the tree. The program was held on the evening of December 23 with a fairly limbless tree proudly displayed in front of the classroom. Dad played the part of Santa Claus. The children performed nicely and were so proud and happy. Quite a few people from Shageluk and Holikachuk attended and all had a grand Christmas celebration.

Dog Sled and Team

Chapter 9
1943 - OUR DARLING

Friday, January 1, 1943. Dad: "The war conditions are looking much better for the United Nations. I am feeling fine with less eating and drinking great amounts of water."

January 2, 1943. "We are having warm weather. It is raining. Manila has fallen to the Japs. Hitler is on his downward stretch, so his road to fame is reversing to disaster. The plane does not come to get the army recruits. They are supposed to go to Bethel for a physical examination."

Dad got up early each morning to exercise, then went out to chop wood, carry gas, empty toilets and the slop buckets. He found that his health improved when he exercised and worked hard. When he felt better, his temper flew less readily and the students took a greater interest in school.

January 5, 1943. "It is 42 degrees below zero. The attendance is pretty good. We had sewing, which Mae is teaching, and shop. The students are doing very well in both. We put up the drill and worked on building a forge. We didn't have any metal for the legs of the forge, so we made them out of wood. There is still no plane to pick up the army recruits."

January 9, 1943. "Bella started having her baby last night at midnight. Mae went over there at 9 o'clock this morning. Bella didn't want me there. She is having trouble with the afterbirth. Mae applied ice to her abdomen, and then injected 1 c.c. of petuatrin into her arm. That worked some, but I believe it is the ice that did the trick. The placenta came late this evening."

January 18, 1943. "Mae is teaching. I am feeling tough again. Yvonne can say 'up'. She has started to crawl up on chairs and is so cute now. I must begin exercising again. I will quit drinking coffee. Matilda is over here working."

January 26, 1943. "It is a great day. It is somewhat warm and it's Mae's 33rd birthday. The Germans are losing. President Roosevelt just got back from Africa, where he was with Winston Churchill and the great general, working on further war strategy. The army boys from Shageluk and from Holy Cross are here for a check-up. Most of them are O.K."

Saturday, January 30, 1943. "It is dripping in the schoolhouse just like an ocean. Yesterday we had a big party for the kids. Matilda is here working and chewing tobacco. Hitler did not deliver his own speech – Goering and Goebbels did. Bombs dropped over Berlin while they spoke. They promised a fearful retaliation. I bought 60 pounds of moose meat from Eli for $9.00."

February 1, 1943. "The kids are infested with lice and the school is like a lake. It drips and drips. I broadcast to get social welfare for Matilda. It should help her."

February 5, 1943. "The mail plane came from McGrath. Miss Anderson, the nurse, came along on the plane. We had only one delivery of mail in January. Schultz, the bush pilot is in really good humor now."

February 7, 1943. "The mail plane returned from down river. The postal inspector, George, Dennis and Schultz came for coffee. George asked if I was an ex-preacher."

February 8, 1943. "I taught and had shop. The kids are a little tough, but they are O.K. with me. The school building is a terrible wet mess. It is raining all the time."

Sunday, February 14, 1943. "I decided I had to go to Anvik. I got Mike's dogs. They were pretty slow. One of them bit me. I got to Anvik at 10:00 p.m."

February 16, 1943. "I visited with many around the village. There was a big dance tonight. I danced until midnight, then went to bed."

February 17, 1943. "I got up to get ready for the trip home. Bertha was at the dance, so she will go home with me. We hooked up the eleven dogs and got on the trail. The trail was really tough. The lead dog was very slow but I got some good exercise. We got home at 8:00 p.m. We found there will be a dance in Shageluk on Friday evening."

February 19, 1943. "Many people came for the dance. It was really fun. There was some drinking and fighting, but we had a swell time until 3:30 this morning. Eli brought candy for everyone."

Sunday, February 21, 1943. "The Germans are making a big drive in Tunisia. The Americans lost heavily."

Friday, February 26, 1943. "Yesterday I made a medical call to see a small girl in the village. She has yellow jaundice [hepatitis]. Today she is here for an examination and is much better."

February 28, 1943. "It is a beautiful day. We have not had any mail for almost a month. Mae and Etola went out for a long walk. Yvonne woke up and I am taking care of her while listening to evangelist Charles Fuller."

Etola with Fred and Martha Howard

Etola "arming" Yvonne

March 1, 1943. "There are some students in school, but most have gone away for beaver."

March 4, 1943. "There was great excitement in school today. Matilda came with Celene in a sled. I had to break the sled apart to get her loose. Celene didn't want to come to school today because she and her sister Agnes don't get enough to eat. We fed them."

March 9, 1943. "The troops of the United Nations are on the offensive. There has been trouble with Ambassador Admiral Stanley, because he is so outspoken. There is no plane for mail."

March 14, 1943. "It is another fine day, but we still have no mail. We don't know what has happened to the mailman. It has become cold and now we have the stomach flu again. I don't seem to care about school. The kids are a little wild."

March 20, 1943. "The mail finally came. He left much mail at McGrath so he will get it and fly back soon."

March 24, 1943. "Etola is not feeling very good. It looks as if she is getting this sickness—jaundice."

Thursday, March 25, 1943. "Etola is beginning to get very ill. I gave her insulin injections. The acetone acidosis is getting worse. I have been up all night."

Friday, March 26, 1943. "I was treating Etola all day. There is nobody to talk to. It's been a terrible day. Etola passed on to her Saviour very quietly and peacefully at 5:30 p.m."

Saturday, March 27, 1943. "We tried to fix up Etola. Mother fixed her tenderly and lovingly as always, but how tough!"

Sunday, March 28, 1943. "The natives are here. Jonas and Roland are making a coffin for our darling. The natives are coming and going."

March 29, 1943. "Etola is put in a box ready to go to Rev. Chapman in Anvik. Gachidle is taking her over by dog team. It is so cold. This is a tough life!"

Mother then sat down to write a letter to her sister Emma, the most difficult letter of her life.

Shageluk, Alaska

March 29, 1943

Dear Emma,

I don't know how to write you—it's the worst thing I could ever do at this time as we have had an awful loss…

Our darling Etola has gone home to live with Jesus on March 26 at 5:30 pm. She came down with some sort of liver trouble that's been going around and acidosis set in so fast that nothing we did helped. She went into a coma and went to sleep for eternity. Oh, I thought we would go crazy.

The missionary nurse came over to help us with the funeral, etc. She sure has been wonderful. She held a little sermon and prayed. The natives took it sort of hard. A native here took the coffin over to Anvik for burial by dog team. She will be buried from the church on Wed. The cemetery is in a very pretty place on the mountain side. Both white people and natives are there.

I think God took Etola to keep her out of sorrow and this terrible world. She was just too wonderful to be in this world. Herman is writing Momma. I can't seem to say the right thing as telling this grief to my mother is such an effort but you explain [everything] to her. Vonnie is such a darling that I hope she can fill the empty spot in our life and if the Lord is willing Vonnie will have a sister or buddy in July. We hope it's a girl to help take Etola's place. Etola always said she hoped she would die before I did and she got her wish.

The nurse has been such a comfort and sister to us that I dread seeing her go back. But as soon as we can travel we will go to Anvik—leaving Shageluk for good and stay there for the first boat. We are not having any more school. Herman couldn't stand to teach. We sent [a] telegram to Juneau. We expect [an] answer soon. They just have to give us a good job or we stay out of the service.

Hoping this letter will not upset you too much. Things always happen for the best. We had too big plans, I guess.

Lovingly,
Mae and Herman

March 30, 1943. Dad: "The mail returned early. Brother Feltes came up from Holy Cross. We got some letters of condolence. Tagging is on now."

March 31, 1943. "There is so much work to do with these natives, helping them with skins, tags and orders."

April 1, 1943. "I am very sad. There are too many things to remind me of Etola. I'm working on reports but I feel far from good. Many people are here for help with beaver tagging and social welfare work."

Friday, April 2, 1943. "It's a nice day, but I am very sad—horribly sad. I'm working on reports but it's awfully hard to do. People are coming here for help at all times. The sun is higher and the days are longer."

Saturday, April 3, 1943. "It's a beautiful day. I worked on reports all day. Marcia was here for a long time trying to console us. I gave her cod liver oil. Most of the villagers are out trapping."

On Thursday, April 15, everyone in Shageluk was awakened by a terrible earthquake. The school building was just shaking. Dad went around the village to see if everyone was O.K. The earthquake shook the village again at 12:20 p.m. It did not cause much damage but all were frightened and made aware of the power of the earth.

Saturday, April 17, 1943. "The people had a meeting to retain us but we are not staying. There is too much sadness here. I made out an application to teach at Eklutna."

Roland got the wood contract for the following year for 20 cords of wood. He had been so kind to the Larsens in their time of grief by building Etola's coffin. Gachidle came to have his tooth fixed. Dad paid him then for taking Etola's body by dog team to Rev. Chapman in Anvik. Mom and Dad did not want a four day long native ceremony in the Kashim for their daughter as was suggested by some in the village. They chose to have her burial service at the Episcopalian Church with Rev. Chapman officiating.

The flu hit Shageluk again. Dad was well occupied giving out medication day and night to all who were afflicted.

April 30, 1943. "All are sick yet. This is a regular influenza epidemic. First we had jaundice, now we have influenza. It is a terrible sickness. Yvonne is very ill. She requires constant care."

Yvonne improved throughout the week and by May 13; Mom had her out all day while preparing the garden for planting.

By May 16, Sunday, Mom and Dad started to sell many of their belongings. They took inventory of all government supplies, cleaned, completed the annual reports and tagged beaver. Dad felt that Mom seemed to be O.K., so he decided to make one last trip to Holy Cross.

Tuesday, May 18, 1943. "I left for Holy Cross traveling through ice and cold. I slept outside and froze like a dog down where two sloughs, Lucky Point and Railroad City, meet."

May 19, 1943. "I made it across the Yukon, poling through heavy floating ice. There was a big ice jam at Nulato, but I made it to Holy Cross. I am staying at the mission. They are very understanding of my situation."

Friday, May 21, 1943. "It is very stormy, so I can't get across the Yukon. I am visiting here and there but am so very nervous."

Sunday, May 23, 1943. "I went to church. There were quite a few people there. Then I went to see the show 'Wolf Lairs' based on Jack London's novel. Now I am planning on going home."

Monday, May 24, 1943. "I left for Shageluk at 5:30 a.m. and got home at 5:15 p.m. We started to pack at once. It's a lot of work, work, work."

Wednesday, May 26, 1943. "We are still packing and giving out medicine. We are checking the entire inventory in all places. The people received seeds for gardening. All of the villagers are doing a lot of talking. I gave out many magazines."

Friday, May 28, 1943. "We had to tag beaver all morning. We are still packing. The people are putting on a big show about our going. It is raining hard. We worked on reports and the mail. Many people came. We are selling many of our belongings."

Saturday, May 29, 1943. "We are in Holy Cross on our way to the outside."

Sunday, May 30, 1943. "The war is raging. We left Holy Cross on the 'Steamer Alice' on our way to the 'Nenana'. WE ARE SAD!!!"

Chapter 10
THE INTERIM YEARS
SHAKTOOLIK AND CIRCLE

D ad, Mom and Yvonne (Vonnie) left Shageluk on May 29, 1943. They boarded the steamer 'Nenana' at Holy Cross on May 31. They arrived in Anvik at midnight. Mom and Dad were never to see the village where their daughter was buried again. From Anvik they went to Kaltag, Nulato, Koyokuk, Galena, Ruby, Kochrines, Tanana, Hot Springs, Minto, Nenana, Fairbanks, Juneau and then Petersburg. As Mom states in her itinerary, "On June 17th, we arrived in Seattle at last." She was anxious to get back to Mandan, N.D. to give birth to her third child. A son, Robert Edward Larsen, was born on July 1, 1943. He weighed 6 lb., 7 oz. There aren't many pictures of him as a baby because it was war time and film was not readily available. Yvonne called him her "little buddy," which he is still called today in the shortened form, Bud. He was to be our only brother, and all agreed, a very good one.

Mom and Dad could not go back to Shageluk, because everything reminded them of Etola. Dad obtained a new teaching position in The Alaska Native Service in an Eskimo village called Shaktoolik. Shaktoolik is located on Norton Sound of Alaska's west coast about 140 miles north

Bud and Yvonne in Shaktoolik

Bud and Yvonne Playing on the Seashore

of Shageluk. On July 8, 1943, my parents received correspondence from
the outgoing teachers regarding what they should expect in the village
and a few important necessary details. The letters follow:

UNITED STATES
DEPARTMENT OF THE INTERIOR
OFFICE OF INDIAN AFFAIRS
FIELD SERVICE

JULY 8, 1943

To the incoming Teacher,

I am enclosing keys to all the buildings in a separate envelope. The storekeeper, Simon Bakoalook, has a key to the warehouse #1, #2 and to the padlock for the residence. The store had to use warehouse #1 to store the emergency supplies and I suppose they want to continue to use it. #2 is used only for the school. All keys are marked except the #6 door, which is used for gas and fuel oil. I wish to inform you that the oil shed should be locked at all times if you do not want the gas to evaporate. I enclosed the oil shed as too much gas and kerosene disappeared the first year we were here. Some of the fuel oil can easily be used for their outboard motors and is liable to disappear when gas is scarce.

The native store had stored their milk and perishables in the school basement. I do not approve of the store to clutter up the basement and it requires a considerable amount of the teacher's time to unlock it and allow them to get supplies out. They should have their own basement under the store. You can do as you like but I have found to my own satisfaction that there are some natives that cannot be allowed to enter the government buildings and get store supplies. Some store keepers will send anyone to get milk, etc., and they consider the teacher responsible for supplies stored. For some time warehouse #1 was not locked and I had to look after it because, in my own mind, I find not all natives to be honest.

Destitute supplies are being sent in this year. Four families have been getting destitute supplies from the store. There is great demand for skin sewing and every one that is getting destitution supplies could easily make sufficient money by sewing for the army men and the CAA.

The natives of this village are about like the common run of them in any village. Most of them are very accommodating. A few cannot be trusted too far. All will try a teacher to see how much they can get out of them. Some like to peddle and tattle but as the general run of Eskimo they mean well—but one must not allow them to borrow, etc.

Some garden tools are out, as they are still using them, and it is well to gather them up as soon as possible. Natives are not so prompt in returning tools. This village is very bad in holding tools as long as possible and most of the time I have to remind them several times before they return them. I generally tell them to bring them back as soon as they are through with them. It is a good policy to keep a paper handy and mark down all tools when they borrow them. They realize then that one is looking out for any who may in time become owners of government tools. I am leaving the shop open with sufficient tools in it to accommodate them with tools for emergency. I am leaving many tools in the basement and I do not believe it is necessary to put more into the shop. Tools have a mysterious way of disappearing, so one should always be on the alert. A little precaution will make them more careful and less liable to pick up tools.

The chimney in the annex will have to be put up and funds are already available for putting up a new chimney. There is ample cement in warehouse #1 for any necessary construction.

You will find an inventory in this enclosed envelope. Instructions are found in the file and on the wall along side the medical closet. You will find the new authorizations on a nail by the wall.

Several natives can be trusted and they can furnish you with any information. Mrs. Brown, George Aliye, Eric Tatpan, Frederick, Simon Bakoalook, I have found quite reliable. John Kotongan probably is among the most advanced natives. He would probably be glad to do anything but generally charges very much.

The gardens in back of warehouses #1 and #2, also below the road, and the one down below the greenhouse, also the large one below the church, I planted for the incoming teacher and it will furnish you with all the vegetables necessary. Aliye has a small patch below the church.

We had the light plant running for school work, but generally used the gas lamps for our home after school. The oil will have to be watched carefully, as it seems to use considerable oil. Mr. Payne had cut the battery up and used it for his radio. He claims it would not charge, so he used his little plant to charge the six volt batteries. They were run down and I was unable to start the engine with the batteries. This winter the batteries fell to pieces. I start it by hand. It starts easily. Should you have any trouble, turn the needle valve open just a very little, as it pops. Be sure and close it, just where I have it, for you may have trouble. Be sure to have all the lights turned off until it runs smoothly. Oil the dynamo; be sure to look at the oil gauge every day. Change the oil every month. It is not necessary to change it more often. There is ample gas here to run the light plant another year without using the supplies coming in, providing you use gas lamps at nights. Most teachers, except extravagant ones, prefer to use gas lamps for it does not interfere with the radio. I am not suggesting anything the incoming teacher is to do. The locality from which they come and the home environments, city life, etc., very largely determines their success or failure.

We have enjoyed the few years here; however, there are better places, but the natives are the common run of them. The only reason we are leaving here is that the school is too small for two teachers. There is plenty of work for two teachers, but the rules do not allow two. Our children need a year in the States to regain their health and then back to Alaska we will hike. Here is to your success.

Sincerely yours,

Tom W. Schultz, Teacher

To the incoming teachers at Shaktoolik:

July 8, 1943

Dear Friends:

There are just a few things that I would like to tell you about before we leave the country, so I will proceed to put them on this slip of paper.

We hope you will enjoy the flowers in the sun porch as much as we have. Many of them were there when we arrived two years ago.

The gardens all looked fine when we left there last week. We hope too, that they will provide you with plenty of vegetables. The little garden right by the schoolhouse was dug by our girls and Henry and Edward Pitmatalik. We told the boys that whatever grows in it is to be theirs. There were only a few plants up when we left, so we do not know that it will have anything in it.

In that cupboard by the stove in the back room you will find some toys, quilt scraps, pencils, etc. Those are things left from a Junior Red Cross box that came the first year we were there. You can do as you please with them, of course. Another box was to have come last year but it did not arrive.

Just before I left there, I misplaced two birth certificates that should have been given out long ago. One family now lives in Unalakleet and when the mother came a few days before we left, I could not find her child's certificate. They were for Edward Phillips and Melvin Brown.

You will find the older children much farther behind in school than they should be, but they were when we came too. They have been neglected, but you will find that they are very bright children. The little children are nice and quick, too. I had one three year-old and one four year-old in school because they wanted to come and there were so few children for two teachers.

We wish you lots of good luck in your work there and hope you will like the people as we did.

Sincerely yours,
Mrs. Martha Schultz

Another thought: Mrs. George Aliye owes the school six yards of print cloth. She will return it when she can get the material. She is about the best skin sewer in Shaktoolik if you ever need a teacher.

Mrs. Schultz

Because the war was still raging, Mom and Dad had to stop at the Alaska Travel Control to fill out a detailed application for permission to enter Alaska. Permission would be granted by the Western Defense Command and Fourth Army. Our parents had to swear that they were not enemy aliens or persons of Japanese ancestry or persons dangerous or potentially dangerous to the military security of the Territory of Alaska. They were photographed and thumb printed. The applications were accepted and they left Seattle by ship on August 23, 1943, with Yvonne, almost two years old, and Bud 2 ½ months. They disembarked at Seward on Sept. 14, 1943. From Seward they boarded another ship on their way to Shaktoolik. It was a frightening journey. The passenger ship had been outfitted with warheads. The captain spotted a Japanese submarine, so in total darkness the warheads exploded through the night.

The family arrived safely in Shaktoolik. The Eskimos helped them move their supplies and hauled their large trunks into the schoolhouse. Here Dad's duties were to teach school, oversee reindeer herding, tend to medical calls, handle the mail, attend the village council meetings, tend to legal matters, order groceries and supplies for the destitute, themselves and the reindeer camp, write letters for those who couldn't, loan government tools for gardening and woodworking, keep the oil burners going, complete and file government reports, tag skins, and serve as captain of the Shaktoolik branch of the Territorial Guard. Mom helped with all of this in addition to being a mother and housewife and playing the piano for church services.

Schoolhouse in Shaktoolik

Teacher's House in Shaktoolik

The oil stove in the school room was very bad. Most of the time the teacher and students squeezed into a very small room because Dad couldn't get the stove to work. At the end of November he reported, "The annex chimney is smoking like a monster." By the end of December the stove in the big room was frozen solid and he had to take it completely apart. It never did work properly. The stove was his greatest teaching problem. The students he found to be "somewhat smart." But then again, while practicing the Christmas program, he complained that "the students were having plenty of trouble learning things." Attendance was pretty good and severe illness did not rage through Shaktoolik this school year as it did each year in Shageluk. On occasion Dad would get notes from parents to excuse their children from school, such as: "Mr. Larsen, Please I want Clara absent for hooking Tomcod this afternoon for us and for dogs," and "Mr. Larsen, Please excuse Gilbert this afternoon. I want him to go fishing Tomcods." This was excusable because it was necessary for survival in the North.

Reindeer herding required a lot of work: trying to get men to go to the camp, ordering groceries and supplies and filing government reports on the status of the herd. George Aliye, the lead man, had much trouble with the herders as shown by this letter written from Reindeer Camp on Dec. 6, 1943.

Dear Mr. Larsen,

[I] just [want to] let you know I want to get off from Reindeer herding today. I'm getting tired of them talks from different men. Another great trouble is my feet. I can't walk this month like before. Last [time] I was going down and I turn back when my feet get worse. I don't mind if anything comes to me this time. There's somebody waiting for me to take my place this month. You send that man up today, not later. I told when I go down last time I want to get off. Well that's about all for [now]. I'll see you if I [come] down myself. Very truly yours,

Dan Savetilik

As soon as a replacement was found for the herders, each and every one who was relieved was off hunting and fishing and totally forgot their sore feet or other complaints.

Reindeer Corral

Reindeer Herd

Butchering Reindeer

Reindeer Hides

Mae Larsen in a Kayak

"Captain Herman L. Larsen" created quite a Territorial Guard Unit to protect Alaska's coast in that area. Each man was issued a parka, shirt, shoepacks, belt, 30.06 rifle, bayonet, 71 rounds of cartridges, canteen, cup, oil, soldier's handbook, drill book and a military training book. Mom enjoyed watching them train and march around the schoolyard. With shoe laces untied, parkas unzipped and basically with a totally disheveled appearance, they marched and did their best to follow orders. Once, Mom laughed so hard because they all marched directly into her clothesline. Dad received a fine letter from E. L. Bartlett, the acting Governor of Alaska, for his work with his unit.

TERRITORY OF ALASKA
OFFICE OF THE GOVERNOR
JUNEAU

December 7, 1943

Captain Herman L. Larsen
Alaska Territorial Board
Shaktoolik, Alaska

Dear Captain Larsen:

Two years ago today when the Japanese attacked Pearl Harbor, there arose the necessity for the creation of a Territorial Guard to replace the Alaska National Guard units, which had already been called into federal service. During the months since the Guard was organized, you of the Shaktoolik unit have performed outstanding service, which has earned you the gratitude of all Alaskans. You have given freely and unstingingly of your time in this patriotic task and your devotion and enthusiasm have been inspiring.

I should appreciate it if you would extend to your officers and men on behalf of Governor Gruening, Commander-in-Chief of the Guard, who is now in Washington, D.C., on behalf of Lieutenant Colonel J.P. Williams, the Adjutant General of the Territory, and on my behalf our sincere thanks for all your accomplishments. Joining in these expressions are Major C.F. Schreibner and Major H.R. Marston, who have been detailed to work with the Guard by the Alaskan Department of the Army. Also please accept our best wishes for a Merry Christmas and a Happy New Year.

Sincerely yours,

E. L. Bartlett
Acting Governor

Now that Mom was in Shaktoolik, her family at home in the States was beginning to express their disapproval of Dad's work in Alaska. They did not appreciate Mom and her family being so far away. Her older sister Emma in Seattle wrote:

"Poor Mama! I feel so sorry for her. She seems so alone and at her age she should at least have one daughter around...I received your most interesting letter on Saturday. I sent it on to Mama. I imagine how she enjoys every morsel of news she can gather from you. You, no doubt, sent her a letter, too... I hope you don't stay away too long. Maybe something will let Herman out of Alaska. There should be something in the scientific field for him instead of herding Indians and Eskimos.

I know it is going to be a lonesome Christmas for you. But, as Mama wrote, Etola will celebrate Christmas with Jesus and the Heavenly Hosts. She is most fortunate. Life at present hasn't much to offer young folks of today. It is the Lord's will."

Love, your sister

Throughout the school year Dad's health was not very good. He often said he was "feeling rotten." With the too recent death of Etola, he was unable to help himself emotionally, which took a toll on him physically, so in the spring he received this letter after having requested to be transferred out of Shaktoolik.

UNITED STATES
DEPARTMENT OF THE INTERIOR
OFFICE OF INDIAN AFFAIRS

Herman Larsen   Alaska Indian Service
U.S. Gov't Teacher   Juneau, Alaska
Shaktoolik, Alaska   April 3, 1945
Via Unalakleet

Dear Mr. Larsen,

I regret that I cannot offer you a transfer to Southeastern Alaska as you have requested. However, there is a vacancy in Circle on the upper Yukon. I think you would find this a desirable station. There is no reindeer work and no store at Circle, and I am sure you would find this a relief after the extremely heavy program at Shaktoolik. Mrs. Larsen would, of course, be transferred as special assistant. The position at Circle is now vacant and we would like to have you transfer as soon as river

navigation is open in the spring. This transfer would be for the conven-
ience of the Service and transportation costs would be borne by the government. Will you please wire a reply to this inquiry so that we may make
the necessary recommendations to the Chicago Office at an early date?

Sincerely yours,

Don C. Foster, Gen Supt.
By: George A. Dale
Director of Education

Dad did accept the position in Circle and there he experienced
another difficult assignment. They arrived in Circle at the end of August
in 1945. The school and residence were in total disrepair because the
government property had suffered much damage in a spring flood. Dad,
in somewhat of a desperate state, wrote the following letter:

Mae and Children in Front of the Teacher's House in Circle, AK

Mr. Reinholt Brust   Circle, Alaska
Chief Clerk, ANS   Sept. 17, 1945
Juneau, Alaska

Dear Mr. Brust:

In reply to your letter of September 6, last received, I find it difficult to properly advise you at this time whether I shall need all the money allotted for repairs. No repairs had been done when I got here. The cleaning attempted here when Mrs. Larsen arrived, she informs me, was of poor quality. There is a rumor current that the engine, now here, was at Fairbanks. No bills for repairs or transportation filed. No lumber for repairs has come. We have a promise of some lumber coming in from Fairbanks. The last boat of the season, the "Casca," brought no shop lumber, though ordered. I take it that kind of material is hard to get.

The trouble here, even before the flood, is that there was nothing to work with—unless the natives and whites here stole the supplies that should have been here. The flood did a lot of damage, but it did not carry off things in buildings that remained stationary after the flood ceased. I cleaned off and oiled up the few remaining tools when I got here. As for repairs and new buildings, we need the school repaired, part of the $450 allotment—we need an extra building for oil, gas, wood and other supplies. The chimney flues are now standing on the front porch (which is ready to fall down), and must remain there all winter unless I can get erected an extra storage place of some kind. I have no tarpoling.

The medical division needs to erect some form of medical unit, enough to take care of the work that needs to be done. Just to illustrate: the other day a mother came in with her small daughter, who had cut one finger off and partly cut the other off. I had no place to work and practically nothing to work with. The flood, I believe didn't create this condition. My experience has been that cases of an emergency nature present themselves quite often among the native people.

Another thing here. The natives and whites alike won't do anything unless they get $1.50 per hour. That part is not in accord with my way of thinking, but I have no booze to feed these people, so I either have to do the work myself or pay the price if I want someone to work. As soon as the men get back from hunting I shall have a general meeting and see what wages the folks are willing to accept. I have not enough school seats. If thirty pupils come as they ought, lumber has to be used for repairing seats and building new ones or making tables. Some school supplies, enough to get along with through the winter, have to be bought locally.

If I do all the repairs and building myself, I shall need only enough money to pay for supplies. I have already put in way more overtime (I didn't put it down on paper) than regulations call for, but the work has got to be done in spite of rules and regulations. Again, I don't know how much money I shall need. What bothers me is: How I am going to get the work done?

Most sincerely yours,
Herman L. Larsen
ANS Teacher

P.S. I shall let you know as soon as I find out about the money proposition.

On October 30, 1945, Dad reflected on his life so far in Circle as he wrote to a young acquaintance, Pfc. Vernon L. More, and his wife, who were staying at the Baranof Hotel in Juneau, Alaska.

Dear Folks,

I (appreciate) the fine company we had over the radio and the fine service you rendered our station at Shaktoolik.....

In a way we like it here. Mrs. Larsen likes it pretty well here. I can't say I like it too well. The kids are very nice and attend school regularly. But then I like all kids. I do not like to teach little tots, but I love to work with them. I had my training in the executive field and Senior High School. But my work is plenty varied to keep me interested.

Picture to yourself the old country physician and you got old man Larsen. Looking at my diary, it is a funny one.

Back to this place. It was one of the worst holes I can picture to myself, even worse than Northway by a long shot. Miss Alma Carlson, our Field Nurse, came when we were busy cleaning up. That made me cross, for we had no decent place to put her. However, upon her recommendation, I built a little dispensary. I would have built it without her suggestion. I hired the minister here as first class carpenter (he said he was). He practically ruined my lumber, or rather the Govt. lumber, and I fired him. As a result, I did the work myself with practically no tools to work with. This darn place didn't even have any teaching material. No materials for the little kids. The poor kids in this place certainly have suffered for lack of competent teachers. All they could do was to write big reports to the office about the wonderful things they had done—all B.S. —brown sugar....

And now I shall tell you, Vernon, some of the more pleasant things of life. It seems to be my luck to somehow or another get into some of the more cultural things of this universe. One evening about two weeks ago close to 10 p.m., I was listening to Tundra Topics—per 9:30 p.m.—put on by the Bank of Fairbanks. I fell asleep. In walked one of these Indians and, all excited, asked me to come over to his place and bandage up a fellow Indian, who had gotten shot in the "nose." I got up and walked over, administering first aid and getting the victim upon the small bed in upright position to prevent much bleeding. I could see no hope for him. Then on a rampage for the slayer, a white man, George Rakosky. Through a drunken brawl lasting some days, a quarrel had ensued and the Indian victim, Hobo Bill or William John, Sr. got shot, I would say accidentally. The victim died about 2 a.m. that following morning. Then coroner's jury, later autopsy, yours truly was on all of them, examining witnesses in Commissioner's Court, burial—I did not have to act as minister for the first time in years—what a life. Next to Fairbanks on the witness stand. I don't know how long I'll be gone.

That is the life of a Federal School Teacher. Then they say we are supposed to work every day, 8 hrs. per day, for five days a week. 40 hours per week. Who said so? Secretary Ickkes. I have worked every Saturday & Sunday inclusive but one Saturday and then I went to Circle Hot Springs, where I found the Govt. Typewriter, in bad condition from the flood here, which before had been sent to Fairbanks for repairs, but the fellow had left it at the Springs, claiming he had no room for it. I got so darn mad I took the thing back with me and decided to fix it even if I ruined it. Mrs. Larsen and myself worked all night on the thing and Sunday morning we had it together again, after spreading it all over the front room rug, two small screws were left over. Mrs. Larsen has more patience than I have and found where they belonged. The typewriter works like a new machine. Thank goodness.

I sure enjoyed your letter. Talk about the Army. I was in it many years ago – in the Hospital Division attached to the 3rd Infantry. I wonder where the old timers are now. We had quite a time and at Shaktoolik I was faithfully drilling those guys of the Alaska Territorial Guard. What a life, but I like it fairly well.

> Write again please,
> Best wishes.
> Herman L. Larsen

After all the hard work preparing the school for students, it wasn't long before attendance began to drop off drastically. In October Dad wrote a letter to the parents of the children not attending school:

> Circle, Alaska
>
> October 22, 1945
>
> Dear Parent,
>
> Your child is out of school too many times. Unless he/she attends school every day we shall contact the U.S. Commissioner at Circle Hot Springs. The Juneau Office, Cir. April 24, 1945, has put the responsibility of sending the children to school regularly when there is school upon your shoulders. It is illegal to keep the children out of school when in the village unless sick in bed, which can only be ascertained from this office. You will, in all other cases, send the children to school or get a written permit from the Juneau Office. Please comply with the contents of this letter.
>
> Sincerely yours,
> H.L.Larsen
> U.S. Government Teacher

In November and December he wrote similar letters. In the beginning of January he made a list of eight students who had been consistently missing. From these letters he received many excuses: "My daughter did not come to school this morning because she was helping me washing," "My son can't come to school because he hurt his leg," "My son can't come to school because he is hauling wood with his father," "My son is not coming to school cause he is going out to get caribou," "My daughter can't come to school because she got to sew her moccasins." Dad replied to this last note by saying, "We have only excuse for sickness in bed and getting food for the family if one is starving to death. No excuse for sewing moccasins." H. L. Larsen, U.S. Gov't Teacher. The mother replied, "She can sew and go to school in the afternoon. I think that's the best. Her moccasin is full of holes."

On January 25, 1946, Dad made a long list of children not attending school and sent it to the General Superintendent in Juneau. He wrote another letter to the parents stating, "Why are not the children in school?" The parents replied by writing, "All the kids don't go to school so I let my kids stay home," "I let my children stay home. I thought you was sick," "I'll keep my children home until we heard from the General Superintendent." He did not realize at that point in time that 22 parents had signed and sent a damaging telegram to the General Superintendent with the following allegations reported by the Juneau Office:

Allegations as reported in Telegram

1. Children's faces washed outside in the snow between 25 and 40 degrees below zero, causing frostbite to some ears
2. Brushes their hair with scrub brush, which is said to have been used to scrub floors with
3. Has taken our daughters one at a time in dispensary, made them strip to the waist for inspection
4. Made boys and girls smoke cigars
5. Will not permit children to have drink of water in school hours
6. Or go outside to toilet, making it necessary for the younger ones to have a complete change of clothes when they come home

Mom was outraged by the accusations in the telegram. She wrote a letter to Dr. George Dale, Director of Education, Alaska Native Service, Juneau, Alaska on Jan. 28, 1946.

Dear Dr. Dale,

Much emphasis has been given to Mr. Larsen's having the girls stripped to the waist in the dispensary. The word "stripped" is a strong word to use in this case and refers to evil thought. I had full supervision of that case last fall, and I did exactly as our field nurses have taught me, nothing different. Mr. Larsen has tended to so much sickness in his lifetime that to him those things are perfectly natural, and I know, in these eight years in Alaska, many, many people have been mighty thankful Mr. Larsen has been able to do something for them. I have an idea Mr. Larsen will start refusing to go out on sick calls when people don't appreciate his services any more than this telegram indicates. I know that whenever something baffles him, he is upstairs studying medical texts till way out into the night. If the people don't like the way we are doing things why don't they come to us and tell us about it, and that goes for Fred Powers (Northern Commercial Company), too. Why let things go for almost half a year and then dig up something?

Take this washing referred to. I had full charge of that, too. The parents can keep the kids clean. We can much better spend our Government time than to wash kids in school. One sure thing it has never been 25 to 40 below in the schoolroom since we got here, and that is where those few dirty kids were washed. I even used my own good towels on them. No kids were ever washed outside. That would be cruel. We never wash our own kids outside. Neither do we wash anybody else's kids outside. And some of these things happened once last fall just as has been stated and nothing but good was said about it at that time.

Yours truly,
Mae Larsen
Special Assistant

Mr. Carlos W. Holland, a field property clerk from Fairbanks, was sent to Circle to investigate the allegations in the telegram and was to report to the General Superintendent, Mr. Don Foster. He found that the village schoolmaster had been "framed." Upon inquiry at the District Attorney's office in Fairbanks, it was found that the people of Circle had filed an application for a liquor license. Fred Powers of the Northern Commercial Co. encouraged the petition signing, as he was to be the license holder. The petition was denied. Keeping the children out of school and the telegram were an attempt to intimidate Mr. Larsen "for any part he may have played in preventing the issuance of the license." A village meeting was held. The natives agreed to again send the children to school.

On April 22, 1946, Dad wrote to the general superintendent stating:

> In view of the fact we have a fairly large school enrollment and a fair interest shown in school activities, I would recommend the continuance of the school. True, we have had some trouble here in the past, but I feel this should be forgotten. What bothers us more than anything are the poor living quarters as well as poor schoolroom and teaching equipment. I have, and the whole family has, never frozen so much in our lives as we did last winter. Then, too, there is the flood to think about. That is not a very pleasant thought. Talking about freezing: I had to get up every morning about 2:00 a.m. when cold to fire the stoves. The kids were shivering in bed whenever they kicked their bed-clothes off. This, continued in the future, is not conducive to good health or to good teaching. We, therefore, have had in mind a transfer to better living conditions.... However, if all the supplies come and the living conditions are corrected in the near future, we will remain at Circle another year or two, maybe more. We really like Circle and know that local conditions will correct themselves in the near future.

> Most sincerely yours,
> Herman L. Larsen,
> U.S. Gov't Teacher

Dr. George Dale, Director of Education sent a letter dated April 25, 1946.

> Dear Mr. and Mrs. Larsen:
> With a great deal of pleasure we read Mr. Starling's [passed to him from Mr. Holland's field report] very favorable report of his visit to Circle on March 12 to 15. You people indeed have had a stormy session at Circle this winter, but I feel that the reasons for your difficulties are, in general, complimentary to you. We are certainly glad to support our employees in the field when they are having difficulties when it is so plain that their difficulties result from their effort to do a sincerely good job. Attempting to combat the use of liquor among the Natives of your community and to help them to improve their own economic status are certainly important elements of your assignment, and we appreciate the

vigorous attack that you have made upon these problems.

As a result of your experiences this winter, you may have discovered ways of getting desirable results that will produce less commotion as the community has suffered during the past winter; be that as it may, we feel that you are getting results and that you should be commended for your vigorous and successful efforts. We appreciate particularly the fact that you are willing to remain at Circle for another year. Now that you have "weathered the storm," I feel that you have done a desirable and effective service to this community.

Sincerely yours,
Don C. Foster
General Superintendent
By: George A. Dale
Director of Education

There must have been much discussion in the education office in Juneau. They certainly were aware that the inhabitants in Circle were persistent in getting a liquor license. Dad received a telegram from the general superintendent, Mr. Don Foster, at the end of April, to which he replied.

Dear Mr. Foster:

Received your recent telegram, though it was held up a day here at Circle and had no date on it.

I am positive you are doing the right thing in closing the school in Circle. Here are my reasons: Last night and this morning, Mrs. Seller, the missionary, circulated the counter-petition to the recent liquor petition. She canvassed the whole village and dropped into our quarters this morning. All signers she could get were 4 or 5. Some of the natives said, "We rather have liquor than school, we don't care."

Most of them stated to the missionary that Fred Powers had promised them school in return for their signatures on the liquor petition (which, by the way, was also circulated last night but earlier than the missionary's).

Under these conditions, this is no place for honest teachers.

There probably will be no applications of children to other schools, as the parents have been told to "sit tight and they will get school through Washington."

Most sincerely yours,
Herman L Larsen
U.S. Govt. Teacher

The school year in Circle certainly was a difficult one. Mr. George Rakosky was sentenced to a term of 18 months in the United States Penitentiary at McNeil Island in the state of Washington for the "accidental shooting" of Hobo Bill or a "violation of a Territorial Statute." Dad applied for a position in Levelock, Alaska, and for a passport to go to Norway (he hadn't been there in 13 years) to check on his family since the war was over. Mom, who was stressed by the entire year, spent a few days in the Fairbanks Hospital with what Dad described as "some kind of stomach disorder." In truth, Mom, at the end of the first trimester of pregnancy, lost my fraternal twin in a very painful miscarriage. I was still with her.

Chapter 11
1946 – 1949
LEVELOCK, ALASKA
ELAINE'S STORY

On June 14, they left Circle at 1:00 p.m. on the SS 'Yukon'. The ship loaded up 24 cords of wood at a nearby wood camp and went to Coal Creek the next morning. There they loaded empty oil barrels on board. At 5 p.m. a cow moose swam in front of the boat, so the pilot blew the whistle at her. As they continued on, the scenery became much like the inside passage. On June 16th at 6:45 a.m. the SS 'Yukon' arrived at a cozy place called Eagle. The boat was short of fresh meat, so everyone had mostly canned ham and eggs to eat. They saw a large brown bear on the beach. Again the pilot blew the whistle and the bear took notice. Yvonne and Buddy were so excited and wanted to see more bears.

They came to Dawson about 5:30 p.m., where the passengers had to stay in Hotel Regina. The boilers of the steamer were cleaned out, so there was no toilet system and they were unable to stay on board. Dawson looked like a ghost town after the gold rush days. There were many old closed-up hotels and whiskey parlors. Most of the houses were old and

72 - S.S. Yukon at Columbia Glacier, Alaska

S. S. Yukon

crooked. Mom bought a dress for herself, overalls for Vonnie and both kids got new shoes. They left Dawson on June 18 at 12:20 a.m. after piling on more wood. The people on the boat thought Yvonne and Bud were such good kids.

Stewart Island was the next stop on June 19. All the thirsty people rushed off to get beer and, according to Mom, "including my old man." There an old horse was used for hauling freight from the boat. Every time he heard the boats coming, he would rush off into the woods. Twenty cords of wood were loaded on the boat. As the journey continued the water became clearer and swifter. At Whitehorse they took a train to Skagway. From there they traveled by ship on the inside passage to Seattle and again on a train to Mandan, North Dakota. At the end of July, Dad wrote a letter to friends in Circle saying, "We are here at last. The trip was long and tiresome, but very interesting...lot of beautiful scenery. Traveling on Canadian boats was wonderful... the service was excellent. It is terribly hot here in North Dakota but a good climate for people with rheumatism or arthritis...We expect to be in Levelock the last part of November or maybe a little before."

Mom, Yvonne and Bud stayed on Grandma Hendrickson's farm until I was born. Dad made arrangements for all of our trunks and supplies to be sent to Levelock from Circle, then went to New York and left on the Swedish American Line's 'Gripsholm' on Saturday, August 10, 1946, to Gothenburg, Sweden, then to his family in Forde, Norway. The Germans occupied Norway from April 1940 until the end of the war in 1945. During that time Dad lost contact with his parents, brothers and sisters. Now he felt he had to go "home."

Mom was in town (Mandan) at her brother Arthur's home, eating fresh cinnamon rolls, when she had her first labor pains. Our Aunt Bessie took care of Yvonne and Bud while Mom was in the hospital. I was born on November 23, 1946, at 3:16 in the morning. Dad came back from Norway after Thanksgiving and was told by the Alaska Native Service to go directly to Levelock. The rest of the family was to go by train to Seattle and then by ship, but the ship had hit a rock and was damaged quite badly, so we flew to Anchorage, where we stayed for three days waiting for a bush pilot to take us to Naknek. Yvonne and Bud had to sit on a frozen butchered pig in the back seat while Mom held me on her lap. With a different bush pilot we flew from Naknek to Levelock. Mom had hoped that Yvonne and Bud would be more comfortable on this leg of the journey, but in the back seat was that same frozen pig.

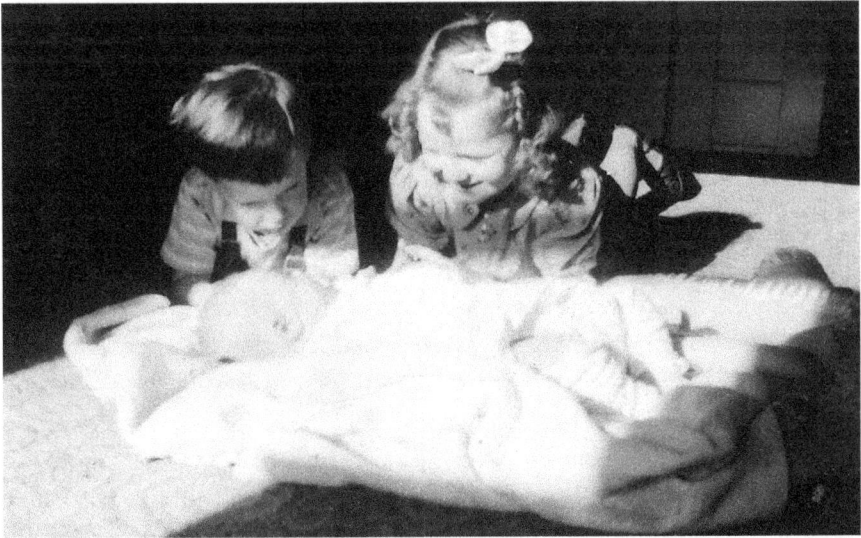

Bud and Yvonne looking at their new sister Elaine

We landed on the ice with skis on the plane. It was a very long slide. A sure-footed Eskimo carried me up to the house while Mom helped Yvonne and Bud on the slippery surface. This was the nicest house the Larsen family had ever lived in, in Alaska. Mother finally had a washing machine. Levelock was a growing village where several new houses had been built by prominent people. It even had street lights from the new warehouse down to the beach. Along with new houses, it had new roads throughout the town with a very long airfield and a new fish cannery. It had a new movie theater, a store, and a cafe with many frequent patrons. The people were Eskimos, half-breeds, and there were more white people living there than in most other villages. Most of the people fished for a living.

In the fall when fishing season was over there was much celebrating, drinking and gambling. One evening two men, Nels and Shorty, came to our house drunk. They put another bottle on the table and managed to drink all of it. When it was empty Mom filled it with water, flavored with maple extract. They drank all of that "good stuff" too. Shorty couldn't hold all he drank, so he wet the floor under the table. Dad and Nels tried to get him to the bathroom, but it was too late. Mom didn't want to see what was going to happen next, so she took us over to the neighbors. After a long argument with the homeowner, Nels was allowed to join us in the neighbors' house. He said he wasn't drunk and "could think just as good as anyone else." Mom left with Yvonne, Bud and me. When we got home, there was Shorty lying on the front steps outside the door. His wife came to get him before he froze to death. Mom had to stay up most of the night scrubbing her floors.

In the fall Mom netted over 50 salmon. She borrowed a canning sealer from a friend and canned 400 tins of fish. Each can cost three cents, which was very inexpensive. It was a big job but well worth her time. The Larsen family had plenty for the year and she was able to send some canned salmon back to her mother in Mandan, N.D. The game warden would fly over the beaches to see if any fish were being wasted, so all the fish had to be put to good use or one would be in trouble with heavy fines or some form of reprimand. We had canned salmon throughout my early childhood and it still is one of my favorite foods.

Mae Larsen Catching Whitefish

The school was well attended with Dad being "the great disciplinarian" as usual. Along with reading, writing and arithmetic, he taught basket weaving, sewing, shop, chorus and art. In addition he started a school newspaper, called *The Levelock Reporter.* The school newspaper included community news such as the comings and goings of the community people, visitors, plane crack-ups, news of births and illnesses, jokes, cartoons and creative stories. He started this newspaper for the benefit of the older children. It was to be a weekly paper, but because of the lack of cooperation of the students, it was printed once a month. Dad wrote frequently in his diaries, "Scolding kids on account of bad school paper. Kids are very lazy. I typewrote all of the school paper—working all evening."

As if Mother didn't have enough to do with all the childcare, cooking, cleaning, and entertaining, she applied to be the postmaster of Levelock on August 14, 1947. *The Levelock Reporter* article states as follows:

New Post Office Established

A new post office has been established at Levelock. It is an all-service post office and is open all days, except Sundays and holidays (unless the mail plane doesn't come in), from 9:00 a.m. to 5:00 p.m. The postmaster is Mrs. H. L. Larsen, the teacher's wife. She tells us that soon the post office will handle international money orders in addition to regular money orders.

It was a way for Mom to earn money of her own, because Dad was very touchy about the little funds Mother spent.

The following is an example written on November 1, 1947, of the entertaining entries of the newspaper:

Up-River Bachelors Searching for Cooks

The Up-River bachelors sent to Naknek for some cooks. They are going to have their cooks sent to them for special services. The cooks are supposed to be pretty young, good-looking and it's rumored, they are to be regular New York models as to form and shape...Most of [the] Levelock fellows will be up-river most of the winter. Andy went down to Naknek with his boat a day or two ago to get them.

It was later reported that "the cooks who were beautiful, gay and willing to travel up the scenic Kvichak River had to be returned because of the heavy floating ice on the river. A plane took them home so the bachelors had to cook their own meals this winter, too."

Dad had hired several older boys to do the janitor work in the school, but because he was fussy and particular and they weren't doing the job well, they were dismissed and he took the position.

On Nov. 1, 1947, *The Levelock Reporter* wrote: "Mr. Larsen, our teacher, is the new janitor for our school. He is doing it because he does a better job than his pupils did."

Dad was more cerebral than he was mechanical, so his janitorial service was not the greatest success. In the first entry of his diary he wrote, "Doing general chores—janitor work." For each day of the following week he was "working on the engine (generator)" or "working on the engine in the basement." On Jan. 8, 1948, he was "still working fixing the engine which uses three barrels of oil each week. The pipes froze up in the girls' and boys' bathroom. Filled in two barrels of oil and ten gallons of gas." For the remainder of the month he continued, "Teaching and working on engine." Finally after replacing the fuel pump diaphragm he wrote, "Almost blew up the schoolhouse. I can't tell how much gas the tank holds." Later on the school newspaper reported:

Our Fire Fighting Squad

John Meggitt and Virgil Hanson are civic-minded citizens. They came rushing into the schoolhouse one day to fight a big fire. The fire had been lit early in the morning. The teacher went out for an early walk. When he came back, the fire was out. Just after school started he went downstairs to light the fire. After a while the two men came in a hurry. They brought a lot of fire equipment. A lot of water in the oil had tripped the carburetor. A lot of unburned oil was in the firebox when it was lit, sending very much smoke up the chimney. The firefighters were thinking of the school burning down. We appreciate that the civic-minded citizens are on their toes.

Here is another example of Dad's janitorial excellence as reported on March 1, 1948:

"Troubler"

The library book shelf is finally made. The oldest school boys and Mr. Larsen made it in the school basement on the 5th of February. After they nailed it together they had to take it apart again since it could not be taken up the steps. They worked one evening until after twelve mid-night only to have to take it apart and rebuild it in the schoolroom the next morning. The book case has the name "Troubler," because it caused Mr. Larsen and the boys so much trouble in the making.

We did not escape our share of illness in Levelock. At the end of October in 1947, all three of us kids came down with whooping cough along with everyone else. I, not even one year old, was especially ill. The following report was in the school paper on December 1, 1947:

Levelock Postmaster Leaves

Mrs. Herman L. Larsen, Levelock Postmaster, left for Seattle with her three children on November 12. She arrived in Seattle on the 13th, in the morning. The reason she left is that her baby (Elaine) wasn't feeling well. Too, during whooping cough Mrs. Larsen had many nights without sleep and needed rest. Mr. Larsen informs us he does not expect her back before Christmas, depending on her health. In addition to his many other duties, Mr. Larsen is taking care of the mail until the Postmaster gets back.

Elaine on the Kitchen Table in Levelock

Elaine sitting on a Crate

Along with whooping cough, I had developed a glandular boil on my lower right jaw. Dad could not handle lancing the boil so I was taken to a physician in Seattle. Dad spent Christmas alone that year. He held the school Christmas play with the following statement on the program: "Due to much sickness and interruptions this play is not perfectly rendered, but the children are trying hard to do their best."

We returned after Christmas pretty much rested and recovered, with the remainder of the year being fairly normal, but Dad's troubles weren't over yet. Our grandmother on the farm in Mandan, N.D., had broken her hip. Mom's older sister from Oregon, Alma, went home to take care of her. Alma had to return to her own home, so she hired another lady to be Grandma's caregiver. This didn't work out very well because our Uncle Nels, an older bachelor, fell in love with her. After their marriage they moved to Oregon. Now the pressure was on Mom to leave Alaska to take care of Grandma.

Yvonne recalls boarding the plane on the tarmac in Levelock. Dad was crying as we flew away. She had heard him talking about being so lonely. We flew with a red-headed pilot named Babe Ellsworth. Dad trusted his piloting skills the most of any bush pilot in that area. We arrived in Anchorage on March 17, 1949. There we stayed at the old Anchorage Hotel. In the evening Mom warmed a can of soup on the radiator and gave us bread and apple butter. After we were put to bed there was a knock on the door. A man who had taken interest in Mother wanted to spend the evening with her. She told him to go away many times because she had three little kids sleeping. Yvonne was very frightened, but finally the man went away.

The next day we flew to Seattle where we stayed at our Aunt Emma's house. We all slept on her Murphy bed. Later that evening Aunt Emma came home. She was so happy to see her youngest sister and the three of us children. She had always insisted that Mom leave Alaska. There were others who could have taken care of Grandma, but all of Mom's brothers and sisters felt it was time for her to leave the untamed territory.

The first words I remember hearing in life at age two and a half were "Close your eyes and go to sleep. We'll soon be there," as Mother was tucking a fuzzy blanket around me. We were sitting next to the strangest window with rounded corners. It was night and there were many bright lights moving by quickly. I don't remember what was happening nor where we were, but with my mother's loving arms around me, I must have felt secure and did indeed fall quickly to sleep. Certainly we were on a train going back to Mandan, North Dakota, never to live in Alaska as a family again.

Chapter 12
MANDAN, NORTH DAKOTA, USA

Dad stayed in Levelock until the fall of 1950, to wrap things up for the Alaska Native Service, then again went to Forde, Norway, on December 8, 1950, to be with his parents and siblings. In the spring of 1949, life must certainly have been different for my older sister Yvonne, then seven and a half years old and my brother Buddy, five years old, to live without their father on a farm so far away from the home they knew; but I, being only two and a half years old didn't remember having a father, nor what a father was.

Mae and Children
Back on the Farm
in Mandan, ND

We were free on the beautiful farm called Fair View, nestled amongst the rolling hills with the sight of buttes on the horizon. We were surrounded by loving but seemingly old aunts and uncles. Our first cousins were close to Mother's age. Grandma, then 83 years old, was a nice old lady with a cane. We had a section and 80 acres of land as our playground. There were dogs, cats, turkeys, chickens, Angora rabbits, geese, Holstein cows, Black Angus cows, range cattle, Guernsey cows and a big old Black Angus bull. Fourteen huge Percheron workhorses were still used for farming. On the less domestic side, to name a few, were prairie chickens, prairie dogs, pigeons, hawks, meadowlarks, bull snakes, garter snakes, blue racer snakes, songbirds and coyotes, whose howling lulled us to sleep at night. Also we had the most feared and deadly rattlesnake. Our first lesson on our new playground was to look down as we walked to watch for rattlers. We had gardens, trees and Indian burial grounds. The trail that Custer's 7th Cavalry traveled in the spring of 1876 to the Little Big Horns in Montana went right through our farmyard. There were two barns, two chicken coops, a laundry house, a milk house, a wooden granary, a steel bin, a windmill, a shop and a very large farmhouse. The outhouse seemed to be a mile away, especially during the middle of cold winter nights. Only Grandma was allowed to use the modern but minimally functioning plumbing upstairs in the house, because she had broken her hip.

The house was divided into two separate living quarters. The main part was for Grandma, Mom and us three kids. On the other side lived Uncle Ted, Auntie Erna and their daughter Luane. By the time summer came Uncle Nels and his new bride moved back to the farm with an 18-foot trailer, which was parked out in the yard by the windmill. The entire farm was a child's dream, with so much food to eat and so many places to explore, while surrounded by so many caring family members.

The Horse, Jimmy

Yvonne and Bud did not have to go to school the remainder of that year, nor the following. Permission was granted by the school district for them to be home-schooled because there was no means of transportation to get them the three and a half miles to Highland School. Yvonne had been in second grade in Alaska. Since Dad was the schoolteacher, he had passed her on to the next grade in his final reports to the Alaska Native Service. Both Yvonne and Bud were very good students, so they weren't hindered in learning in any way by studying at home. Mom had had much experience teaching in Alaska when Dad had other things to do. She never let us be idle. Also we were often reminded of how bright and talented our older sister Etola had been. This presented a challenge to us throughout our learning years.

Mom worked hard milking the cows, separating the cream from the milk, picking eggs, cooking and helping Grandma. She found the time to take us for long walks through the pastures and coulees. It was obvious she knew every square inch of that farm. When she watched the sheep as a child, she built large pyramids of smaller stones on every large rock in the pasture. We thought the pyramids were beautiful and never disturbed them. She took us to the ravines to pick chokecherries, June berries, buffalo berries and wild strawberries. Once when we were picking chokecherries, Mom spotted a large snake in the brush. She thought it was a rattler because it made a rattling noise as it crawled through the sagebrush. We all grabbed rocks and stoned it. When there was no life left in the snake, Mom went to take a closer look. She sat down and cried because she had killed a harmless big bull snake. Mom loved all creatures. She had always kept two bull snakes in the coal bin in the basement, because rattlesnakes would not come into the basement while bull snakes lived there.

Uncle Teddy was also very entertaining. He was Grandma's second youngest child, nine years older than Mom. We all sat on the porch in the evening just visiting. Sometimes he would put a caterpillar on the end of a stick and twirl the stick slowly, pretending the caterpillar was getting dizzy or drunk, causing it to lose its balance. We laughed so hard at his antics and commentary. Once he tied a string to a piece of caramel. The dog willingly swallowed it and Uncle Ted pulled it back out again. Then the dog obediently swallowed it again. Finally after several retrievals of the caramel, the string came back empty because it had melted in the dog's stomach, and we cheered for the dog because he won the caramel. Uncle

Ted was always gentle and kind. Once a week he went to the Mandan Creamery to sell his cream. He always stopped at the co-op store to buy a pint of strawberry ice cream. Yvonne, Bud and I split it three ways; we had never tasted anything so delicious.

Uncle Ted twirling a Worm

We played often in the pond below the hill not far from the entrance to our farm. It was a shallow pond and a great adventure. We caught tadpoles and small turtles. The cattails around the pond grew so tall. I enjoyed rubbing my cheek on their fuzzy exterior. Buddy actually found a good use for them. We took them home, pulled them apart and dried them. Bud found some red wool and hand-sewed a pillow, then stuffed it with cattails. I was so impressed with his creation.

Mom spent time with us in the evening after chores and supper were done, teaching us to develop our artistic talents. She drew animals, flowers, birds and trees as we sat in the kitchen near the warm cast-iron cook stove. Our only light was a kerosene lamp above the kitchen table. The Sears Roebuck catalog was a storehouse of fun. For paper dolls we cut out the models from the bra and girdle section, then pasted them on cardboard with flour and water or syrup. Then we cut out hats, dresses, shoes and coats from the front of the catalog. Whatever was left of the catalog was used as toilet paper in the outhouse. We were happy when Mom or our aunts canned peaches, because the paper wrapping from the peaches was much softer toilet paper than the Sears catalog.

All of us had to take baths on Saturday evening. A large laundry tub was filled with water which was heated in a big boiler on top of the cook stove. We bathed in order of age, from oldest to youngest. We were covered with a white bed sheet in order to stay warm and have some privacy. By the time it was my turn to bathe, the water was dirty and cold and

Grandma's homemade lye soap floated like a sticky mess on top the dirt. I probably was never too clean, but it was certainly better than a week's worth of dirt.

Yvonne, Bud and I slept together in a big iron bed with a heavy mattress on top of open springs. The bed made an excellent trampoline when I was misbehaving. In winter it was very cold because the coal in the furnace would burn out before morning. We were covered with Grandma's homemade wool quilts stuffed with the wool from her sheep. Along with the howling of the coyotes, the intermittent flashing of the beacon light sitting on the south end of the farm lulled us to sleep. It was hard to get out of bed in the morning in below-zero temperatures. Frost hung thickly on the windows. The first order of business each morning was to throw on our heavy coats and overshoes to make the lengthy trip to the outhouse.

Heavy Snowfall in the Yard

At the end of April 1951, Dad came back from Norway. Yvonne and Bud jumped up and down excitedly repeating, "Daddy's coming home! Daddy's coming home!" I'm sure I joined in the ceremony not knowing who this person was. A large heavy-set man walked through the door. He had a loud commanding voice and talked without ceasing. Mom finished making supper and we all sat down to eat. Dad had purchased a carton of cottage cheese which was opened and set on the table. Mom gave me a small taste of it. It was pretty good, so I asked for a little more. She put a teaspoon on my plate, and with the second bite I found it to be awful, so I said I didn't want any more. Dad got up from his chair, came behind me and picked me up by the shoulders. He repeatedly banged my legs and bottom so hard on the heavy oak chair hollering, "You will finish the food on your plate and will learn to behave from now on!" No one told him to stop this horrible behavior. Obviously he was acting as he usually did and this was expected. If he wanted to be abusive he was allowed to do so. When the beating was over, I could not eat the cottage cheese because I was crying so hard. Yvonne left the table and went to the piano in the parlor. She had always been such a kind and protective big sister to me, but this time she looked at me out the corner of her eye as I was crying violently, trying to walk on my sore legs. I had always been surrounded by kind and gentle people. Now I met my Dad and feared him.

Dad had bought a new shiny black car and hid it in the barn underneath some blankets. Mom found it one day and was rather upset because it was not affordable. Yvonne and Bud still needed transportation to get to school, but Dad had a new car. I liked it because he put his belongings in it and moved to Fargo, ND, leaving us on the farm. He studied to become a Swedish masseur and would send for the rest of the family when he was making good money.

In the summer, Dad sent Yvonne a new blue bicycle and Bud a red one. This was their means of transportation to school, 3 ½ miles from our farm. I was only four years old and had to stay at home one more year. I remember one day in the spring, I was so excited to meet them. We had a big Black Angus cow named Sally. She let us ride her and sit on her back when she was lying down half asleep. I yelled at Yvonne and Bud as they were coming over the hill, "Sally had twins! Sally had twins!" We named them Jack and Jill. They sucked on our fingers and were so beautiful.

On September 1, 1952, I started school. Yvonne's bicycle was outfitted with a straight hard bumper seat over the back wheel, where I sat while she peddled up and down the hills. My bottom was so sore and her legs were so tired. Highland was a one room schoolhouse with grades 1-8. I was excited about starting school, but that changed in a hurry. The

Bud and Yvonne with their new Bicycles

Elaine on the Porch

teacher was another abusive disciplinarian. I had two boys in my class, a nice German boy in front of me and a mischievous Bohemian at the desk behind me. He wasn't even potty trained, so his older sister had to change his pants during recess. One day he pulled my hair and poked me in the back. I turned around and told him to quit bothering me. The teacher came over, grabbed me by the shoulders and shook me so hard I thought my head was going to fall off. I cried very hard. My sister across the aisle could not help me and felt so bad. I had to suffer through the hair pulling and poking through the rest of the year without saying a word.

There was no school lunch, so we had to bring our own. We usually had chokecherry jelly sandwiches and a pint jar filled with milk. By the time our military-like school marm would let us eat, the sugar had crystallized out of the jelly and the salt had separated out of the homemade butter. The cream floated to the top of the milk and it often tasted like whatever the cows had eaten the day before, like French weed or wild onions. The school's drinking water was stored in a cream can in the basement. We all shared the same dipper, which was floating in the water. If one person was ill with a cold, we all became ill.

During the winter when it was many degrees below zero, I did not go to school. Shortly after I returned, when the weather was warmer, there was a bad snowstorm. We couldn't get home and had to stay at the teacher's house next to the school. I was scared. I slept on an old army cot with a green wool blanket that made me itch all night. The teacher's husband was nice, but she was like a major character from Halloween on a daily basis. I felt she disliked me because I finished my work and went ahead in my workbooks, leaving the boys behind. On my report card she wrote, "A good worker, attendance needs improvement. Try to improve attendance." By the end of the school year I had attended 138 days of school and was absent 42. On May 22, 1953, the school year ended and I was fortunately promoted to second grade. I did not look forward to having the same teacher the following year, but summer brought a new twist to our lives. Dad was finally ready for us to join him. Grandma was able to get along fairly well, so we packed our belongings and moved into a tiny upstairs apartment, which also served as Dad's massage office, on 4th Street North in Fargo, North Dakota. Our freedom was gone.

Chapter 13
FARGO, ND
1952 - 1958

O ur first apartment in Fargo was the upstairs of a small home owned by Mr. and Mrs. Skaar. They were an elderly Norwegian couple that had been Dad's friends for many years. One of the two rooms was packed with books, magazines, and massage equipment. The other room was a very tiny kitchen and a small bed. We finally had indoor plumbing at the top of the stairs. Mom, Yvonne, Bud and I brought a few articles of clothing and we each had something in the form of entertainment in our possession. I had a small shoebox filled with doll-house furniture and my doll Tudy. The apartment was inadequately tiny and crowded for a family of five. The three of us children slept on the floor next to the massage table. Every morning we had to roll up our quilts and put them in the corner of the closet in case Dad had clients coming for a Swedish massage. The worst part of living there was that we had to be so very quiet. We tiptoed up and down the stairs and spoke to each other in a near whisper. Neither the elderly couple nor Dad could tolerate any amount of noise. It was so stifling because on the farm we spoke loudly, laughed heartily and sang at the top of our lungs.

Mom got a job as a cook at the Graver Hotel working Monday through Saturday, nine hours a day for less than minimum wage. She could have had better employment because she was a gifted pianist, skilled in clerical work and had many other qualifications, but she always said meekly, "I'm no good," a notion instilled in her by her controlling husband, so she did not attempt to get a higher paying job. Dad worked sporadically, depending on how many clients came for a massage, and was often away from the house. He made many trips to the post office and was a member of the Eagles, Elks and Sons of Norway clubs. Yvonne, then 11 years old, was left to watch over Bud and me.

In September, Yvonne walked a little over a mile to Ben Franklin Junior High School, where she was in seventh grade. Bud and I had only seven blocks to Horace Mann Elementary, where he was in fifth grade and I in second. I was so frightened to be in a large classroom with so many pupils. The girls were especially scary. In my young life I had never seen nor played with a girl my age. It didn't help when one of them bit me and often scratched my arms and face, but the teacher, Miss Elofson, was watchful and kind and corrected my classmate's dog-like behavior. The rest of my classmates were very nice and I felt comfortable in a short time.

As soon as we were able to print the alphabet, Miss Elofson gave us a form on which we had to record our personal information. We printed our name, date of birth, sex and nationality. She printed the word "American" on the board for us to copy, but I insisted I was not American so she had to show me how to spell "Norwegian." Dad spoke Norwegian often with his friends. Mom didn't care for the language (though she was fluent), but made it plain that our family was full-blooded Norwegian. The teacher could not talk me out of the notion that stuck in my head so my nationality was entered differently from the rest of the class.

Attending a large school with one grade per classroom was quite an experience. The school even employed a nurse who was responsible for each student's health record. Yvonne and Bud and I did not have the required vaccinations to attend school. The nurse encouraged my parents to send us to the clinic to get our shots, but Dad would not allow us to do so. I had a scar on my upper left arm from an old burn. When I was four years old I ran into Mom when she was carrying a kettle filled with boiling water. Some hot water spilled on my left arm and left a scar in the perfect spot. So when the nurse asked me if I had been vaccinated for small pox, Mom told me to tell a little white lie and simply say "yes."

At the beginning of school, every student had to have a Mantoux test to check for tuberculosis. We Larsen children tested positive. Again we were supposed to go to the clinic, this time to have our lungs x-rayed, but Dad would not allow us to have any form of medical treatment other than his own. He told the public health officials who had received the reports from the school nurse that we had small inactive spots of tuberculosis on our lungs from living among so many T.B. victims in Alaska. He claimed the spots were inactive, so we couldn't possibly infect other students. I was so afraid I would be sent to a sanitarium for a few years to recover. The thought of being far away from my family was traumatic, but Dad was insistent and a smooth talker, so we managed to stay in school.

Horace Mann was a great school. I often claimed that I lost my sack lunch on the way to school, but the truth was I forgot it at home since there wasn't an adult to remind me to bring it. I was frequently invited to different homes to eat lunch with my new friends. There I learned some minimal social skills and a bit of confidence, which had been missing in my life. The school playground was a full city block with potholes everywhere for playing marbles. I became quite skilled in marbles and was very proud of my collection of moonies and cat-eyes. Oftentimes I stayed too late after school, which worried my mom and sister, but I was winning a great collection of marbles and didn't see the necessity of being accountable. The only embarrassing moment that comes to mind from my three years at Horace Mann was in physical education class. One day our teacher demanded our strict attention as we sat on the bleachers. A boy behind me pushed me off the bleachers. I was accused of being disruptive and had to stand bent over in front of the class while the teacher paddled me three times with a ping pong paddle.

We lived at Skaar's for one year. Mr. Skaar made his wife promise that if either of them became ill he or she would not go to the hospital. That summer Mrs. Skaar became very ill. I went downstairs with my mother, who tried to give her a few sips of water. She was too weak to drink the water and died in her bed. It wasn't long after her death that we found a larger apartment on Broadway above Kresge's Dime Store next to Dad's close friend, the violin maker Gunnar Helland, and his wife Edith. Later we heard that Mr. Skaar took ill and went straight to the hospital where he died. Because he did not keep his promise to his wife, Dad was very upset. The rest of us thought it was a good decision, otherwise Mr. Skaar would have died alone.

Our Broadway apartment was quite a bit larger with two rooms and a bath. Dad used the first room closest to the hallway door for his massage practice. Along the walls were huge bookcases containing his many law and medical books. We lived in the other room, which had a kitchen with a table and chairs and a couch. The bathroom off to one side was where we bathed occasionally and where mother washed clothes on a washboard in the bathtub. It was nice to have more room, but not so nice to have so many cockroaches. They scattered all around the floor when the lights went out. I was fully aware of their presence as we still had to sleep on the floor in our sparsely furnished apartment.

It wasn't long before Mom purchased a Singer treadle sewing machine from J.C. Penney for seven dollars. At age seven I was supposed to learn to sew all my own clothing. It was simply unaffordable to purchase any-thing. My first sewing lesson was a gored skirt imprinted with "Lady and the Tramp." It was a circular skirt with so many seams. As I sat at the sewing machine encouraged by my mother and big sister, the tears ran down my cheeks in frustration. I was a tomboy and felt that sewing was for sissies. I finally accomplished the unattainable and wore that "Lady and the Tramp" skirt until the brown dogs were almost white and the former black background was gray. To go with my skirt, I had second-hand shoes and a white blouse purchased from the Salvation Army Store for 25 cents each.

Since leaving Alaska, Dad tried to find a comfortable niche in life. Along with his massage practice he studied law through correspondence from the "College of Law" in Chicago, Illinois. He worked part time as a law clerk at J. E. Hendrickson's law office in the Fargo National Bank building next door to our apartment. In 1955 he received his master's degree in Education Psychology from North Dakota State University. He also took the bar exam but never did practice law. In the fall he became Superintendent of Schools in Maxbass, ND. Mom was not interested in moving again, so we remained in Fargo.

Living in Fargo, we spent many hours with Gunnar Helland in his violin shop. He was a gentle man. Bud learned how to re-hair violin bows and began to learn the skill of violin making. We often went over to his place in the evening to watch his television. We watched Groucho Marx and Lawrence Welk, but the most impressive television event during those years was the coronation of Queen Elizabeth II, on June 2, 1953.

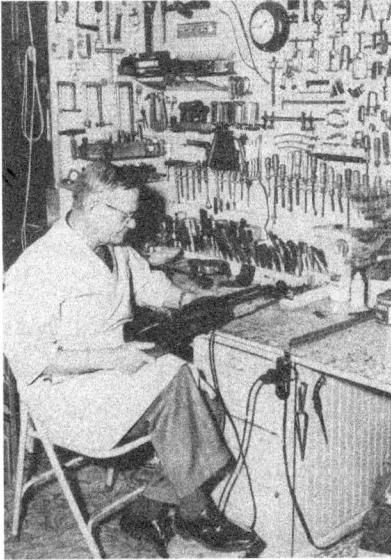

Gunnar Helland, Violin Maker

Gunnar had a favorite chair in front of his T.V. He allowed us to search through the cushion and sides where we found the change that had fallen out of his pockets. He laughed so hard at the three of us and he let us keep the precious coins for our piggy banks.

Dad worked in Maxbass, North Dakota, for one year. The following year he talked Mom into moving to Hendrum, Minnesota, where he was again the Superintendent of Schools. Our house was across the street from the school. A young teacher, his wife and young children lived upstairs. Dad could not tolerate the noise, so he asked the family to find housing elsewhere. Then we had the whole house to ourselves. Dad bought beds for us to sleep on, which was so wonderful, because we had not slept in beds since leaving Grandma's farm.

As the daughter of the superintendent, I felt honored. I had many friends and the teachers paid close attention to my well being. One friend's parents owned the cafe, so there was endless access to free candy and ice cream. Bud was the town's paper boy. He talked me into assisting in the delivery of the Sunday Fargo Forum. I hated getting up at 4 o'clock in the morning when it was still dark to deliver those heavy papers. Bud delivered on the south side of town and I had the north side. It was especially bad in the winter because some people forgot to leave the screen doors unlatched, so I had no place to put the paper except in the snow on the front porch. Once I was so frustrated I sat down on the snowy steps for a long time and got my pants all wet. I had a long cold walk home, but it was worth it because Bud gave me a quarter every Sunday.

Life in Hendrum was good for me but not for Dad. He wasn't feeling well and developed a big boil on the back of his neck. He went to a doctor in Fargo and was diagnosed with diabetes. He refused to take insulin and because of the excess sugar on his brain he got angry easily. He felt that doctors knew nothing and he refused to adhere to their advice. Etola took insulin injections when she was alive so when her condition was complicated by jaundice she did not recover. He was not about to make the same mistake. He felt he could cure himself with fasting and exercise. After the diagnosis he was disappointed with himself and with his situation. He had many disagreements with the people of the town and with the school board so at the end of the school year he resigned.

We moved back to Fargo and rented an apartment above Jarvis's Candy Store on south Eighth Street, close to the Northern Pacific Railroad Depot. When we went to pay our first month's rent, a little girl was standing next to her mother in the candy store. Her mother, older brother and she were going to live in the apartment on the street side of the building and we were renting the apartment on the back side which faced the alley. The little girl turned to look at me and stuck out her tongue. I thought we were going to have a questionable relationship, but soon Patti and I became close friends, more like sisters, even though she was only seven years old and I was ten. We thought it was so cool to live where the smell of chocolate and caramel permeated the whole upstairs, but it wasn't long before the odor was sickening—I cannot eat chocolate to this day.

Patti's mother worked in the afternoon at the American Legion and at the Eagle's Club in the evening until closing. Mom went back to work at the Graver Hotel during the day. At the beginning, Patti was often alone because her brother was out and about with his friends. In the evening she slept on our couch until her mother came home. Soon we were together every day, generally outside on the city sidewalks where we played hopscotch, or out in the alleys where we did chin-ups or hung upside down by our knees on the bars, which surrounded the windows and the staircases going down to the basements of the brick buildings.

Together we enjoyed digging in other people's garbage to find discarded treasures.

We befriended every bum and drunk on the street. Many times the drunks slept in the hallway between her apartment and mine. We simply stepped over them in the morning to go out to play. There were no locks on our doors, but somehow we felt safe in that environment. The summer went by quickly and I started sixth grade at Hawthorne Elementary school while Dad went to Holloway, Minnesota, where he was superintendent of schools.

Yvonne was a junior at Fargo Central High School and Bud was in ninth grade at Agassiz Junior High. Bud went back to Gunnar Helland's Violin Shop in the evenings and weekends to further his education in stringed instrument repair and construction. Hawthorne had an orchestra and, because Dad was happy when he played his violins, I wanted to join in the fun. Bud found some parts for a violin in Gunnar's scrap pile. The neck of the violin had a beautiful lion's head carved at the end, rather than the normal scroll. Bud inlaid some bright green eyes in the lion's head. The inscription inside had Gunnar's initials with the date of 1931. I learned to draw the bow across the strings and without the benefit of lessons, which were unaffordable, I joined the orchestra with my beautiful scrap violin.

Bud Learning the Art of Violin Making

Winter was great fun. Patti and I went ice skating every chance we had at Island Park three blocks away. I loved to play hockey with the boys, but when the rink police discovered I was a girl, I was kicked out. When he wasn't looking, I went back into the rink for the heat of the battle. The boys thought it was cool to have me on the team and warned me to get out when they saw the rink police coming. I loved the game and managed not to get hurt without the proper padding and helmet.

Island Park also had a pool, so when summer came Patti and I went swimming every day. Her mom was happy that I was her companion and gave me the ten cents necessary for admittance. We took lessons and became great swimmers. The park had a lot of playground equipment which allowed us to stay there when the pool wasn't open.

In the fall Mother took her one-week vacation and we all took the train back to Grandma's farm to help with haying. It was so nice to be back even though the work was hard and the weather was hot. We had to be very careful as each bail was lifted onto the hayrack because often the bailer cut a rattlesnake in half. A bale may contain the tail or the head of a snake, and all work stopped until our uncle got rid of the poisonous nuisance with his pitchfork. After a long day in the field Bud and I walked three miles to the Heart River for a bath and a swim.

Yvonne and Mae Larsen
sitting on a hay wagon

One day while we were haying, Mother told us the story of a Mandan Indian Princess who was buried with a leather gown decorated with a thousand elk's teeth. Anyone who found her would become instantly rich. Immediately Bud and I made plans to find the young princess. When the haying was done we took two shovels to the south end of the pasture, where there were signs of Indian graves, and we randomly dug large holes in search of the Indian princess. Uncle Nels discovered what we were doing and at supper time spoke his mind, "Tomorrow morning at the crack of dawn the two of you are going out to fill in every one of those

Yvonne, Elaine and Uncle Nels bailing Hay

holes before I lose one of my expensive cows." We spent the entire next day backfilling. At the end of the day we were returning home exhausted when a rattlesnake startled us. With newfound energy we stoned it until we thought it was dead. Bud picked it up by the rattle and suddenly it came to life and coiled up to his hand. He dropped it quickly without getting bit and we raced home as fast as we could. We had had enough punishment and excitement for one day.

Chapter 14
JUNIOR HIGH SCHOOL
1958 – 1961

A few days after we returned from haying at Grandma's farm, I started
seventh grade at Agassiz Junior High School. Bud was a sophomore
at Fargo Central High School where Yvonne was a senior. Dad
went to Henderson, Iowa, and Mom returned to the Graver Hotel.

That year 31 of us were used as guinea pigs and were placed in an
experimental accelerated class. We were expected to face the challenge of
going faster than the rest of the students and spent all our time with each
other in reading, English, spelling, arithmetic, social science and general
science. We met other students in art, home economics, shop, physical
education, band or orchestra. I felt special to be in this class, but felt at a
disadvantage when the teachers discussed matters of normal living, such
as taxes, life and health insurance or banking. Mom did not pay taxes,
have insurance or use a checkbook. She kept her minimal funds in her
purse hidden in a closet at our apartment. She earned $180 per month—
$100 went to rent, the phone and lights, and the remaining $80 was used
for food and whatever else the four of us needed. She would have been
better off on welfare, but Mom was proud, so we had to live within our
means. Dad's financial situation was private. He contributed zero dollars

to the family and we were taught not to ask for one thin dime.

My next disadvantage was my hatred of reading books. Dad left all his belongings, tables, chairs, massage equipment, desks, typewriters and files tightly packed into the largest bedroom of our apartment. The walls had bookcases lining the entire perimeter and were filled with his expensive books. When he left for the next town each year he warned us, "Don't touch my books!" I despised all his precious belongings, especially his books, because we had to carry heavy boxes of books each time we moved. Because he took one of the bedrooms, Mom, Yvonne, Bud and I had to sleep in the small bedroom where there was a double bed, a set of bunk beds and several dressers. I felt it was unfair to be so crowded because all Dad's junk and disgusting books took up so much space.

In spite of my disadvantages, I worked hard in school trying to keep up with the others. The teachers loved our class and we often launched into great discussions unrelated to the subject matter. We had loads of homework every evening. I didn't get enough hours of sleep and on top of an already heavy schedule I went to orchestra or trampoline practice an hour early each morning. We had to prepare for concerts and other functions performed for our parents and the community.

As a special group our class became haughty and too confident at times. Our social studies teacher was a single woman who we thought was elderly. She kept her gray hair up in a perfect knot on the top of her head, her clothes were neat and colorless, and her large wire-rimmed glasses sat squarely on her wrinkled face. She demanded discipline and performance. One day we decided to pull a trick on her. The bell rang on the hour, so we planned to drop our pencils at exactly two minutes to the hour before the bell would ring. She was writing on the board at the time when 31 pencils fell to the floor, making a terrible racket. She turned around in horror and blurted out with a loud shrill voice, "I thought this was the cream of the crop, but now the cream has soured!" We were punished with a long quiz, a long lecture and it was a long time before she forgave us for our transgression.

In the spring we were studying the Territory of Alaska, when the very same teacher arranged to have my mother come to show her Alaskan slides. Mom explained what it was like to live there and answered many questions, "Yes, we ate moose meat. Seal blubber tastes best when mixed with fresh berries. No, it was not an easy life and I would not want to live there again." I was so proud of Mom and although I had no choice, I was proud that I had lived in Alaska also.

At the close of school Patti and I again hit the streets. I was getting a bit too old to play hopscotch, so we did a lot of exploring. We went through piles of garbage just like a pair of alley cats. Next to the drug store was a liquor store. The drug store's garbage was mostly boxes and crates and the liquor store's garbage was filled with the most beautiful colored bottles we had ever seen. We made couches, tables, chairs, end tables and cupboards out of the crates and boxes. Often the boxes contained packing material which we spread out for tablecloths and doilies. We decorated our "house" with all the beautiful colored bottles. The back alley looked spectacular, but at the end of the day we had to throw everything back into the garbage cans.

When Bud joined Patti and me in exploring, we certainly graduated to a higher level. He took us out to the alley behind the grocery store for the new experience of dumpster diving. Patti and I stood guard when he climbed in for the big search. He brought out many heads of lettuce and bunches of old grapes. The produce wasn't fresh enough to sell to the public, so it was tossed. When we brought it all home we took the outer leaves off the lettuce, washed up the grapes and had the finest meal. Bud taught us a great lesson on how to scrounge for food since the supply at home was meager.

Yvonne had a summer job in a secretarial office on Broadway. She knew it was difficult for Mom to make ends meet, so she helped all she could. She knew that the teachers had sent notes to Mom saying, "Elaine cannot see the chalkboard in the front of the room." Yvonne made an appointment for me to see an optometrist and a week later I picked up my glasses with her money. When I put them on, the world became so clear! I cried for joy because I could see again.

Unfortunately I forgot to take my glasses off when Dad came home from Iowa. He took one look at me in disgust and hollered at me for not exercising my eyes, making it plain that if I had been responsible, the dumb glasses would not be sitting on my face. His verbal abuse was hateful and I disappeared with Patti just to be someplace where he was not.

In the summer Dad stayed in bed for many days at a time—in our family bedroom. We had to serve him breakfast in bed or sandwiches, which he requested from anyone who happened to be in the apartment during the day. He always complained of feeling nervous and ill with his breath having such a fruity odor, typical of an uncontrolled diabetic. In the fall Dad had to get out of bed. He went to Molson, Washington for the year.

Eighth grade was much the same as seventh with some different teachers in different classrooms. I became more involved in after school sports. The eighth graders played basketball against the ninth graders and we battled like a pile of maddened chimpanzees. One of the ninth grade girls, who I thought was a bully, was out to get me after we won that evening's game. As I was standing by my locker, just having put on my heavy fake fur coat, she and three of her buddies tackled me and stuffed me into my locker, slammed the door and left. The air holes of the locker were in the door above the shelf which was above me. I hollered a few times but no one was around. Even the janitor was gone for the evening. I was quickly running out of air when the bully finally came back. She taunted and threatened as I told her that I did not want to die. She said if I told her the numbers of my combination she would let me out on one condition—I had to quit the basketball team. She wanted to win at any cost and found me to be a threat. After a few attempts at the combination, I was freed. Fresh air had never felt so good. She made me promise not to tell anyone and I never did, because the thought of suffering her revenge, supported by her immoral cronies was unthinkable. I finally went back to playing basketball, but with half the effort and spirit.

When school was out for the summer Dad wrote a letter to Bud asking if he and I would please take the train to Seattle to help him drive back to Fargo, because Dad was too nervous to drive the entire way by himself. Bud dutifully got his driver's permit, Dad sent money for the tickets and we boarded the Northern Pacific Railway. It was a beautiful trip. We found seats upstairs in the Vista Dome, which was surrounded with windows for serious sightseers. We saw many species of wildlife and soaked up the beauty of Cascade Park and the Rocky Mountains. The train itself had some wildlife aboard. There were several couples kissing and fondling each other. I was mortified and kept my eyes glued to the scenery outside. After 32 hours of travel, we arrived in Seattle, Washington, where Dad met us at the depot.

After one night in a hotel, we went to visit our cousin and her family at their vacation home on Puget Sound. When the tide came in we went swimming and boating in the ocean. I managed to ingest a few big gulps of sea water. When the tide was out we picked oysters for supper. Dad ate a large quantity of oysters and became very ill, which made us realize it was not the time of year to pick oysters because they can be poisonous in the wrong season. We stayed two more days waiting for his health to improve, then went to Aunt Alma's home in Pilot Rock, Oregon, where our elderly Grandma from the farm was staying.

Grandma was still a beautiful lady at age 93. She walked with a cane and chose to speak more Norwegian than English in her old age. Her clothes were so attractive. She wore silky dresses imprinted with turquoise flowers on a navy blue background. At the top of the row of buttons she wore a rhinestone pin. I loved sitting next to her because she always smelled of freshly brewed coffee, which she drank from a saucer. How I wished time could reverse itself so we could all be living back on the farm together!

Our Aunt Alma and Dad did a bit of arguing. Alma thought it was terrible that her little sister had to work so hard cooking in a hotel restaurant and didn't have a house. Dad claimed he had nothing to do with Mom's decision to stay in Fargo. Alma thought I looked terrible. My hair was cut wrong and my clothes were so homemade looking. She offered to let me live with her for the rest of my childhood years but Dad wouldn't think of it. We soon got on the road for a long nerve-wracking trip home. We had to sit so quietly so Dad wouldn't get nervous. I was happy to get home to Mom, Yvonne and Patti.

In the middle of the summer Yvonne announced that she was going to marry a fellow she met while attending North Dakota State University in north Fargo. I wasn't too happy about the announcement because Yvonne was our chief cook and housekeeper. I didn't know a thing about cooking and cleaning and Bud wasn't expected to know.

Yvonne sewed her wedding gown on the old treadle sewing machine. She entrusted Bud to decorate her cake because he was so artistic. The ceremony took place on September 3, 1960, in the hottest weather possible. My light blue maid-of-honor dress turned two shades darker because it was completely wet with perspiration. Dad did not attend because he was on his way to North River, Washington for his next school position, so Bud gave Yvonne away.

The day after Labor Day I started ninth grade at Agassiz, Bud was a senior at Fargo Central, and Yvonne and her new husband went to live in western North Dakota. Patti, her mom and brother moved to a bigger apartment one block further south. Our new neighbors were very strange. They were a brother and sister who had lived together all their lives. I thought they were old, but the brother was still working. He went to the stockyards every day to slaughter sheep. I saw him coming up the stairs a few times and he was covered with blood. I didn't want to know these people, but some of their little friends became quite acquainted with us. Our entire apartment became infested with bed bugs.

Mom and I wrapped towels around our noses and scrubbed every-thing with buckets of water and strong ammonia, but the bed bugs were everywhere. I was embarrassed in school every day with bites over my whole body and face. The bed bugs left an odor on my skin that faintly smelled like skunk or roadkill. I told everyone that I had a strange skin condition because telling the truth was like admitting to poverty. The bed bugs stayed for several months when finally they must have all died by infecting each other.

At Christmas Dad came home on the train and we celebrated with our usual Norwegian food of lefse, lutefisk, flatbread, cranberries and potato dumplings. Generally Dad received dried mutton legs and a keg full of gammelost from his brother in Norway. The gammelost, which means old cheese, smelled up the whole apartment. When Dad went back after Christmas vacation he promised that if I worked hard in school he would pay me a dollar for each "A" I earned.

By the time Dad came back for the summer, I showed him my report card. I had gotten straight "A"s. He looked at it and reluctantly gave me seven dollars. I had never had that much money in my possession. Of course he pointed out that I must have thought I was smart, but in no uncertain terms would I ever hold a candle to the intelligence of Etola. He never offered to pay for any achievement again.

That summer Bud and I had the great opportunity to go to Bible camp in Cooperstown, ND, with many others from our church. We brought our suitcases to the dormitories, where we met our counselors, then were given a short tour of the camp. Later we all met at the outdoor chapel for services and a pep talk regarding the rules of the camp. Next was supper, then free time to get acquainted with the others.

That evening my friend Carol and I met a couple of nice boys from another town. The four of us decided to go for a long walk in the woods since it was still daylight. Our curfew was 10:00 p.m., so we had a few hours to enjoy the evening, but we simply lost track of the time. We ran back to our dormitories and arrived four minutes late. My counselor had her pajamas and robe on with her hair up in curlers. She was pacing the floor. "Oh there you are, young ladies," she said, "I was looking for you and now that you are disrespectfully late, you will pay dearly for this." Carol and I were up early every morning peeling potatoes for breakfast, dinner and supper, day after day. We were required to go to church services in the evening, then straight to bed. I know Carol's parents had to pay her way to camp, but our church paid my way because Mom couldn't afford it. There was no money lost; I just became an expert potato peeler.

Chapter 15
HIGH SCHOOL AND MARRIAGE
1961 - 1965

B ud graduated from high school in the spring of 1961, but continued to live at home while he attended Concordia College across the river in Moorhead, Minnesota. Dad went to Aberdeen, Washington, where he taught math at a junior college. Finally I got to go to Fargo Central High School, only three blocks from my apartment. All the students who finished ninth grade at Ben Franklin Junior High on the north side of Fargo and all who finished ninth grade at Agassiz Junior High on the south side of Fargo finally came together to form one huge class of 576 sophomores. The school building was huge, but there were so many students that we had to attend language classes across the street in an old elementary school building called Emerson Smith.

My subjects as a sophomore were art, the second year of Latin, biology, rapid English and experimental geometry. Physical education that year was so exciting because Fargo Central had an Olympic-sized indoor swimming pool. The school board made a mandatory requirement that all students had to learn to swim or would not graduate. I couldn't believe my luck. Patti and I had been swimming every chance we could get at the

Island Park Swimming Pool in the summer. We were like fish and this requirement was a done deal.

Experimental geometry was difficult because it encompassed both plain and solid geometry presented to us through a new teaching method. The first couple of weeks we raced through squares, rectangles, triangles and circles, then went directly to the lateral area and cubical contents of cubes, cones, cylinders, pyramids and prisms. Some of us were lost, but the teacher was exceptionally patient and gave us help after school. We even felt free to phone him in the evening. Although I thought I was flunking, I got a "B" on my report card as a gift for my involvement in an experimental class.

The rest of my courses were fun and interesting, except for rapid English. The grammar portion was fine, but we were expected to give an oral book report every month. It was obvious to the teacher that I had not read the books I reported on, as I stuttered and shook in front of the class. Shakespeare, Chaucer, Tennyson, Hemingway, Steinbeck and Poe didn't impress me much at that time because I hated to read. I was told so often, "Don't touch my books!" that I didn't care to touch any books. I mastered the art of good listening and note taking.

My counselor understood my difficulty with the rapid English class and arranged for my transfer to a normal English class in the second semester. There we focused on grammar and a bit of writing with only one required written book report for the semester. I was no longer miserable nor challenged, but very happy.

Dad returned home from Aberdeen, Washington, for the summer. I began to take interest in boys but was not allowed to go on dates. When invited to go to the movie theater, I arranged to have my date pick me up at Patti's apartment. I knew I was breaking the rules of the household. Mom thought it was fine that I go out on occasion but Dad was adamantly against the whole idea. Patti promised not to answer the phone in case Dad was looking for me and since her mother worked in the evening, all angles were covered so I could have a bit of a social life.

That summer I tried to do some babysitting to earn some money to make school clothes, but it was a disaster. Patti's mom knew of a single divorced mother who had three young children, ages two, four and six. I went over to their apartment one Saturday to take care of those cute little blonde children. The children were very thin and the apartment reeked of stale cigarette smoke and dirty diapers. The children complained of being hungry, so at lunch time I opened the refrigerator only to find a six-pack of beer. I searched the cupboards frantically to find something to feed them, but there wasn't even one slice of bread. I poured them each a glass of water and one for myself and told them that maybe their mother would bring some food home.

When the mother arrived she was empty-handed. I told her that if she could afford beer and cigarettes she could certainly afford some bread, peanut butter and milk for the children. She tried to slap my face but I was quick and ran out the door without pay. After that bad experience I decided to earn money by sewing and doing alterations, which worked out well.

Grandma died on Oct. 2nd, 1962, at the age of 95. We all went to her funeral at the Heart River Lutheran Church in Mandan, North Dakota. It wasn't so terribly sad that she passed away, because she had lived a long, wonderful life. Our Uncle Ted had long since moved from the home farm to Arizona and Uncle Nels was past retirement age and simply could not handle the hard work anymore. The farm was sold and all the belongings were auctioned off. I was so sad over the fact that I no longer had a place where I could escape and run freely over the hills and prairies.

Heart River Lutheran Church

For the school year of 1962-1963, Bud switched colleges and went to Moorhead State University. Dad went back to southeast Alaska to Hydaburg. He enjoyed being back with the native people but could not stand the living conditions. His house leaked like a sieve and the mice ruined many of his belongings. He returned home in the midst of my junior year. I was studying U.S. History, English, experimental chemistry, phy. ed., highway safety, orchestra and German. Of all these subjects, German was my favorite.

With Dad back home, I became a very nervous person. I was responsible for cleaning our apartment every Saturday morning, which was never good enough. He complained that there was dust on the telephone or dust on the coffee table or dust someplace else. If we left our cereal bowls and spoons in the kitchen sink he hollered at me for that too. There seemed to be less money for food, so I tried to help Mom by not eating lunch in the cafeteria at noon. It was too expensive. I got by with a few cups of coffee which the teachers were kind enough to share. I don't believe any of them knew how little I had to eat and probably just assumed that I was addicted to caffeine.

I continued to sneak over to Patti's in order to go on a few dates, but by summer I felt that I would never have a future. My boyfriend announced that he was going to quit high school because he had enough credits to go to college, so we broke up and went our separate ways. I hadn't dreamed of marrying this young man or anyone else at the time, he was just very kind and I considered him a close friend. I spent quite a bit of time with Bud that summer trying my best to stay away from our apartment where I was continually confronted with Dad's anger.

Before school started I had a long discussion with Mom. I wanted to quit high school and get a job. I also begged her to let me join the Navy, but she convinced me that I should stick it out for just one more year and I agreed.

When Dad walked out the door to go to Ortonville, Minnesota, for the year, I was never so happy to see anyone leave in my life. He had become so uncontrollably angry and nervous. He was difficult for our family and was especially mean to Mom. I loved her so much and could not stand to see her hurt in any way.

I went back to Fargo Central for my senior year as I had agreed. I took English, phy. ed., psychology, world history, art, orchestra and the second year of German. I knew we were going to have a new German teacher this year, but did not know what to expect. I envisioned an elderly person with white hair and a cane, maybe some old person who had escaped from Germany during the war. The name written on my class schedule was L. Gunderson, which sounded like an old European name to me.

With a bit of apprehension, 30 classmates and I ran over to room 390 in the old Emerson Smith building for the third hour. I took my seat in the first desk of the first row by the door. The teacher hadn't arrived yet, so we tried to guess who it might be. As the bell rang he limped into the classroom and, most assuredly, he had very white hair. "Sure enough," I thought, "This is the old guy from the war." But as he turned to face the class I realized that he was young. "Is this your first year of teaching?" I asked. He nodded and I said, "Well, how about that." The rest of the class started laughing. When we settled down, he laid out the rules of the class and what he expected of us. I felt him glaring at me because I had been disrespectful. He assigned massive amounts of vocabulary for us to memorize for the next day, and I couldn't wait to get home to tell my mom about my new German teacher.

It wasn't long before Mr. Gunderson had students coming in to his classroom after school just to visit. He was just 21 years old, single and had just graduated from Concordia College in Moorhead, Minnesota, the previous spring. We found that he had worked in the summer for California Packing Company, a subsidiary of Del Monte, picking peas. One night he fell off the pea picker and broke his leg. He had his cast removed the day before school started, so that is why he limped into the classroom on the first day. His hair was naturally blonde but had turned white from so many hours in the sun.

The janitor was often upset by our presence in the classroom. He tried to clean the classroom but there were many of us students just hanging around after school. I can still hear him, "Gunderson, could you please get these damn kids out of here so I can get my work done?" Mr. Gunderson told him to go on to the next room because ours was clean enough. He didn't want to tell us to go home.

By October, I was thoroughly smitten by this young teacher. In art class we began painting on canvas with oils. My subject was a bust of Mr. Gunderson with our German textbook in the foreground and a German castle in the background. I was not secretive about my crush on this teacher.

One day my counselor called me into her office. She said, "Sit down, young lady." I sat down and she pointed her fingers at me saying, "There will be no student in this high school falling in love with a teacher." I was mortified but left in agreement.

On November 22, 1963, I was in art class painting a different subject when the news blasted on the intercom. "President John F. Kennedy was killed by an assassin in Dallas, Texas." We were all shocked and numbed by the news. We were dismissed from school because no one could concentrate anyway. The next day was my birthday and I didn't celebrate at all. Everyone was too sad.

I made it through the year but kept a low profile. I didn't want the year to end and since graduation was just around the corner, I felt horrible because I would never see Mr. Gunderson again. When classes finally ended we went to the Fargo Civic Auditorium to practice for the graduation ceremony. When we finally received our diplomas, I was happy and sad. Later I got a phone call from Mr. Gunderson. He explained that he was going to Europe in a few days, but was free Saturday and did I want to drive around the lake country in Minnesota for the day? Oh, yes, I certainly did.

Dad wasn't home yet, so I left a note for Mom and Bud telling them where I went and with whom. I borrowed a nice shorts outfit from Patti, along with her brand new red Angora sweater. Somehow I thought this had all been a figment of my imagination, but finally he picked me up and we drove for miles through the lake country. We went to supper at a resort and I could barely eat my salad. By the end of the evening I had his Concordia ring in my possession. I wrapped some strings from my graduation tassel around it to make it fit and to hide it. For a graduation present he gave me a coat pattern and some camel-colored wool to keep me busy while he was in Europe. He also kept me busy while he was away reading the letters which he wrote at least twice a week.

When Mr. Gunderson came back from Europe, Dad was back from Ortonville, Minnesota. I dared to invite my teacher to meet Dad.

Unfortunately it didn't go so well. Dad asked him how he liked Norway. Mr. Gunderson teased him and said he thought Norway was a hopeless mountainous country and that all the people should move out so the place could be bombed flat. Then when the people moved back they would have some fine farmland and a better spot to live. Dad did not accept the fact that Mr. Gunderson was teasing. When he left, Dad told me that I was to have nothing to do with that cocky teacher. I was never supposed to see him again. So until Dad left for a position in Osnabrock, North Dakota, I was picked up for dates at Patti's apartment.

In the fall I went to Concordia College. On December 18, 1964, Mr. Gunderson and I got engaged. Not until then did I call him by his first name, Loren. When Dad came home from Osnabrock he was fighting mad about our upcoming marriage. Dad was in Fargo, but chose not to attend our wedding, so Bud gave me away. While two very large men stood guard at the church door watching for Dad in case he decided to show up, we were married on August 14, 1965. Loren was 23 and I was 18. The principal and his wife and some of the teachers from Fargo Central High School came to our wedding. The counselor who had warned me not to fall in love with my teacher was there and congratulated us heartily.

I felt sorry for Mom because she cried after the ceremony, but Bud wasn't married yet and was still living at home, so I knew she would be okay. I was very happy to leave the poverty of home and the angry man who was to blame for our hardship.

Elaine's Wedding Day

Chapter 16
THE GRAVE - FIFTY YEARS LATER - 1993

M other always told us she did not want us children, Yvonne, Bud and me, to return to Alaska. She said it was not a good place to be, as she remembered the hard times she endured along with the painful memory of losing Etola. Yet Yvonne, having just received her master's degrees in special education and guidance and counseling, found there was a need for her skills in Alaska. She left North Dakota and went to teach in Kipnuk, Alaska, in the fall of 1993.

Mom had been living alone in Mandan, N.D., since Dad died in January of 1981. She enjoyed being back at the place of her birth, where she was able to return to her family farm on occasion. There she could view the beautiful hills and prairies and relive her wonderful childhood. She loved her family history and frequently went to the Heritage Center at the capitol in Bismarck to see her cousin Nancy Hendrickson's original homestead cabin with many of its original contents. I asked Mom often if she wanted to have a home in Fargo, N.D., to be closer to me since Yvonne was no longer near her. She stated she had very bad memories of living in Fargo and wanted to stay in Mandan.

Now that Yvonne was in Kipnuk, she was anxious to find Etola's grave in Anvik. No one in the family had ever been there, including Mom and Dad. She also wanted to see her first home, Shageluk, Alaska. She arranged to go on Saturday, September 19, 1993. She flew from Kipnuk to Bethel, then from Bethel to Aniak. Aniak is a town of about 450 people. The airport provides flight service to most of the small villages in the Lower Yukon. On Monday morning she flew to Anvik in a Markair single-engine 207 through wind and fog over thick forests and many lakes and winding rivers. As prearranged, she was picked up by the school pickup and met the school principal, Mr. Don Yates. He had located an elderly lady, Alta Jeru, who knew the whole story of Etola's funeral and where she was buried.

She proceeded on to Alta's home, where she had to climb up the hillside to get to the pink-painted dwelling. Yvonne knocked on the door and when Alta opened it, they had an instant liking for each other. Alta invited Yvonne into her immaculate home, where she told of Mom and Dad's influence on the village and how everyone adored Mom and Etola. After she told Yvonne that she looked so much like Etola, she launched into the story of Etola's funeral.

Episcopalian Church in Anvik

Mom and Dad hired Gachidle Workman to bring Etola's body to Anvik by dogsled. The trail from Shageluk to Anvik was 25 miles long and took about 4 hours to make the trip. Alta's children were playing outside when they came to tell her that a team of nine dogs had arrived. There was a white covered load on the sled and the team carried it to the church. Our parents were in such deep sorrow they could not make any of the funeral arrangements and asked Rev. Henry Chapman to take care of all of them. The next day the grave was made ready and the funeral was held at 2 p.m. Alta heard the funeral bells at the Episcopalian Church ringing but she could not attend since she had two small children.

Etola's Grave in Anvik

Alta and Yvonne then walked the path through the woods to the cemetery. The trail was covered with gold leaves, high bush cranberries and rose plants. Surrounding them were birch trees, evergreens and elder trees, whose roots grow above the ground. The air was cool and crisp and smelled of fallen leaves. They walked to the grave, its fence now broken down and in need of repair. It had been cared for at one time by Elizabeth Krueger Walker, Alta's niece and a friend of Etola. Elizabeth died in 1988 or 1989 and is buried next to Etola.

On September 22, Yvonne decided to walk to our sister's grave one more time. She wrote, "I went up the path where my sister's body was carried. My feelings were of disbelief and I was somewhat overwhelmed as I thought of 50 years ago and today. I thought of how part of my bloodline is buried here on this hillside, so far away from my own existence. It's an awesome reality to think that a half a century can easily be erased by a single trip to a gravesite."

Then Yvonne walked down the pathway to the church. There she watched the river that flows past Anvik and saw a float plane taking off the water. She returned to the school where she was picked up by a four-wheeler and taken to her waiting airplane. She was flying to Shageluk.

Chapter 17
THE DISCOVERY

In Shageluk, Yvonne went straight to the school. It is a new and very modern school, as the old schoolhouse where Dad taught had long since been torn down. The principal had told the people of the village that Herman Larsen's daughter was returning for a visit. Yvonne met many people that day and was able to go blueberry picking with some of the school children and their chaperones. On the large hill one of the residents told Yvonne about how Mom was held in such high esteem and said of her, "When she was with us, we never saw her." While Mom was there she dressed as they did, picked berries, made moose skin moccasins, ate with them and ministered in such a way that, unlike other white people they had known, she didn't stick out in the crowd, so they always said, "We didn't see her." They were all sorry about Etola's death and wished Mom could still be with them.

After school was out for the afternoon, Yvonne walked down the hill and across the dirt road. Just then, a woman came out of a little yellow house to empty her big white dish pan. She was slowly emptying the dirty water out when she looked up and saw Yvonne. She was shocked at seeing a white person with light blonde hair. She threw the dishpan and all on the ground, shouting, "Who you is?" Yvonne introduced herself and the woman, Mary John, invited her into the house, saying it was nice to see her as she had not seen her since she was a baby. Mary apologized for the lack of electricity in her home. She couldn't afford to pay the bill, so it had been disconnected. She made tea for Yvonne and herself on the wood-stove, and then served fresh blueberry pudding and salmon strips. She remembered the Larsen family very well and they talked for several hours. Then she and Yvonne went to play bingo. After bingo they returned to the house. Yvonne asked if she could stay with Mary for the night. Mary was a bit surprised that she would want to stay in her old house but said it was fine. She told about how her son passed away and how drinking helped to ease the pain. She cried and performed a few sorrowful looking Indian dances in the middle of the floor as she wailed. This made Yvonne somewhat uncomfortable. They finally went to bed at one o'clock in the morning. Yvonne's bed was so lumpy and from the fear that Mary would get up again to dance and cry, she barely slept the whole night. Yvonne also pondered the new information Mary shared with her that evening. The next morning after breakfast Yvonne ran back to the school to give me a call.

"Elaine, are you sitting down?"

"No," I said, "What is going on?"

"I made a discovery you are not going to believe," she said.

I returned with, "Oh, I suppose you are going to tell me that we have a half-sister or something."

"How did you know?" she asked.

"I didn't know," I said, "Just knowing Dad, and how Mom always told us not to go back to Alaska, I always suspected something funny went on."

"Well, you are right!" she said.

"Yvonne, you are kidding me. I was just guessing."

As my heart was pounding with excitement, Yvonne emphatically stated, "Elaine, I am not kidding. We have a half-sister and her name is Lori Woodford Christiansen. She is a special education teacher and lives in Metlakatla, Alaska. I'l fax a picture of her when she was about twelve years old. You won't believe how much she looks like us. I'll tell you more of the details when I get back to Kipnuk. I'm using the school's phone, so I have to cut this short." Before we hung up, we agreed not to tell our 83 year-old mother of the discovery she made at this time. Perhaps there would be a better time at a later date.

The principal in Shageluk was so excited and happy. She had taken the picture of Lori off the wall and helped Yvonne fax it to me. Lori certainly looked just like Yvonne and me when we were that age. I, in turn, faxed the photo to our brother Bud with a note saying he should not tell Mom of our exciting discovery. Then the principal and Yvonne went to the school kitchen to meet Lori's other half-sister Agnes Woodford, who was the school cook. Agnes said she was sorry that Mary had told her about Lori. Everyone agreed not to tell Yvonne about her half-sister before she arrived in Shageluk because they thought she would be so angry. Yvonne said she had the right to know and was not angry; she was happy, confused, in turmoil and delighted all at the same time. Her mission was to find the grave of her dead sister and now she found a sister who is alive.

Yvonne went back to Kipnuk with Lori's phone number. She had been hesitant to give Lori a call. Then the assistant superintendent of the Alaskan school system, John Weiss, came to Kipnuk to hold an in-service for the teachers. Yvonne told him how she discovered a new half-sister on a recent trip to Shageluk. John asked, "Lori Christiansen is your sister?"

"Yes," she replied. John then encouraged her to give Lori a call because she was such a good teacher and a nice person.

That evening Yvonne called Lori. Lori was in shock. She had just watched a television program not an hour earlier where someone had found her family. Lori had told her husband, Arne, that she would never find her white family even though she had been searching for years. She knew that Yvonne was five months older than she when the Larsens left Shageluk, but she was stunned to hear that she had a younger brother and a younger sister. She had never had a brother before. She was happy to hear that Mae Larsen was still alive and was sad to hear that our father had passed away thirteen years earlier because she still wanted to find him and get even with him for denying her existence. She thought he was a highly educated, rich person who could have helped her escape her difficult childhood. She was assured that we didn't have it so easy either.

I had borrowed Dad's Alaskan diaries from Mother's home and busied myself for a week making four copies of his daily entries from all the years he was in Shageluk. I was to keep one, then give Yvonne and Bud each a copy and send one to our new-found sister in Alaska. I then called Lori to introduce myself and to tell her she was going to receive a copy of our Dad's diary. Of the four of us, the diaries would be the most meaningful to Lori, as she would know all of the people mentioned and could read about the events prior to her birth and the few months afterward when her father left the village. Shortly thereafter I received Lori's first letter.

October, 1993

Dear Elaine,

Thank you again for all the work you did in copying the diary. I am so enjoying it! I've been experiencing such strange emotions. When I first heard from you and Yvonne I suddenly felt whole. I can't describe the feeling! I never knew I was running around this world as a half-person, but when I first heard from Yvonne it was though the whole right side of my body started filling in. I was all of a sudden whole. Weird. I only read about stories like this, but I actually felt the feeling.

Also while reading the diary I really felt a strong emotion toward our "father." I could feel the emotions he was feeling. I knew the people he talked about and, strangely enough, I felt in my life the very same way he felt toward those very same people. The way he perceived those people was the same as I did.

When I read about Etola I sure felt a great sense of loss. Strangely, I felt completely sad all day. I don't know if I'm also grieving for all her friends who are all dead now, just in the last few years: Ida, Bertha, Genevieve, Riley, Anna, Matilda Mom, Albert, Dorothy, Robert, Johnnie, Arthur P., Grace, Bella, Billy P., etc. They were all great friends and last year when I went home the loss was greatly felt. It was like wandering in a ghost town. This diary brought them back for a while. It was great! (And sad.)

Anyway, I love talking to you and can't wait to meet you. We have to make our meeting very special. Wouldn't it be nice to plan a big family reunion? I envision Seattle along with my husband's great family. They haven't seen each other since we last were there about six years ago. Oh, well, a person can dream, can't he?

I am enclosing an extra old Christmas card for brother Bud so his family can get the idea of what our bodies look like. I find that women are more emotional and guys stand back and get a kick out of us being our wonderful selves. Silly, huh? I enjoyed seeing Bud's family (from Yvonne). I have never in my life had a brother and that knowledge alone is pretty overwhelming. I wouldn't know what to say or how to act toward a brother. Imagine that?

Well, I hope this letter finds you and your family well. We had very bad news today. Arnie's son by his first marriage died this morning. He was 30 years old. We always think our children will outlive us. One never knows. I was married at 18 to my first husband (8 years). Arnie and I will be married 22 years in June. We are old people now. My son from my first marriage is 33 years old.

Love,

Lori

Chapter 18
LORI'S STORY
OLD GRAMMA CECILIA

It was a cold morning in the third month of the year on the third day of the month in 1942. The Grandmother was having difficulty starting the day. She should be thinking about making plans to make the Announcement soon. This meant that she should begin to put all her worldly possessions together and start to plan for her final journey to the Big Village. It was nice to think of all the relatives and all her people, no matter what village they were from, who had taken the journey before her and it would be so nice to see all of them again. She, of course, presided over all the burials and knew the ceremony by heart. Along with her other thoughts there were a few requests she needed to make known to the family, then she would be ready to follow the well-worn sacred trail to the land of the Big Village. She let herself imagine how her family would react when her final day arrived. Her daughter Matilda would be in charge.

The first day of death, after the wailing of mourning ceases, the women chosen by the daughter have to clean and purify her body and put on her best clothes. The men make a platform on which to lay her body, which is propped up six inches high under the head. When the family decides to place her body on the platform, either on the floor of her house or the floor of the Kashim (a semi-subterranean building where all Indian ceremonies are held), this begins the first day of her journey.

Old Gramma Cecilia

The journey to the Big Village lasts four days. These four days are used by the people of the Big Village to prepare the biggest potlatch (feast and celebration) to welcome the deceased to join them forever. In this land there will be neither hardship nor suffering, only happiness.

After she is laid out on the platform, a small cloth is placed next to her body that holds all of her favorite belongings and everything she needs to make her journey, such as matches and snacks. Also on the cloth is a cup and saucer. The women of the village start cooking immediately. This is the time to share the last meal with her and to give her the nourishment she needs to complete the first day of her journey. A portion of all the food and drink that is served beside her is placed into the cup and saucer so that all the onlookers can see that their donations are being shared. Because she is an elder, the older women are served first. If a man dies, the men are the first to share the meal and if a child dies, the children are served first. The people make sure the deceased is fed three times a day. A "sign" is made over the food and all other items that come in contact with the funeral ceremony. The "sign" is made four times by a motion with the hands as if one were picking feathers off a bird or picking a piece of food and throwing it to the wind. The "sign" is made to ensure that everything is going with her on her journey.

There is an oil lamp or a candle placed next to the body and lit so she can see the sacred trail. Should this go out during the viewing, she may wander off the trail in the dark and never find her way. She may be destined to wander aimlessly through all eternity or her spirit may come back to the village as a ghost and she will never see the Big Village. If an observant person notices the light going out, he must quickly put his hands over her eyes until the light is replenished. By doing so, the light of her journey is not disturbed.

The women spend the first three days of the ceremony sewing a beautiful fur parka, boots and gloves that she will wear on the fourth day. When she crosses the river between the outer world and earth she is the center of attention. Entering the Big Village, she will be dressed so beautifully and the Great Chief there will look down kindly on the village that made her so fit to join the perfect Big Village. During the same time, the men are busy making her coffin and a fence to put around the grave as a marker. The fence is the final tribute to the loved one and on it is carved all of her favorite things.

On the third night a big farewell potlatch is held. The people from the neighboring villages are invited. Everyone brings the finest dishes and many gifts are shared in her honor. The potlatch lasts well into the night.

Early in the morning, at about 4:00 a.m., the entire village is awakened, including the small children and newborns. This is done so that the spirits of those who are sleeping do not turn into the eternal sleep of the deceased. This is a special time to say farewell and help with the final leg of the journey. She is now placed in the coffin dressed in her furs and fine beadwork. All the members of the family sing a farewell song in the Indian language. In this case the song will be sung by her daughter and grandchildren. After this is done, all the people start clapping sticks together and stomping their feet extremely loudly in unison. The sound is deafening and by doing this they have chased her spirit away from the earth. She has reached the Big Village. All her belongings from the cloth are placed in the coffin. One has to make sure there are no pictures of anyone or the spirit of the person in the picture may follow the spirit of the deceased. The coffin is now sealed and ready for burial. There is only one window in the ceiling of the Kashim and the coffin is removed through it. The coffin can not be taken out the door because the body cannot retrace its steps in the land of the living. Once outside, the coffin is taken to the cemetery by sled or by boat. After the coffin is lowered and the fence is in place, food is placed in the plate and the cup for the birds. If any food somehow did not get to her by the "sign," the birds would let the people of the other world know that the traveler had plenty of food.

All personal effects are burned at the cemetery and the smoke brings them to her new residence. Some effects are put up as shrines so, when viewed, the loved ones are not forgotten. Grandmother made a mental note to make sure her daughter Matilda did not forget any part of the burial ceremony. Like all her ancestors, death was a part of life. There was no fear, just something inevitable. Death this morning seemed inviting.

She quickly put this thought out of her mind. This was a new day and there were things which had to be done. The small cabin needed a warm fire for her family, who was still sleeping. At 5:30 a.m. she slowly removed the bear skin covering and felt the blast of cold sink into her very being. Although it was soon spring, the weather still had the lingering effects of the cold winter. She moved quickly to stay warm. The walls and windows were covered with frost. She scolded herself for not getting up in the middle of the night to keep the fires going. She grabbed her fur parka and went to the wood box next to the fifty-gallon oil barrel stove in the far corner of the cabin. GHUTRZ AH EE! The box was completely empty!

She was past seventy years old and was wondering who of her sleeping family could help get wood. She did not want to disturb her sleeping granddaughters, Agnes, who was eight, and Celene, who was ten. She had already pushed them to the limit as they helped with day to day survival and the extra sleep would do them good. Her daughter Matilda was also sleeping fitfully, as she was near her time to deliver a baby. Matilda's husband Woodford was in the last stages of T.B., which was ravishing his body. The only special boy of the house was two year-old Ralph, and it would be a long time before he was able to help, so she resigned to face the dark alone and get the wood by herself.

The family was living in a village called Shageluk, Alaska, a small Athabascan Indian Village located on the Innoko River, a tributary of the great Yukon River, sixty miles from the Innoko—Yukon Junction across from the Grandmother's hometown of Holy Cross. Life was difficult for the Athabascan Indian people. At this time tuberculosis was raging through the villages and the disease was taking its toll on the people regardless of age. Her daughter Matilda had already lost eight of her children. The population was down to approximately 150 people. Gramma Cecilia wondered if there would be enough people remaining who would be impacted by her life's experience. She did her best to pass down everything she knew to her only daughter and, as far as she knew, Matilda was an excellent artist in beading and skin sewing. She was also a good listener to the stories of the past. Gramma wished Matilda had not been so restless. It would have satisfied Old Cecilia so much.

Sometimes life wasn't fair! Gramma remembered when she was so happy with her mother and father and the life she had in her village of Holy Cross. She loved the cold winters when animals were abundant for hunting and trapping. The winter fishing was excellent, with plenty of blackfish, pike and whitefish. Spring was a fabulous time of year with all the ducks, geese, swans, cranes and the delicious bird eggs. The whitefish and chee were so good after finishing all the winter dry fish. Beaver trapping was in full swing in the spring and the excitement of going to summer fish camps was glorious.

At the fish camps were thousands of king, silver and dog salmon to harvest for winter eating. There was plenty for the dogs who were used for transportation hitched to sleds over the frozen land. Berries were everywhere! There were salmon berries, blueberries, black or crowberries, low and high bush cranberries, red currants and her favorite gahg a veeda (black currants). Of course there was the moose! She could almost taste the wonderful stew on cold winter days. She felt better recalling the good times.

A furrow came over her brow when she started thinking of when she met the first white men. They were Russians who came to her village and completely changed the life she loved. She absolutely hated them. She was a young innocent girl when she was taken advantage of and they were abusive to her people. They forced their lifestyle on her people and she would never forgive them in her heart. They even tried to force her family to speak the unspeakable language of Russian. This was one thing no one would force her to do. She loved her language too much. She never let the dreaded white people know she could understand Russian and sometimes used this to her advantage. First the Russians came, then the traders, then the Catholic priests and nuns to Holy Cross.

She had just entered her teen years when she was put in the Catholic Mission to learn the white ways. She could never forget one early fall when the nuns brought all the mission girls on a berry picking expedition. She strayed farther into the woods to be by herself with her own thoughts and to find the bigger berries that grew further inland where no one was allowed to go. As she was picking the berries she heard a noise behind her. She turned to look and there she saw the enemy. He was a member of the down-the-river people who had been enemies of her people for quite some time. Before she could call for help, he put his hand over her mouth and dragged her over the hill where he met the rest of his band. They were taking her as a slave. Her mother had told her about these people and she was taught never to show fear even though her heart was racing rapidly. She glared at them as they spoke in their own language, which she could not understand. She held her head high and followed the leader down the other side of the hill to a nearby waiting birch bark canoe. Once she was shoved into the canoe, she knew she was going to be taken to their home down river. After they reached the village, which is the present day St. Michael, they brought her to their chief to find out what they should do with her. They knew several families who needed a slave, but when the chief laid eyes on her he was so smitten with her beauty that he told them to leave her with him. He was going to take her for a wife, even though he was forty years older than she. The people she was with were Eskimos. They were not pleased with his decision, but as long as she was with the chief she was to be respected.

The chief taught her his Eskimo language, along with many of their ways and customs, and treated her wonderfully. She respected him and grew to love him. They never had children, so she had all of his attention. She lived a happy life for a few years. She never lacked for anything. The women showed her how to make baskets and sew skins. She soon became a skilled artist.

Her happy life ended when he died. One of her husband's relatives told her to escape and go back to her people, because the Eskimos were going to make her a slave because she was not one of them. She was provided with a canoe and escaped back to her home, Holy Cross. Everyone was so surprised to see her because they all thought she had died.

Now she turned her thoughts to where she was in Shageluk and remembered when the white teachers came and then the Episcopalians arrived in nearby Anvik. How she wished they would all go back to where they came from. Now she was forced to learn the English language. She learned it to stay one step ahead of her family, but she refused to speak it.

Getting back to the matter at hand, she opened the door and the blast of cold air was frigid. She used the one good thing that white man provided, a flashlight, to guide her to the wood stack to get the wood her granddaughters forgot to bring in the night before. She quickly gathered an armful and went back to the house. She took the butcher knife, which was lying next to the stove, to make shavings for kindling from one of the pieces of dry wood. She knelt down, stood the wood on end and tucked the other end into the firm part of her abdomen, then started the smooth whittling of the wood, watching it form into little curls of shavings. She opened the door of the stove and placed the shavings on the bottom, then stacked a few pieces of wood on top of the shavings. She lit the shavings with a match and gently blew on the tiny flame to help it ignite. Then she added birch wood, which would prolong the heat for several hours. This done, she closed the door of the stove and opened both dampers. The sound of the roaring fire took the chill from her bones and already the small log cabin began to feel its warmth.

This completed, she took the dipper that was hanging on the wall and dipped some water from a pail, poured it into a kettle, then set it on the stove to boil for morning tea. In another pot, she boiled more water to make mush for the family. She had to wake up her granddaughters soon, as they had to go to the white man's school. Matilda should also be aroused because she worked for the white teachers in exchange for some food and clothing for her family.

Old Cecilia angrily thought that going to school was a waste of time. Why should her granddaughters want to have a white life when their own was sufficient? They sat locked up in the schoolhouse all day and by the time they came home in the evening it was already dark outside. She didn't think they learned one thing that could be of value to their daily living. She wished they would soon reach age 16 so they could quit school and get on with their lives. They weren't helping at home and still had to be fed. In her day, she wasn't allowed to come to the dinner table unless she put in a full day's work. Sometimes when there was too much to do, she showed the white teacher that she was still in charge of her family and kept her granddaughters home. The fact that Celene and Agnes tried to speak English in the house really made her angry. She forbade this. She knew her daughter Matilda spoke English, which she learned at the Catholic Mission in Holy Cross, but because she was employed by the white teachers, she had to. In exchange for her work she brought home enough food to feed three adults and three children. Now that she was going to have another baby there would be another mouth to feed. The man of the house, her son-in-law, was unable to work because he was too ill with tuberculosis.

The Grandmother wondered whose baby her daughter carried. It was not unusual to have another man when your own husband couldn't provide for you. She herself had had a close personal relationship with her son-in-law for several years. Her husband talked her into choosing this man for her 14 year-old daughter. He was their age and after a big battle with her daughter she married this man who was forty years older than she. Matilda was an obedient daughter but no one could force her to love this old man whom everyone called "Woodford." Matilda resented leaving Holy Cross to move to Shageluk. She left her friends, aunts, uncles, cousins and her brothers and sisters. Holy Cross was a Catholic village and Shageluk was Protestant. To make matters worse, most of her children died in Shageluk as toddlers.

Grandmother would never have believed that after her husband Michael Dixon died, she too would move to Shageluk for her remaining years. She lost all contact with her husband's family at St. Michael. While Matilda wasn't terribly happy with Woodford, Cecilia found she had much in common with this gentle man. He loved children and allowed his wife her freedom because he understood that she was still a very young woman. He was a good provider and often spoiled her until he contracted T.B. He meticulously carved a real chair for her. Most everyone sat on wooden boxes in which five-gallon gas cans came. Matilda wished the chair had been painted blue, her favorite color, but it was painted orange because that was the only color of paint available. Because of this chair she was the envy of all her friends. He was an excellent craftsman and furniture maker. Woodford, Old Cecilia felt, contributed to Matilda's wildness by not making her behave like a wife. He allowed her to go to the white man dances while he watched the children.

Grandmother hoped the father of the new baby would help her daughter, as she knew Woodford would not be alive too much longer and she would follow him soon after. Usually the girls refused to reveal the father of the baby if they were not married to them, but since she was a midwife she would get the answer to her question during the most painful part of her labor. Two years previously, Matilda finally gave birth to a son. Woodford was so happy that he made a beautiful high chair for him. Now that Ralph was past his second birthday there was hope that he would live. Matilda could do no wrong in Woodford's eyes.

Gramma awakened the family and they all washed in a small basin before breakfast. Ralph was sitting on Mama's lap and Papa Woodford felt well enough to join them at the small table to eat their oatmeal mush. After breakfast, Celene and Agnes went out to chop and carry in wood before school. Mama was quiet and didn't seem very happy. She was even somewhat intolerant of Ralph's baby ways. This was contrary to her behavior, because she loved Ralph so much and wouldn't let him out of her sight. She even "armed" him (wrapped the baby on her back with a blanket so her hands were free) and brought him to dances so they would not be separated except when she went to work. She always left the girls at home.

This morning Mama said she wasn't going to work at the school-house. Gramma was glad because Ralph was a handful for her and for Woodford. After the girls finished their chores, they left for school. Mama was still trying to coax Ralph to eat his mush. Papa felt quite well today, so he thought it might be good to go out in the village to visit a friend. The medicine (Brown's Mixture) that he got from the teacher for his T.B. seemed to be working. Woodford's friend had some wood for him so that he could carve some real bowls like he saw in the schoolhouse. He tried to take advantage of all of his good days. He was already 69 years old and was in the class of a small percentage of people who lived past 40. He wanted to use his talent and get the bowls done for his family.

Chapter 19
THE BIRTH

After Papa left, Mama announced that she was in labor and told Gramma to take Ralph over to the neighbors. She was glad the girls were in school and Papa was out of the house because this was a private time. She already had been through this eleven times before and knew what to expect. She should have her baby sometime in the afternoon. To have an easier time, she would go out to chop some wood. The house had to be heated to the fullest capacity when the baby was born. She might even have to saw some logs if the girls had chopped all the remaining wood. She went out to greet the sun-filled day.

Celene, Ralph and Agnes Woodford

Meanwhile, in the cabin, Grandmother was preparing for the birthing process. First she tied a rope to one of the logs in the ceiling over the bed and tied four knots in it. This would keep the hands from sliding down the rope when the contractions became unbearable. She put the basin within reach so she could set it under Mama when she squatted while hanging on to the rope. Then she prepared the bed and found a blanket in which to wrap the baby. She placed a second basin within reach and on the stove she put kettles of water to be used to clean the baby. When this was done, she took out her small stool and sat down to work on a willow basket she had started.

Outside, Mama was looking for the ax to start chopping some wood. In the distance she heard the faint sound of dogs barking. Someone was getting ready to go beaver trapping. It would be so nice to have some fresh meat. Beaver was one of her favorite dishes. She wouldn't mind being out in the wilderness for several weeks feasting on the tender and tasty beaver meat. The air was so fresh. The beginning of spring always makes one feel so jubilant. She loved the challenge of skinning the beaver and stretching the prime skins perfectly round with hundreds of nails in just the right places. She knew how to prepare the fur just right. She only submitted prime fur so the buyer would not consider her family lazy and dumb and would pay top price. Oh well, it was no use to think about this in her condition and with her husband dying of tuberculosis, it was never meant to be.

Just then she was hit with an intense labor pain that almost took her breath away. She knew her mother had prepared the house for birthing, so after the pain subsided she grabbed the ax and chopped a few more pieces of wood. She began to feel afraid of having this baby. She only wished it would be a boy to justify having another mouth to feed. She hoped the baby would look like her, pure Indian, so that she would not have to reveal who the father was, even if the pain was unbearable. She knew her mother would be so upset if the baby looked like the father. No one needed to know that the father was the white schoolteacher who employed her. She never meant to love this handsome Norwegian, but he was kind to her and with her husband dying and the schoolteacher's wife having been in North Dakota for the birth of their own daughter, these things happen. It was not unusual to submit to a man to satisfy his needs. She was taught to do so. Even if the Catholic Church believed it was sinful, it was not sinful in the Indian way. The sun was bright and it was a beautiful zero-degree day. She hated to leave the outdoors, but it was time to go inside.

She slowly set the ax down and started for the house, pausing when a contraction hit. She reached for the door of the porch. Holding on to the handle, she stopped for a moment before continuing into the main house. The heat hit her as she opened the door. It was so warm that she felt a bit lightheaded. She went to prepare herself, then lay on the bed. She would soon have her twelfth child. Her mother came up to her and, in a soothing voice, asked who the father was. She did not answer and another contraction hit her. It was so severe that she almost cried out but that is not the Indian way. By now the sweat was pouring out of her. Her mother told her it was time to get up and grab the rope. She shakily got up to cling to the rope. Her mother asked again who the father was but she did not answer. After a few minutes, which seemed like an eternity, she glanced at the Big Ben clock ticking away. It was almost three o'clock in the afternoon. Finally her mother said the baby's head was showing and she prepared to catch it. Soon the baby was born. The gramma looked at it and Mama never heard such a shriek in her life. The baby was totally white! The gramma started using language that Mama had never heard in her life. Then another contraction hit her. This time she barely muffled a cry. Her mother shrieked again and the rage in her voice was frightening. She saw her put the first baby on the blanket in time to catch the second. Twins! This was a bad omen. Mama asked if they were boys. In her rage Gramma could barely control herself as she cut the cords. She screamed that they were girls and they were white! Since there was only one white man in the village, the idiot Norwegian schoolteacher, there was no doubt who the father was. What a disgrace! Mama glanced at the first-born twin and saw how healthy and beautiful she was, then reclined in the bed, totally exhausted, and listened to the babies cry. She listened to her mother screaming uncontrollably, saying this was not meant to be.

Always with twins one had to die. It was the Indian way. These were two half people who could never function as a whole person since their spirits were totally split. Who would want to feed these worthless creatures? They would always be sickly since they were twins and wouldn't live long. In that split second Gramma made the decision that no food would be wasted and one had to die. Mama hoped it wouldn't be the beautiful first-born. Even though they were identical, she felt the second baby was smaller and inferior. Swiftly Gramma put her hand over the mouth of the first crying baby and snuffed the life out of her. At that moment, the second baby became a whole person as the spirit of the first baby entered it.

Suddenly the door opened and in walked Aunt Sarah. She was coming to see what all the commotion and screaming was about. She looked down and saw the two babies lying on the blanket. One was crying and the other was so still. She asked Gramma what happened and she told her that since they were twins she exercised her right as a medicine woman to get rid of the first-born. Now that she had time to think about it she was going to get rid of the second white baby since it was going to bring nothing but disgrace to the family. An argument erupted and Aunt Sarah grabbed the remaining baby. She told Gramma that she had done the right thing with the first baby, but the second baby had been made whole and she was not going to allow her to take its life. Aunt Sarah reminded her that her medicine was stronger than Gramma's and she had to allow this baby to live. She would take total responsibility for the baby and Gramma had to agree that the baby would become a slave to Aunt Sarah. This was the Indian way when someone saves a life.

Sarah Benjamin, the one who saved Lori

Aunt Sarah saved me. Mama could hear them talking from what seemed to be a dream. Arrangements were hurriedly made to dispose of the first baby before the family returned home. Since the house was at the edge of town, no one would see them walking down the road to dispose of the baby. At this time of the year the ground was frozen, so the baby was put up in a tree and would be buried when the ground thawed. As they got ready to leave, another elderly aunt came in the door. They told her about the twins and swore her to secrecy regarding the disposal of one of the twins. She was to send word to the teachers that twins were born but not to mention what had to occur. The teachers had to report the name of the new baby to Juneau. They wrote that twins were born, but one of them was too weak to survive.

The remaining baby was placed in a burlap swing that hung from the ceiling. Gramma and Aunt Sarah gave the swing a push and went out with the bundle. Mama was feeling humiliated and ashamed. Little Auntie, as she was called, went over to look at the new baby and said that since she never had children of her own, she was going to give her very own Bear Song to the baby. The child would have the temperament of a bear. This was a very high honor and doing this would make her have control over this baby. Mama would have stopped this had she been in a better frame of mind because the baby was already going to be Aunt Sarah's slave. Both women were strong willed and had high demands, so she allowed each woman to have a part in this baby's life.

Mama decided she was not going to nurse this baby. The white teacher would never acknowledge this baby, so why waste precious bonding? She told Little Auntie to go over to get the cousin next door to help feed the new baby. The cousin's baby was old enough to have food chewed for it, so there would be plenty of milk for both.

Soon after Little Auntie left the cabin, the girls returned home from school. As they came in the house they saw the swing. Mama was sleeping and they knew the baby was in the swing. They carefully tiptoed over to peek at the new baby. Since the older girl, Celene, was taller she could see the baby plainly. When she looked she was horrified by the pure white skin. The baby opened its eyes for a second but it was long enough for her to see the color blue. She got so scared she grabbed the younger Agnes' hand and rushed out the door. She told her sister they had to wait outside for the family to come home and Mamma needed her sleep. She could not get the sight of the new baby out of her mind. All the other babies she saw were dark and beautiful, but this one looked like a total freak. Its eyes looked like they had been cooked. How could she invite her friends over to admire this thing? Was it a girl or a boy? It looked like it should belong to the teacher's family. Their baby had white skin and blue eyes and was crawling around. She wondered if Gramma knew about this baby. Certainly Gramma would never allow this thing to live with them. Agnes kept pestering her to go back in to see the baby, but Celene would not allow it. She said they had to wait for Papa and Gramma to come home first, and then she could see the baby.

Soon Celene saw her Papa coming down the road carrying their baby brother. He was smiling. She could not run to her father as she normally did and stayed sitting on a block of wood. Agnes ran to greet him, but Celene could not move. She loved her Papa so much, but was so afraid of what he would say about this new baby. Agnes told him there was a new baby in the house. They all went in and Papa picked up the tiny little infant and rocked her. She had no fingernails and no toenails, and when she cried the girls thought she sounded like a little mouse. When Mama woke up, Papa told Celene and Agnes to take Ralph outside to play for a while before the sun set.

While outside, the girls saw Gramma coming up the road with Aunty Sarah. Agnes ran to Gramma and told her that they had a special baby in the house. Someone came to the school and she overheard her telling the teacher that Mama had twins, whatever that was. The teacher let school out a little early. Gramma was glaring at her demanding to know where Papa was. Just then Papa came out of the house smiling. He told the family that the little girl born to Mama was special. His great grandparents had a little Russian blood in them and the baby must take after that part of the family. Everyone had to help Mama take care of the baby because she was so small. Celene was mystified. How did her younger sister overhear someone telling the teacher that Mama had a baby when she didn't hear? Is that why the teacher told them to leave when she hadn't finished her schoolwork? He practically chased them out of the school. She felt he was a mean man and was glad that her Papa didn't have his ugly disposition. If Papa was happy with the new baby, then she would be too. She was taught to respect her elders.

Chapter 20
ETOLA JEAN LARSEN

The entire village was talking about the strange baby born to Mama. It was obvious that it belonged to the schoolteacher, because the baby resembled his daughters as she grew older. She had blonde curly hair and blue eyes, but Mr. Larsen accused the villagers of being gossips and thought the baby looked really Indian. He didn't want his gentle wife to think that he was capable of committing adultery. He felt, in this primitive land, isolated from the rest of the world, that no one would find out about his behavior. He had his ways to convince his wife that he was always free from wrong doing.

He had a weakness for Indian women and Matilda was his favorite. He did not count on her giving birth to twins. He usually assisted in the births in the village because he was the village doctor and the teacher. He wasn't called for Matilda's time probably because her mother hated white people. Gramma did not want white people to come into her house and she held Mr. Larsen in low regard. He wondered what went wrong with the other twin. He wished he had assisted in the delivery to know why one of them died. He also received the message that Matilda was a proud woman and wasn't one to scorn as she sent word to the schoolhouse about the birth of her twins and since the remaining twin was nameless, she left it up to the teachers to give it a name. This was her way of not acknowledging his daughter in her household. If she thought she had him in a corner to name this child, he would show her how wrong she was. He had his wife name this baby. This way it would prove that he had nothing to do with the child in his wife's eyes and it would convince her that Woodford did indeed have some Russian blood. Mrs. Larsen wasn't fooled and dutifully named the baby Marene Ethel, signed the birth certificate, sent it to Juneau and hoped this innocent child would have a chance in life. She would do all she could while they lived in Shageluk to help the child, but nothing beyond that.

A few days after the birth of the twins, Mr. Larsen went to see Matilda. There was great tension in the cabin and Matilda refused to talk to him. He visited with Woodford. Woodford told the people that he made medicine and wished for a baby that looked like the Russian part of his family. If Mr. Larsen thought the people were ignorant and believed the story, there was someone who did not underestimate the natives' intelligence. It was his eleven year-old daughter Etola. She was his pride and joy.

Etola and Martha Howard

Martha Howard, Herman and Etola Larsen

The Larsens allowed Etola much freedom in the village. The Shageluk people accepted her as one of them. She was taught not to thumb her nose at the native food by saying it smelled bad or that she didn't like it. The villagers explained that the spirits of the animals they were eating must not be offended or you will go hungry or starve to death. She also learned the Athapascan language and listened to the Indian stories and superstitions. She was very intelligent and learned quickly. She was also talkative and was welcome in every home. This was a great honor, as most outsiders were not welcome in every home. They didn't feel she was a spy for her parents and she was rewarded with gifts of native clothes and art-work. Etola was invited to the Kashim for the special dances that were held. She was not a stranger to the Lucky Dance, Mask Dance, Stick Dance or the Doll Dance. She was a special child to everyone as well as her parents. They even allowed her to have a cat in the house, which for Mr. Larsen, was simply unheard of. Although she showed much loyalty to the natives, she was fascinated by the graveyards and did not put much stock into the idea that one can die if the rules regarding the graveyards are abused.

There were many mischievous things that Etola did in the village that were not told to her parents because they knew Mr. Larsen had a bad temper. Many things she did were not accepted by the Athabascans for their children, but they realized this was a child of a different culture. Indian children were taught to be quiet and listen to their elders. Etola was talkative and asked many of the elders about their culture. She kept everyone awestruck with her many questions and antics, mimicking different people in situations that amused her. People were entertained seeing a white person acting like an Indian. She even had her first puppy love experience—which Mr. Larsen would never allow—with a local boy and another from the neighboring village of Holikachuk.

Her fascination with the graveyards was causing great concern among the people. She had several playmates in the village and these girls were telling their parents about the things she had done that were forbidden in the Indian culture. One of her best friends was a girl named Dottie, who lived a mile below Upper Shageluk across the Innoko River in another village called Lower Village or Lower Shageluk (shortened by the kids to Lore Village).

One day Etola visited Matilda, who lived at the end of Upper Shageluk, just before the trail leading to Lore Village. She saw the new baby and was so excited that this baby looked just like her baby sister Yvonne. She carried the baby all over the house and proudly showed it to the neighbors announcing this also was her baby sister. She made a mental note to tell her mother Mae that this baby wasn't very clean and she would ask if she could bring Yvonne's outgrown clothing for the baby to wear. Etola did everything she could for this baby and she was trusted. She thought having little Marene and Yvonne was like having little twin sisters even though they were five months apart. While visiting Matilda, Etola looked out the window and saw Dottie walking down the trail. She knocked on the window and told Dottie to wait for her. She hurriedly put the baby down and ran out to walk her friend home to Lore Village. Etola was not afraid of walking home in the dark. The Indians were much too superstitious, but nothing frightened Etola. She showed respect for the villagers' superstitions, but did not believe in them herself.

Just before crossing the river to get to Lore Village, Etola spotted the cemetery across the river. She asked Dottie to join her in looking around the cemetery. Of course Dottie emphatically said, "No!" She knew that entering a cemetery without an adult was prohibited and then only for burials and special occasions. This was a sacred place, the resting ground of her ancestors, that should never be disturbed. One should only speak in a low whisper while near the reverent place. Some of the older graves had fallen decayed fences. One can never step, not even on the edge, onto what resembled the outline of a sleeping person's coffin. Fences were erected around the graves not only to keep the animals out, but to enshrine the belongings of the deceased. Some important people had actual miniature doll-like houses built over their graves. Etola's curiosity overcame her and, against her friend's pleas, she marched over to the cemetery. She was fascinated with the treasures she found and hollered to Dottie to come.

Lower (Lore) Village Graveyard

Dottie was on the trail in the middle of the river between upper and lower village waiting for Etola. Such a fear as she never felt before in her life overcame Dottie as she stared at Etola entering one of the grave houses. Then Etola hollered at her to come to see all the dishes she found. Dottie knew that the spirits would soon be taking Etola to their home because she entered the grave house and hollered in the graveyard. Then Etola offered to bring some treasures to her. Dottie came to her senses and became extremely angry, telling her not to touch one piece of the dead's belongings or she would never play with her again.

Finally Etola came back to where Dottie was waiting and was amazed to see that she was shaking like a leaf. They walked to Dottie's house and Etola was invited in for tea. The mother told Etola it was time to go since she should not be walking past the cemetery in the dark because of the wild animals and the spirits. She offered to have her oldest son escort her home but Etola declined. She had no fear of wild animals or spirits and walked home by herself as she had done many times before.

After Etola's departure Dottie told her mother that Etola was playing and hollering in the graveyard. The mother was so horrified that she quickly called her mother-in-law, a medicine woman, to make medicine to protect Etola, as she was practically one of the family. The woman did and was invited to dinner in thanks for her medicine. She advised that Etola's parents should be told to keep her out of the graveyards or something terrible would happen.

The next day Dottie's mother visited the schoolhouse and told the teachers to keep their daughter out of the graveyards. She stated that the village council had been notified and a representative was going to visit to warn them of the spirits' anger. Her playing in the graveyard was the most shocking behavior ever known to the village. No one disturbed the ancestors' final resting place. Since the Larsens did not believe in superstitions, Etola was not punished and was not made to realize how serious an offense this was. She couldn't wait to visit the second graveyard in Upper Shageluk.

She had her chance later when she and several of her friends went berry picking above the schoolhouse. As they were picking the high bush cranberries one of the girls came out of the woods in a state of panic. She felt they were all too close to the graveyard and should leave for home immediately. She didn't know if their presence had already disturbed the Other World. Etola convinced them to go on ahead since she wasn't afraid. She wanted to go home with a full bucket of berries.

After they left, she curiously approached the graveyard. How exciting! She looked at all the graves and found another house where there was a complete set of dishes. She felt so comfortable playing there. The sun was shining brightly and Etola was so enjoying herself when she decided to visit the older part of the cemetery in the dark wooded area. She stood there as if in a trance as she spotted a part of a skeleton beneath her feet protruding out of a decaying coffin. She picked up the skull and her berry basket and walked toward the outer edge of the graveyard. When she was back in the sunlight she examined the skull. She decided it would be fun to place it on the doorstep of one of the villagers just to scare him.

She chose a man who was normally a quiet person. She couldn't wait to see his reaction. She put the skull on the steps, knocked on the door then ran to the side of the cabin where she could peek at him as she opened the door. He was so shocked and enraged. Etola was frightened and ran for home. She didn't escape fast enough as the man kept calling her. She didn't stop and kept running as fast as she could.

Her parents greeted her warmly at the door. They didn't notice the fear on her face. She was a well-disciplined child and did very little wrong in their eyes except for a few childish pranks. They asked her about her day and she related everything except the graveyard incident. She went to play with little Yvonne while waiting for the special dinner her mother was preparing, Norwegian potato dumplings (raspeball).

During dinner there was a loud knock at the door. Her father got up to answer the door, irritated by the interruption. The main medicine man was standing there. He looked past Mr. Larsen directly at Etola. He told her father that Etola stepped over the line when she removed a skull which belonged to a great chief medicine man from the graveyard. The village was now preparing for a reburial of the skull and was treating this as an official funeral. He informed Mr. Larsen that his daughter was going to have a very short life related to this deed. The Larsens brushed it off as just a prank, not believing in the Indian superstitions.

Chapter 21
DEATH VISITS

U sually by May 4 the spring weather was well underway, but this May was unusually cold. It looked like a very late spring. Finally on May 15, the ice on the river broke up and was on the move, signaling a change in season. For the remainder of the month Papa Woodford made a high chair for little Yvonne Larsen and delivered it to the teachers. Then he decided to work on a fish trap but found he had no materials. He mentioned this to Gramma and she thought it would be a good idea to gather spruce roots, not only for the fish trap but also for her woven baskets. Papa was feeling good, so he decided he could row up the Shageluk Slough and take big sister Celene with them. He also packed a tent, because they planned to spend one night along the way.

They rowed up the Innoko River until they reached the Shageluk Slough. It was a pleasant June day and the waters were calm. Papa let Celene row the boat and he would steer. It was funny to see her row, as she stood up every time she pulled the oars against the water and sat down when the oars lifted out of the water. The see-saw effect made Papa and Gramma laugh. Soon all three were lost in their own thoughts when, off in the distance, Celene could hear the sound of someone chopping wood. They came upon a flat grassy area of land on the riverbank and the noise grew louder. Celene wanted to stop to visit whoever this was because she was getting tired. People always welcomed river travelers and shared their food and tea. Papa asked if she could see a boat tied up on the river bank. She answered no and he told her that the site used to be a huge village but almost everyone died from the influenza epidemic and because the survivors were too weak to bury the dead properly, the spirits continued living and doing their tasks. They had to respect this village of the dead and go past the area silently and respectfully as these were their relatives. They looked among their food items in the grub box and made the "Sign" over what they had to share with the people and went silently on their way. Celene wondered why the noise of ax chopping was so loud when no one was there, but didn't ask any more questions.

They reached their destination just before dark and Papa went up to the woods to check on a tent site. Suddenly he found himself surrounded by five wolves. He yelled to scare them off but they kept staring at him. Gramma and Celene heard Papa yelling. Gramma told Celene to stay in the boat and she flew onto shore and grabbed two sticks from the beach. With her skirt flying she ran up the bank clapping the sticks together. After the startled wolves ran off they agreed to find a different location down the river to put up the tent. Back in the boat they encountered many turnoffs since they had just experienced high water. Finally they found a tributary which satisfied them. There they pitched their tent and set out a fishnet to wait for their evening meal. They had to make smudge pots, the bottoms cut off of five-gallon gas cans found in every village boat, filled with lighted punk from the birch trees, to fight off the unbearable swarms of mosquitoes. Soon they saw the fishnet moving and knew they had caught a fish. It was a nice fat whitefish laden with fish eggs. They cooked the fish over an open fire and enjoyed a most delicious meal, the natural flavor requiring no seasoning whatsoever. Contented after the meal, they went to bed and slept soundly.

After they completed their root gathering the following day, they started for home but found themselves lost in the midst of many turnoffs. Back in Shageluk, Mamma went up to the schoolhouse to report to Mr. Larsen that her family had been missing for three days. She asked him to form a search party to find them. He sent several men out immediately and could not imagine how anyone could survive out in the abundance of mosquitoes. Several days later Gramma, Papa and Celene were sleeping soundly when they heard the sound of a can beating on a frying pan. It was Wilson Charles to the rescue!

The family felt as though they had been lost for an eternity and were happy to be going home on the correct river path. But they had been gone long enough to have missed out on some of the changes in the village. Wilson informed them that one of the elders, Old Rope, passed away in their absence and the village was in progress of an out-breaking measles epidemic. The measles were not just in Shageluk, but all over the country.

For the rest of the summer, Mr. Larsen treated many people who were very ill with the measles. Several people died. Just when everybody seemed to be on the mend, Gramma (Cecilia Dixon Boston Ignatius) died at two in the morning on August 27. As she had requested, she was given a traditional Indian funeral and was taken out the window of the Kashim and buried in the Upper Village Cemetery.

Nine days after Gramma's burial, Papa joined her at 1:30 in the morning on September 6th. Mr. Larsen tried to save him, but tuberculosis won the battle. Mama was still trying to cope with Gramma's death and funeral and now that her husband was gone she appreciated all the help that Mr. Larsen gave. He donated all the new clothes for the burial and after the funeral he helped take inventory of everything in her house because many people wanted her belongings. He also got wood for her because now she didn't have anyone to help.

In September and October there was a mumps epidemic. At the beginning of winter the mumps had afflicted just about everyone and most were recovering. November welcomed many dog teams and visitors from Holikachuk who came to fix Papa's grave. There were so many deaths in September that there wasn't time to make a fence around his grave. Mama was busy preparing food for the visitors with the help of a younger girl who had just moved in with her again. She was the Godmother of Mama's new baby. She had lived with Mama before, but this time she brought her fiancé with her. After Papa's memorial potlatch was over, Mama complained that she had too many mouths to feed. Mr. Larsen held a meeting with all the parties involved and asked the young couple to move out, which they did.

After a successful school Christmas program, the New Year (1943) was welcomed in with a big New Year's Eve dance. It was very cold, but everyone from Holikachuk came and danced until 3 in the morning. Mr. Larsen played his violin and everyone enjoyed themselves to the fullest. Shageluk and the surrounding communities were fairly free of illness at the beginning of the year, so it certainly was time to celebrate. But it wasn't long before jaundice reared its ugly head and Mr. Larsen was out again treating the children for this malady. Little Rina from the village had a tough time with this sickness. It was touch and go for a while, but now she was on the mend. Mr. Larsen toiled with her day and night and it was well worth it.

On March 23, Etola complained of feeling ill. Her parents put her to bed immediately. Mr. Larsen suspected that she contracted jaundice because he had been treating other children in the village for this disease. Now he had to give his daughter his full attention because she also had juvenile diabetes, which could cause complications.

Etola spent a restless night with both parents by her side. Word spread throughout the village that their beloved angel was ill. All the villagers took turns keeping vigil day and night with her parents. This was the highest form of respect they could show when someone was ill. Her mother and father did everything they possibly could to keep her comfortable and to get her well. Even with a blizzard raging, Mr. Larsen kept calling on the radio for a plane to get her to a hospital, but none came. When Etola showed no signs of improvement the next day, they finally sent a dog team to Anvik for the nurse Miss Anderson. Mama and Celene were there with the Larsens, but there was nothing anyone could do but pray for a miracle. Listening to her excruciating cries was more than anyone could bear. Etola died three days after she first took ill. Roland Dutchman and Jonas Fairbanks made her coffin.

The nurse arrived late in the evening by dogsled. She saw that the Larsens were in no condition to go anywhere, as they wanted to bring their little darling to Anvik to have a Christian burial with the Rev. Henry Chapman officiating. Reluctantly, they finally decided to put Etola in the box and hired Gachidle Workman to bring her to Anvik by dogsled.

Everyone came to express their condolences, including Brother Feltes and Father Anabel from the Holy Cross Mission. The nurse remained with them and was concerned about their deep, deep sorrow.

For the next two months the Larsens did their jobs half-heartedly, constantly and separately alone in their thoughts, each thinking about their beloved daughter and blaming themselves for things they could have done. They went through the motions of tagging beaver, teaching school, visiting the sick, taking care of the mail, hosting out-of- town guests, spring cleaning around the school, painting and taking inventory of all the school supplies.

Even though the village had a meeting to retain them, the Larsens did not accept. Everything reminded them of their daughter Etola. May 18th found them finishing the last of their packing and selling their belongings. The Larsens left Shageluk, Alaska, which was their home for six years, never to return again.

Chapter 22
LORI

I have been called many nicknames during my lifetime – Blossy, Half Breed, White Lady, Pusscat, Celia and Lori – but the one that stuck with me for most of my life was 'Blue Eye' or 'Blue Eyes'. When I first became aware of myself, I was living in a small log cabin, next to the Kashim, which was known as a "Government House." My family consisted of Gertie Rope, her daughter Julia, a blind lady named Lilly, my two older sisters, Celene and Agnes, and my younger sister Connie. Julia was also considered our sister. I was about three years old and my younger sister was two. She was named after the teacher who took Mr. Larsen's place, Constance Marie Dickman. Mama always felt sorry for homeless people and it was not unusual to have one or two other people living with us. Lilly came to us from Flat, Alaska. Her mother had died and there was no one to take care of her.

My sister Celene told me I was much loved by our Papa Woodford and he babied me for the first five months of my life until his death. I was the thirteenth child of Matilda Dixon Woodford and Connie was number fourteen. All her children, including her son Ralph, died of tuberculosis except her remaining three daughters, Celene, Agnes and me. Mama continued to work in the schoolhouse in order to feed us.

After Papa died, there really was no one to take care of me. Many times, I was left to cry myself to sleep as my sisters were too young to take care of me. I was usually given a bottle and pushed back and forth in a burlap swing. My mama told me once that when she was on her way home from work, I was crawling around at the top of the riverbank and before she could get to me, I had tumbled down the muddy bank. When she reached me I was caked with mud from the long drop. She thought I surely was blind because my eyes were filled with mud, along with my ears, nose and mouth. She had to suck all the mud off me with her mouth as there was no time to lose. Had I fallen a few more feet I would have drowned, so I am lucky to be alive.

I was also told that Mama tried to give me away several times, but for one reason or another I was always returned. The story I heard the most about was when young Grace Benjamin was a school girl, she asked Mama if she could have me and she said yes. She brought me to her home in Lower Village and had to hide me in her bedroom until she had a chance to convince her mother they could afford another mouth to feed. Meanwhile, she ran out of canned milk to feed me, so she filled my bottle with water. Evidently that didn't satisfy me, so I started crying and her mother found me. I was returned immediately. The main reason for this decision was because Grace wasn't a married woman with a husband to help take care of her. No amount of crying would change her parents' mind. Later in life she became Aunty Gracie to me and I always looked at her as a mother figure. She always treated me as one of her family.

Four other families told me that they wanted to adopt me. A bachelor from Holy Cross, Alphonse, wanted me but because he didn't have a wife, I wasn't given to him. One of the families from Shageluk whom I actually stayed with wanted me because the wife acted as my wet nurse. They even had a meeting with Mr. Larsen before he left to

Grace Benjamin
and Etola Larsen

finalize the adoption but somehow he talked my mom into taking me back. I was already old enough (between two and three) when the other two families came to get me. One family was from Anvik and the other from Holikachuk. I remember hanging onto my mother with a death grip that almost tore her dress as she tried to push me toward them. Even bribes of a nice new house and new dresses would not make me change my mind.

When I was about two years old, my mother decided to pitch a tent next to our house and everyone moved out to the tent. That very night, our house collapsed because it was so old. Then we moved to the 'Government House' along with Gertie and Julia Rope. One of the first things I remembered in this house was always being hungry. It didn't seem that Mama brought enough food home for all of us, even though the leftovers were given to the youngest ones first. After the food was evenly divided between us, there wasn't much to eat. When school started, my mother would take Connie to work with her and since my sisters had school lunches, Gertie would take out her stash of sugar in a small brown paper bag and mix about a teaspoon of the precious sugar in a tall glass of warm water and we would share this together sip by sip all day. If she felt I was an extra good girl, she would put some sugar on the end of a teaspoon and give it to me full strength on the tip of my tongue and that was the most delicious thing I ever tasted!

It wasn't hard to make me behave since we lived right next door to the Kashim, the community hall used for all Indian celebrations and funerals. Gertie told me many scary stories, so I was deathly afraid of the Kashim all my life. If I accidentally walked in front of it for some reason, I always felt that someone was following me. I would feel a sudden urge to run as fast as I could past this strange structure. This was especially true at night. If my sisters wanted to threaten me, all they had to do was mention the Kashim and I shaped up in a hurry.

I was an outgoing, precocious child, talking from the time I got up until I went to bed. I was always asking questions that no one seemed to be able to answer. As young as I was, I was fluent in the Athabascan language, as this was the main language spoken in our household. Also I was forever running around the village visiting with everyone. There wasn't much going on in the village I didn't miss and repeated it verbatim to my mother.

Once, my sister Agnes tried to teach me how to trap birds to bring home as pets. We found an old window screen with a frame and she set it up in the woods where we saw a flock of birds feeding. She propped it up with a stick that had a string tied to it that was several feet long. Next she sent me to the smokehouse to get a handful of worms (maggots) off the dirt floor and had me place them in the center of the trap where she had carved out a little hole. Then we hid behind some bushes while holding on to the end of the string and waited. It wasn't long before all the birds came to eat the worms and she pulled the string. We caught two robins and a blackbird. She wanted to let the robins go but we were going to keep the blackbird as a pet. While she was busy freeing the robins, she told me to hold the blackbird and not let it go. She put it in my arms. I never felt such a warm, soft creature in my short life. I could feel its heart beating and was so amazed at its strange light-colored eyes. Suddenly it started struggling and I found myself squeezing its neck because that was the only place I had a good grip. I had promised my sister not to let it go. She turned and saw me squeezing it and tried to take it from me but I hung on tightly. When she finally pried my fingers off the poor little bird, it was dead. She explained that it would never come back and swore me to secrecy never to reveal what we had done. I didn't know why because I assumed if the bird died we "hunted" it and why not bring it home for a delicious meal? She just told me not to think crazy thoughts, just never mention this incident. As a three year-old I didn't really understand.

Sometime later, our Catholic priest came up from Holy Cross and used our house to say Mass. His sermon was about being nice to "God's creatures." Suddenly, something he said triggered the big secret out of the recesses of my brain and I stood up and loudly confessed, "Ha, ha, Agnes and I killed a blackbird." It seemed to me that everyone around me moved at once, clapped their hands over my mouth and almost knocked me over. Not only had I spoken in church, but I had confessed to wasting a perfectly harmless creature. My sister and I were both properly disciplined after church on both counts. When Mama retold this story to others, I noticed everyone laughing, but I didn't find it one bit funny because I had been harshly disciplined.

Gertie, our babysitter, usually let us have the run of the village while my mother worked during the summer. We loved Gertie because she loved us and she never scolded us. She was lenient, but we had to watch out for Lilly. Even though Lilly was blind, she was aware of every move we made and questioned us endlessly, making us tell her the same thing over and over until she knew our whole day's schedule. Then she would proudly tell my mother everything we did all day when she came home from work. We sometimes thought we could fool Lilly, but that was never to happen.

Julia, our adopted sister, felt she was pretty lucky, as her parents were divorced. Even though this was pretty uncommon, Julia was having a great time running back and forth visiting her dad. He lived next door just in front of our house and down a slight hill. She often dragged me, "Baby Celia," with her. Since her dad was the storekeeper, we often visited him there. Of course I called him my Uncle Mike. He would set us up on the store's counter and give us an orange or some candy. He loved both of us and was always happy to see us. I so looked up to Julia as the most wonderful human being on earth. She must have been about six or seven years old at this time and wasn't afraid of anything. She was always taking risks and had a Pippi Longstocking personality. She had a tremendous sweet tooth and wasn't satisfied with an occasional treat, so she called a meeting with all her friends present. It seems she had a master plan to furnish the whole group of us with all the candy and gum we wanted. Who wouldn't want to be part of such a plan when candy and gum were usually a once-a-year treat and everyone's dream?

Julia and Gertie Rope

Since she was a very skinny girl, she talked the older girls (including my sisters) into waiting until after supper when we would go to the back of the store and remove a window pane. We would hoist her up through it since she was the only who could fit. Then she would give us all the gum and candy we wanted. After answering all our questions as to how she could get by with this, she convinced the gang that this was perfectly legitimate because her dad allowed her to do anything she wanted. After all, this was his store and she was the pride of his life. The proof was, she was his only child and he didn't need anyone else. They all agreed it made a lot of sense, so we proceeded with the plan.

As luck would have it, right after supper, Uncle Mike was called to the schoolhouse to have a meeting. Making sure everyone was present, we started off to the store. While removing the window pane, it broke and almost everyone wanted to discontinue the plan, as now we were extremely nervous. After calming us down with her smooth talk, Julia was hoisted through the broken window. She filled up her pockets and handed candy bars and gum to everyone. She was then helped back out through the window and everyone likened her to an angel. Why then (with her mouth so full of gum that she could hardly chew), thought my sister Celene, did they have to break the window and sneak away from the store if it was okay with Uncle Mike? Oh well, Julia never lied before and Uncle Mike did love her.

All the guilty parties remained unpunished, but the outcome of this incident was totally unexpected. As soon as Uncle Mike unlocked the store the next day, he noticed most of his candy missing and immediately thought of his daughter chewing a big wad of gum when she came to say good-night to him last night after the meeting. He was too tired to question her as he listened to her excited chatter about her day's adventure. With a quick kiss she vanished as fast as she had appeared. She never stayed long, as she always had a million things to do and his new wife was intolerant of young children. After all, they were an elderly couple who should have been grandparents.

Just when he spotted the broken window, he heard a motor boat pulling up in front of the store. This was very unusual, as no one was expected in the village. He went back out the door and walked down to the river bank where he saw two Catholic nuns in a boat. They had just arrived from Holy Cross, sixty miles down the river. They asked him where they could find Mike Rope and he assured them that it was he who greeted them. They informed him that since he did not have legal custody of Julia and did not formally adopt her, her biological family had insisted she be picked up and brought to the Catholic orphanage at the Holy Cross Mission. There wasn't anything anybody could do, so our precious Julia was physically carried out of the house with much commotion from her parents and from her, and was deposited into the mission boat. She was leaving the only home she knew since she was three days old. It felt like there had been a death in the family.

After Julia left, everyone was very sad. I tried playing with my little sister Connie, but it seemed she was always crying and everyone catered to her by giving her anything she wanted. I was always in the way and resentful of the obvious favoritism she received because she got the best of everything and I either got second best or nothing. If I did anything to make her cry, I got a good licking.

One day Uncle Mike's wife, our Little Auntie, came to visit Mama. Everyone seemed afraid of her and didn't like her because every time she came over, everyone suddenly remembered something urgent they had to do to get out of the house. I used to like to stare at her and listen to everything she told Mama until she finally started to scream at me, telling me to quit looking at her. It was disrespectful to look at an elder in the eyes. She was such a negative person and was constantly scolding everyone in sight. On this particular day, I was sulking because I couldn't seem to do anything right. Mama had brought home two sets of play dishes from the school; one set was red and the other blue. I was so excited to play with real dishes and I chose the blue set. I was told Connie had first choice. She picked the blue dishes and I had such a temper tantrum I was slapped and the red dishes were flung into the cellar where I could see them through the cracks between the floorboards. I was told I permanently lost my dishes but I was thinking of ways to fish them out even though I was told the cellar was haunted. After some thought, I decided I didn't want the inferior red dishes, only the blue set, and I was determined somehow to get them back. I hated my Mama for slapping me and I never accepted the red dishes no matter what story I was told. As far as I was concerned, the cellar spirits could have them.

Mama looked over at me and told me she just given me to Little Aunty and since we shared the same Bear Song we should be quite compatible. There was to be no back talk, just go live with her. So off I went to live next door. It probably wouldn't be too bad with Uncle Mike there and I wouldn't have to compete with Connie.

Well, my uncle worked all day and Little Auntie screamed at me all day. She would not let me play outside and forbade me to go to my house. She decided to teach me how to weave baskets. The usual way of learning anything was to sit quietly and observe your teacher, shut your mouth and WATCH. Never ask questions or you will break your concentration and come up with a less than desirable product. After she thought I had done enough watching she gave me the materials: an awl, spruce roots and split willows. After what seemed like hours, I completed my first row of stitches. I proudly showed her my work of art. She examined it and went into a rage because it was crooked. She ripped it apart, grabbed my hair, shook my head and slapped my face because I hadn't paid close attention. That ended my career in basket weaving. A hundred lickings would never make me pick the ripped basket up off the floor. Since my Mama told me never to cry, I glared at her and told her I would report her to my uncle. I spent the rest of the day stacking wood in the back of the stove. I did report her to my uncle and felt pretty good when he glared at her. There was silence for the rest of the evening.

A few days later she reminded me that if I wanted to continue eating, I would have to prove myself useful to the household. I was to learn to braid gunny sack strings into rope, which was used to fasten floats on the top of a fishnet. This was done by unraveling the strands of the fabric from a burlap bag and when there was a pile of hair-like strands, one end was tied to a nail on the window sill and divided into three equal thicknesses. These were braided just like one would braid someone's hair. I don't know many 3-4 year olds who can do this well. She waited until all my friends were outside playing so I could see that they were wasting their lives. I wasn't wasting mine because I was being taught that one should continually work in order to be successful. After what she felt was sufficient time for me to observe, she propped me up on a little stool to start my next career in gunny sack braiding.

The first thing I noticed through the window was that all my friends were playing "cans" (using cans in place of regular dishes). After trying to get their attention with no success, I decided I better get down to business. I could show them the great talent I learned while they were playing "cans," if I would ever be allowed out of this house. Little Aunty might check on me sooner than I expected. I was really getting into the braiding, singing a little Indian song I learned from listening to Little Aunty sing. What seemed like hours and miles of braiding and twisting all the strands around each other, my Auntie finally came to check on me. She couldn't possibly find fault with my beautiful rope.

The next thing I knew, I got slapped on the side of the head! She hit me with such force that I was thrown to the floor. She was screaming at the top of her lungs in our Indian language about how dumb I was. She told me I was stupid because I had white blood in me, just because my braiding was crooked. In my eyes it was a masterpiece! I picked myself off the floor, brushed my clothes off and started screaming the same things back to her in Indian. For the white part, I inserted her name, mimicking everything she said to me, calling her stupid. She was ready for another attack when my Uncle came through the door. I told him she was being mean to me and she told him I wasn't much help and couldn't learn anything and besides I was being disrespectful by talking back to her. The meanest thing I could think of at that moment was that I would never sleep with them in the same bed again.

I insisted my Uncle go to the smokehouse to get Julia's bed so I could sleep on it. With real sadness in his eyes he told me that we had to leave Julia's bed there in case she came back. It could be any day and he did not want her to think he gave her bed away. But this was a fine time to make a new bed for me. I was so excited! We went to the smokehouse and I watched him as he made my very own bed. I never remembered having my own bed. I always slept with my sisters on the floor. This was going to be so wonderful. While he was building the bed, he gave me some tips on how to get along with my auntie. Do not talk back to her was number one. I was too excited to remember the rest. My bed was finally done and he put a piece of bear skin on it for a mattress. It was so nice and soft. He brought the bed into the house and set it next to the head of their bed. I had my own pillow and blanket and as soon as we were through eating, I went to bed. I woke up sometime in the middle of the night and got so scared because I was alone. I climbed out of my bed and almost stepped on my Auntie's head when I climbed in between them. I only used my own bed during the day to sit or play on for the rest of my stay. No one said a word.

I kept asking my uncle if I could go visit my Mama. I was through being mad at her and he always told me he would let me know when I could go. One day after being slapped for talking too much, I ran out of the door to my Mama's house. I flung open the door to report my auntie and there was Mama, holding Connie on her lap. My little sister was vomiting into a basin and all I saw was red blood. Mama looked up and yelled at me to get out and at that moment Little Auntie came up behind me, yanked my arm and ran me all the way down to her house. There she threw me on the bed. I was NEVER to go back to Mama's without permission. I sulked until my uncle came home and told him what happened. He again told me gently that they would let me know when I could go home.

Matilda with Daughter Connie

The opportunity came sooner than I expected. A few days later I was told by Little Auntie to walk back to Mama's house. When I got to the door I noticed a lot of people in our porch and they stepped aside when I came into the porch door. I opened the door and walked in. The first thing I saw was our baby sister laid out on the floor dressed in all her best clothes. Tuberculosis took my sister Connie. She looked very pretty and seemed to be asleep. I noticed the blue dishes were set on a cloth next to her. Mama looked so sad and was crying. I also noticed another blue bowl with food in it. Some women were sewing a parka. I was so sorry I fought with her over the blue dishes. My sister Agnes came in through the door and told me our little sister had died. At this point Mama looked up at me and said "It should've been you." I was so devastated I thought, "I wish it had been me too." Then Agnes told me, "She told me the same thing when my little brother Ralph died." With Agnes' explanation it seemed to be okay. I just glared at Mama. I don't remember her crying in the rest of her life.

After my little sister was buried, it seemed like nothing was the same. Everyone was very sad. Mama started to drink heavily. I was still living with my aunt and uncle and I didn't care to argue with Aunty or report her. Word came down from Holikachuk that a woman, Old Mrs. Keating, was dying and sent for Mama to visit her. For some strange reason Mama took me with her on this trip.

It was the first boat trip I remember being on and I was so excited. We went up the Innoko River with some friends. I sat next to Mama on the boat and was told not to move around or walk in the boat because we might tip over. The water seemed level with the boat as I peered over the side and it almost took my breath away. After the outboard motor started, I watched the water speed by and it was the most amazing thing I had ever seen. The trees whipped by and the hills seemed like huge mountains. By mid-day we tied up to shore and got ready for our dinner. Mama made some tea over the campfire and we all had a piece of dryfish and some pilot bread. It tasted so good! Mama even let me have a sip of her tea. After we re-boarded the boat to continue our journey, Mama told me how to behave when we got to Holikachuk. I was to sit on the floor and not say a word when we visited with Mrs. Keating because she was very sick and I could cause her to become more ill if I misbehaved. We reached Holikachuk just before supper and we camped with our Aunt Belle.

She had pretty children and her daughter Daisy was so nice and kind. She even painted my fingernails with red polish, which I had never seen before. I couldn't keep my eyes off my fingernails as I had them spread out in front of me everywhere I went. Soon it was time for Mama and me to go see Mrs. Keating.

When we went into the house, there was someone sitting on a chair by her bed. She immediately got up to give the chair to Mama and went home. Mama made me shake hands with Mrs. Keating and she told Mama she was so happy to see me after all that she had heard about me. She told Mama I could sit on the stool by her cooking stove. Mama gave me a threatening look about sitting absolutely still on the stool. I nodded my head "yes" then sat down to listen to them visit. Mama's back was to me. Mrs. Keating was propped up on her pillow and would occasionally smile at me. I felt pretty grown-up sitting on that stool visiting with Mama.

Soon I felt something touching my ankle. I looked down and saw nothing. I wanted to let Mama know this but she told me not to talk. I felt it again. I looked down and again there was nothing there. I was nearly in a panic. Since this was a sick person's house there might be spirits here. I was staring at the floor when I saw a furry little paw trying to touch my ankle from under the stove. I moved my foot over and all of a sudden this furry little orange creature came running toward my ankle. I almost fainted but I was told not to talk. It stopped by my foot and looked up at me. It had the kindest, sweetest face. It was too big to be a mouse and too small to be a puppy. It had no wings so it wasn't a bird. I had never seen an animal like this before. Suddenly it jumped into my lap ever so gently and it didn't seem like it would bite me. Our eyes locked as I sat as stiff as a board.

I must have gasped because Mama and Mrs. Keating both looked at me. Mama looked horrified and Mrs. Keating smiled so sweetly, telling my Mom she wanted me to have this cat. She said it could be my pet and I had to take very good care of it. Mama couldn't say no to a person on her deathbed, so the little orange cat was mine. I put my arm around it and had to laugh because it was making such a strange noise from its neck. It was a very small orange kitten and I named it Pussy. I was allowed to bring it home to Shageluk. I couldn't wait to show this strange creature to my friends and sisters. Mama was terribly displeased by the whole situation but she had to go along with this unexpected event. She preached to me about taking care of it and feeding it and I promised I would die for my new pussycat. When we got ready to leave Mrs. Keating's house, all of a sudden there were a dozen cats coming out from under the cupboards, from under the bed and from under the stove jumping on her bed. She seemed to love all of them. To me life couldn't have been better as I boarded the boat to go home to show Little Aunty and Uncle Mike my most treasured possession. I was told later that when Old Mrs. Keating died all the cats were killed so they could be with her in the next life.

Chapter 23
FISH CAMP

When Mama and I returned to Shageluk, Uncle Mike was getting ready to go to his fish camp. I didn't remember going to fish camp before, so this was another new experience. Everyone was busy packing up everything. We would need dishes, tents, bedding and our sled dogs. It was decided Gertie would stay home with Lilly and keep an eye on our and Uncle Mike's house. Of course I had to take Pussycat. The big day arrived with our boat loaded and the dogs barking and howling. What a racket! We were only going about five miles up the Innoko. Many of the other villagers had already left for the huge Yukon River fish camps. A handful of people stood on the bank to watch us pull out. We shoved off, fully loaded, and just as Uncle Mike pulled the rope starter of the old Evinrude, the engine made such a startling loud noise that my pussycat jumped into the water and was swimming to shore. I almost stood up in the boat screaming but Mama pushed me back down. I was still screaming for my cat and Uncle Mike almost went back to shore but Mama and Little Aunty talked him out of it because we were so over-loaded. My pussycat made it to shore and I saw Gertie pick him up giving me a sign she would take good care of it. I was too sad to wave because this was the first time my cat and I had been separated. Now we probably would have a lot of mice because Uncle Mike said the cat's job was to hunt mice at camp.

Boat Building in Shageluk

At the fish camp we were greeted by the Fairbanks family, who was already settled in their cabin and had cleared most of the high grass around the fish camp. I was happy to see their son Herbert, who was my age, whom I could play with along with his younger sister Theresa. There were four kids in their family and three in ours. It was going to be a fun summer. I forgot about my cat while I ran up the bank yelling to play with Herbert and proceeded to take charge of our playtime. The rest of the kids hauled our supplies up the bank. Our tent was pitched on the awaiting floor platform. It was our instant summer home. After cleaning the smokehouses and building some fish racks it was time to take our fish wheel out of storage.

The fish camp was located at the mouth of a small slough, which flowed into a beautiful lake. It was in this narrow slough where the fish wheel was stored for the winter. Soon the fish wheel was towed to the banks of the Innoko River. Here the current furnished the power to turn the wheel. It had two paddles and two meshed wire fish scoopers. When the fish are scooped out of the water, they fall into a chute-like slide and ride into a big wooden box. This box had to be checked twice a day, in the morning and in the evening, depending on the fish run.

When our supper of dryfish and tea was over, we all had to go to bed early, as 6:00 a.m. would soon be here so we could check the fish wheel. I was happy to go to bed early, as Uncle promised I could go with them in the morning. The tent was full of mosquitoes. My sisters and I crawled under the mosquito net to go to sleep. Mama also made a smudge pot for the mosquitoes and I heard Uncle Mike sharpening the Indian knives to be used for cutting the fish.

The next morning after we had all awakened, my sisters had to go pack water from the clear slough to wash ourselves in the basin, then start water boiling for the morning tea. Little Aunty made some pancakes and Mama fried slab bacon. The breakfast smelled so good and our neighbors came to eat with us. After everything was put away, Uncle Mike, Uncle Arthur, Andy, Tony and I went to check the fish wheel. I was told Herbert was sick and wouldn't be coming with us.

When we pulled to up the wooden box on the log raft which held the fish wheel, I had never seen so many fish in my young life. Soon we had four tubs full with some loose ones on the bottom of the boat. The fish who escaped the stunning blow to the back of their heads were thrashing all over the bottom of the boat and sometimes hitting my legs, almost knocking me off my seat. We headed back to camp, which was not far away and still in view from the fish wheel. The short distance saved a lot of gasoline because Uncle Mike needed the gas to check the store in Shageluk at least twice a week. He opened it for the handful of people who remained in the village. He already sold most of the supplies that came on the spring steamboat to all the people who left for the Yukon fish camps, and now he had to wait for the fall steamboat to bring the winter supplies. Now he could devote his time fishing for a winter's supply to feed the family and the dog team.

When we arrived back to the camp with the fish, all the women were ready at the cutting tables. The first order of the day was to examine and pick out the best fresh fish for our noontime dinner and late supper. These were mostly dog salmon with a sprinkle of kings and silvers. The king salmon were the richest fish, with lots of fat. If you ate too much of this fish, you would get an upset stomach. I personally loved all the salmon; it tasted so good. We had salmon fried in lard, made into soup and baked over the fire. We also had dinners of fish heads and suppers of fish eggs, liver and the upper part of the large intestine. Later there would be half-dried fish and fully dried boiled fish called Guhnovartz. All the kids kept busy helping to hang fish and once they were dried in the sun, they were brought into the smokehouses to smoke. When the smoking was completed, the fish were removed from the racks, bundled in bundles of fifty fish, and then stored on storage tables built up against the smoke-house walls.

Lori at Fishcamp

Then Mama showed me how to string the fish hearts on a smoothly carved stick that was used for hanging flatfish. After I strung the hearts like kabobs on a stick, they were hung on the fish rack to dry. It kept me busy all day and I felt I was being useful and earning my meals.

Fish cutting was usually an all-day affair with four very experienced fish cutters. The fish was split and flattened for the dogs, or striped and fancy cut for our consumption. The heads, back-bones, and guts were cooked for the dogs. An abundance of heads was also hung kabob-like on sticks. Not one part of the fish was wasted. After the fish were all cut, the tables were cleaned and it was time to take a break until the next fish wheel check.

Meanwhile all the kids were kept busy turning the soil in the garden and the grownups planted cabbage, turnips, carrots and potatoes. Boiled potatoes were a must for Guhnovartz (dried boiled fish) and moose stew.

We also could go up the slough to the beautiful lake to pick fresh blueberries, which were used to make Indian ice cream. We never knew any other kind of ice cream existed. If there was a pike or a whitefish in our fish wheel, we used this to make our ice cream. First the fish is cleaned and scaled, then cut into chunks. Next it is boiled and cooled. Then the bones and skin are removed and the fish is flaked in a bowl making sure any moisture is squeezed out. Then a little lard or Crisco is added with some sugar and this mixture is creamed with very clean hands in a circular motion until it is soft and fluffy. At this point some cotton from the cottonwood trees may be added to give it fiber. Finally, the fresh picked blueberries are folded into the ice cream. If it's not berry season, raisins are used instead of fresh berries. This was our dessert and the best treat in the world. I would be on my best behavior if I knew Mama was going to make ice cream. There always was an air of excitement and anticipation on "Ice Cream Day."

Sometimes the older kids played "hide and go seek" with us under the riverbank just for fun. I always liked it when Mama would help by hiding me under the blankets in her bed while she was working on her baskets. She gave orders that no one could disturb her. I sometimes fell asleep while waiting to be found and later wondered if Mama planned this to make me take a nap because the older ones were tired of caring for me.

I very much enjoyed the fish camp, but I was also quite excited about going back home to Shageluk. After fishing season we packed up everything, including our fat dogs, cleaned out our fish camp, stored our fish wheel back up the slough and went home. Everyone concerned had a good feeling about our successful summer. Now, I was happy to go home to see my pussycat. Certainly Gertie and Lilly were anxiously waiting for us.

We were home a couple of months when a sad event occurred. My dear, dear, Uncle Mike died of tuberculosis. Many people said he died from a broken heart from not getting his daughter back. I kept staring at him laid out on the floor of his house. He would never carry me on his back again or save me from Little Aunty. Now he would never get Julia back. I moved to Mama's house during the funeral. That night I put my face in my pillow and cried so no one could hear me.

School had already started, so Mama decided to bring me to work with her. In the afternoons I played with the teacher Mrs. Dickman's daughter, Connie Lou. She was a couple years older than me and was a very nice girl. I enjoyed playing with her. One day she gave me one of her old dolls and a red and blue wheelbarrow in which I put my pussycat and the doll when I was at home. I thought these were the best gifts I ever had and showed them off to my friends and anyone else who would look them. I also made Lilly feel my gifts over and over so I could hear her tell me how beautiful they were. She could describe and "ooh" and "aah" much better than anyone else I knew.

My carefree days came to an abrupt halt when Mrs. Dickman told

Mama she thought I was ready to attend school with the rest of the kids. I walked in that school room and fell madly in love with it. I was so proud to have my own desk in the beginning group. The room smelled so good to me, especially the crayons. I had already learned all the colors of the crayons from Connie Lou. I loved school and did my best to be the best. I was learning to read when a Public Health Nurse came flying in on the mail plane and came to our classroom to announce that we were all receiving vaccinations. Mama was there and told me that when my name was called I was not to cry no matter what was done to me. She said she would stand in the hallway and listen. The only thing I remember was when the nurse told me to open my mouth, she let out a little scream and went to find the teacher and Mama. I heard an argument between the three of them and the nurse won. She told them I had all my baby teeth in my mouth so I shouldn't be in school. She said it was against the law for someone as young as I to take up a desk, even though there were quite a few empty desks. I had to be sent home right then and there in front of her. I had the most intense feeling of hatred for that woman. I walked home alone feeling so angry and I wanted to do something to her to get even. Maybe I would lock the door of the schoolhouse the next time she came in the winter. I was to get my revenge a few days later.

When I got home I told Gertie and Lilly the whole story and their sympathy for me was interjected with a few "poors" which made me feel so much better. I even felt much better when Gertie told me I could actually bring a husky puppy into the house to play with as long as I brought it right back to its mother when it looked tired. She also said she would help me read my sister's book when she brought it home from school to practice. It was called Peter and Peggy. In the book was a dog named Tags and a kitten named Twinkle. I knew the cat was my pussycat's relative because they looked alike and I was so proud to show my cat the picture of Twinkle. I knew he felt so good to finally see his relative because he had no one who looked like him in Shageluk. The kids in the book had so much fun with their animals. I shared the same joy with mine.

A couple of days later, Mama told Gertie that the Public Health Nurse was coming to make home visits around the town. Mama wanted to make sure I was clean and wanted my hair braided. Mama went off to work and Gertie told me to come to her so she could braid my hair. I did under strong protest. I was complaining, punctuating with "OUCHES" every other minute. The braid was so tight, it felt like my eyes shrunk. I wanted the braids undone because I told her it hurt and I couldn't see very well when my eyes shrunk (The braids were pulled so tightly that my eyes were like slits). She said it was Mama's idea so why don't I just get the puppy for a while since my cat was doing its morning hunting. I was glad of that and ran off to get the puppy. The mother dog wasn't thrilled to see me, but I talked her into letting me have the puppy. I ran into the house with it and started watching it wobble around the floor. At this time there was a knock on the door. We all knew it had to be someone white because they were the only people who knocked. Just about the time everyone yelled "Come in!" the puppy started to mess on the floor. The door opened and the first thing the Public Health Nurse saw was the puppy. She was so horrified to see a sled dog in the house, all that came out of her mouth was "Stick it out!' and as she lunged toward the puppy, she tripped on a loose board which came flying in her face and her hand ended up in the mess. The puppy was so startled by all of the racket, it started howling. I jumped up, grabbed my puppy, looked down at the nurse, told her she scared my puppy and that she had Tron (crap) on her hand then walked out the door. I was so happy she fell but I felt sorry for Gertie and Lilly having to put up with all her hollering about the house being unsanitary. I couldn't wait to tell Mama and smiled all day long envisioning the nurse lying on the floor.

Shortly thereafter, Gertie and my sister Celene moved to Holy Cross. I guess Gertie wanted to at least be in the same village as her daughter Julia and she considered it her home since she was raised in the Mission. My sister Celene was going to stay with our cousin Jenny to help her with her new set of twins.

Mama was drinking heavily and many times she took me with her to her friends. One night it was below freezing when we were walking home in the dark. She fell in the snow and I couldn't get her up. I pulled and pulled on her arm but she would not move. I didn't know what to do so I thought maybe if I started crying, she would be so upset with me she would get up and hit me. I started crying, but she didn't move and soon I was really crying because I was so scared. I thought she was dead. I kept calling her but there was no response. I stood beside her, hoping someone would come along, but everybody was in bed. It was late at night. She had woken me up at her friend's house to walk home with her. Now I didn't understand why she wouldn't wake up for me. I don't know how long I was standing there but it was so cold and I had just about given up hope of ever being found. I was going to sit down next to Mama when I heard dogs barking. A team was coming from Lower Village and the driver was flashing his flashlight in my face. He stopped the team, jumped out and put Mama and me in the sled. He drove us home and told me Mama would be okay in the morning. It was a good feeling to be in our house again.

Things were going from bad to worse. We again didn't have very much to eat. Sometimes I was able to forget about food while playing with my friend Mary Elizabeth. That was the highlight of my day since we were both so imaginative. One day I remember being alone in the house with Lilly when I heard someone entering the porch. Since no one knocked in those days, the door opened and there stood Gachidle, a friend from Lower Village. He asked where Mama was and I shrugged, "Ah tzrah" (I don't know). He told me that he brought us a beaver for supper. Lilly really thanked him and he left. I looked at the delicious beaver meat and I could already taste it. It had a slit in the tail and I could see the nice white fat against the black leathery tail. That was all I remember, just thinking what a scrumptious meal we were going to have.

Mama had a gentleman friend at this time and when they partied, his son Franklin, who was my age, and I would have fun playing outside with my pussycat and the wheelbarrow. Franklin's mom had died, so now he always followed his dad everywhere. We had a lot of fun, but one day he didn't come over so I went with Mama to his house to play with him. His dad said he wasn't feeling well. They called for medicine from the schoolhouse. When he felt better his dad came to our house and asked Mama if she wanted to go on a boat ride to Holy Cross to see his oldest married daughter. We were so excited. I told Franklin this was where Mama's relatives, the Sims and the Franks, lived. We had been there before and had spent the night at Railroad City across the Yukon from Holy Cross, close to the mouth of the Innoko. There were friends and relatives there also. I was telling him everything my five year-old brain could remember. I told him about the strange animals in Holy Cross called cows and bulls with horns on their heads. The bulls would get really mad at you if you wore any kind of red clothes. We couldn't have been happier than we were that day as we boarded the big gas boat.

Chapter 24
HOLY CROSS MISSION

The boat landed at Holy Cross and I had the feeling of being awakened and rushed out of the boat. Mama didn't say a word, but grabbed my hand and I was running to keep up with her. I was trying to protest, but she jerked my arm so hard. It wasn't possible to say anything because I couldn't speak and run fast at the same time. I looked ahead to see where we were going and I saw a huge cross on what I thought was a mountain. As we got closer, I noticed many "white man" houses—houses not made of logs but from lumber. They reminded me of the schoolhouse at Shageluk.

As we approached one of the huge buildings I suddenly saw a figure walking toward us. I became so petrified that I stopped suddenly. Mama looked down at me, told me to quit acting silly and hurry along. I wanted to ask her what kind of creature was coming toward us, but I couldn't. The figure was dressed in all black clothing and looked like it had a bandage on the forehead. I knew it was an evil spirit who came out of one of the graveyards, as we were always told, and would come to get us if we misbehaved. I looked at Mama. She didn't seem scared and continued to drag me along. Finally we stopped. I was very tired from running for so long. Mama talked to this creature that had a human face and voice. It was a strange and most frightening experience. This was also the first time I had seen a nun. She pointed to a building and Mama continued dragging me along. We reached the building and went inside. Another nun appeared and after a few words, Mama pushed me toward her. The only thing I heard Mama say was "Don't cut her hair." She looked at me and said "Don't you dare cry" and walked out the door.

I had a feeling of absolute terror and tried to run after her but the nun grabbed my hand. The feeling of the strange hand was something indescribable and undesirable. I looked out of the window and saw Mama walking quickly toward the village from where we had just come. I didn't want this strange, cold hand holding me and I suddenly felt the urge to cry. I held back because Mama told me not to. Soon the nun and I were walking down what seemed like a long corridor. I still didn't know who or what she was and she did not talk to me. I was aware of strange smells of what I would consider later as 'mission smells' such as candles, building smells, old pictures and something cooking far away. Again I was being rushed along and was getting scared, really scared, and again I fought the urge to cry. Soon we came to a large room and I could hear voices from another room directly across from the door we came in. We reached the room and two smaller girls were being dressed by two laughing native teenagers. The nun told them to find another set of clothes for the "new girl" and lifted me on a stool. She proceeded to cut my hair and then shaved the whole back of my head. All I had left was hair above my ears and a longer strand on the top right side of my head which could be braided or looped and tied with a ribbon.

I knew right then and there that these people meant business, because they didn't even listen to Mama about not cutting my hair. Mama was always the boss and we had to listen to her. I looked down on the floor where my blonde curls were piled. My hair had been halfway down my back. With that completed, the nun gave the teenage girls instructions and left the room. She told them my name was Cecilia Woodford.

They started to undress me and I was struggling to hang on to my clothes. No one I could remember ever took my clothes off except Mama. One of them held my hands while the other one undressed me, all the time laughing. I was put in a huge tub that had legs. As they were talking to each other, they were scrubbing me with a huge scrub brush. As it scraped across my chest, I could feel intense pain, but I didn't say a word. I just hated Mama for bringing me here and I felt helpless. After what seemed like an eternity, I was dried off and had to choose one of the two dresses held in front of me. I wanted to get dressed in a hurry so I pointed at one. I thought it was pretty and wished my sisters could see it. The final part of dressing was to put on a long apron so you couldn't see the pretty dress. I discovered later that all the girls had the same kind of apron so the dresses wouldn't get dirty. Bathing and getting dressed in clean clothing was to be the first ritual of every Saturday morning for the next four years.

I refused to talk to anybody. Soon the nun came back and told me I could play outside with the rest of the children. There were 26 children living in the Baby Course, as it was called, or the Second Course. This was where the younger orphans lived, both girls and boys. The other part of the mission was First Course, where the intermediate girls lived and then there were the older girls who were referred to as the Heaven Girls. The boys lived in the boy's dorm, a separate building far away from ours.

The nun took my hand again and we went into a corridor that was so dark it took my breath away. I didn't remember experiencing "dark" in a building before. At home we were never in the dark because there was a candle or a kerosene lamp on all night. I felt that being in the dark was like being in the land where dead people lived. Almost in a state of sheer panic, I finally saw a light at the end of the corridor leading outdoors. The hand that held mine was now a comfort that I thought I would never accept.

We got outside and the nun called a girl over to take care of me. She told me just to do what the rest of them did. I looked on the playground and everyone looked clean, happy and all alike. I was glad my family couldn't see me looking so strange, although I wished they could see the pretty ribbon in my hair. As soon as the nun left, the kids came over to talk to me, but I wouldn't say a word. I had the feeling of the most complete sadness and despair. I wanted to go to sleep and never wake up. I just stared at the kids and soon they got tired of trying to talk to me and went back to playing. I kept wondering where my mom and sisters were and what they were doing.

I heard a bell ringing and a little girl came to tell me we had to line up for dinner. From the behavior of the rest of them, they really looked forward to this noontime meal that they called dinner, just like we did. We lined up and a nun came out and brought us to our room. There were many beds lined up head to foot in long lines. At the back of the room was a long table where a basin was placed for each child. I was shown my basin. There was a washcloth, a hand towel and a bath towel on the holder which extended the length of the table hanging above each basin. To the right of the basin was some hand soap in a soap holder. To the left were toothpaste and a toothbrush. There were two metal pitchers at the end of each table. The nun poured water in our basins all the way down one side of the table and when she got to the end switched pitchers and finished the other side of the table. Then she scurried past the partition which separated us from the boys and did the same thing for them. We all had to wash our faces and hands with our washcloths, rinse it and wring it out. It was then put on our towel bar to dry. She checked to see if everything was put back perfectly and then lined us up. The group with the straightest line got to go to the dining room first.

We walked down a long hallway and as we got closer to the dining room, the smell of cooked food was so delicious. I could also hear chatter and the sound of dishes being handled. We then arrived at a huge room filled with all the mission children. The different age groups had their own section. Everyone was smiling and happy as they greeted each other. I had never seen so many kids in one place, not even in the school at Shageluk. We stood behind our benches by our place settings and waited for a cue from the nun before we sat down. Everything got quiet and we all bowed our heads to say the blessing. The girl next to me told me we had to eat all our food. When we were through, everyone was quiet again and we said a prayer of thanksgiving. This was our daily routine, which was the same for breakfast and supper. We had wonderful Sunday dinners, including dessert. On cue again, the nun in charge lined us up and we marched back to our rooms. We had to brush our teeth, go to our bed, take off our dresses, lay them neatly on the foot of our bed and take a nap in our petticoats. I just watched whatever everyone else was doing and copied them. Mama always stressed obedience.

After our nap, we dressed, lined up again, went downstairs and played outside on the playground. I just sat on the grass feeling so lonely and, at the same time, mad at Mama for leaving me here. I wondered why everyone was so happy. I wanted to go home in the worst way. I just sat there tracing pictures in a little patch of sand. Soon the nun came up to me with a bigger girl saying she brought a friend who was from my village. I looked up, and there was Julia! I was so happy to see her! She started talking a mile a minute as only Julia could do and told me in a few minutes the history and rules of the mission. Because she saw how sad I was, she decided to cheer me up with one of her prize possessions.

She carried with her a box of old Christmas cards, which had the insides cut out so all that was left where the pictures. She explained you "earned" these cards from the nuns and all you had to do was be an obedient girl. She let me look at all the beautiful pictures and told me to choose one, making sure she emphasized which ones were her favorites. I had a feeling these were not the ones I should pick. They were all beautiful though and I picked one. I felt I was so lucky to have Julia. She told me to wait there and ran off. Soon she came back with an empty card box. In great detail she presented me with the box explaining that if I stayed long enough I might be able to fill it. I was informed it was okay to trade with the other kids and if I behaved myself, it shouldn't take long to fill the box with beautiful Christmas pictures.

She asked about the family at home and explained that the nuns were holy people who worked for God and all their names started with Sister Mary with different last names. I asked her why they had bandages on their heads and whose sisters they were. She guessed they had no hair. That's why they covered up their heads and they were sisters to each other. I then just assumed that was God's way of making people who were to work for him have no hair. I was not only satisfied with the explanation, I believed it. Julia was so funny jabbering away and introduced me to the other kids as 'Baby Cecilia'. So the first day wasn't so bad after all with Julia there, and the kids gave me the impression they were going to be nice to me since I had a relative on the big girls' side. The Sister came back and took Julia away. Since we didn't live in the same section, I usually could only see her on Sundays. I couldn't wait to be ten years old so I could move there. I occasionally saw her in the dining hall, but she had her own life with her own grown-up friends.

Mission life was pretty routine: get up in the morning, say morning prayers, go to early Mass, go to breakfast, play, have dinner, nap, play, supper, play, sponge bath, night prayers and bed. Sundays were different, because there was a high Mass added to the morning routine and a very good supper to eat. Also, if you had relatives among the villagers, you had the opportunity to visit them on Sundays. We also had benediction services in the evenings.

In our daily routine, I thought sponge baths were tricky and challenging. Each person was given a four-button flannel nightgown. You had to unbutton your nightgown and reach through this opening. With your hands and arms out of the sleeves and with soap on the washrag in the basin, you scrubbed your entire body under the nightgown. Then you rinsed off all the soap and dried with a towel. We eventually learned how to be expert sponge-bathers. I'm betting we could all hold our own in a contest to see who could break the record for sponge baths. After our baths we turned away from our basins holding our hands out for inspection. We had the back of our ears checked also. We were experts and rarely had to re-do our sponge baths. If we did, we repeated the whole process. We helped each other out by giving each other a mini inspection before the sister came.

All the sisters took care of us, but we seemed to have two who were somewhat permanent for our group. Sister Mary Kathleen was our own angel from God. We knew that and liked her so much because she was so kind. We wished she was the only one to take care of us but she had a relief, Sister Mary Delia, who I thought must have been a partner of the devil himself. If there were any repeats of sponge baths it would come from her. If anyone wet his or her bed, she would rip the sheet off the bed and tie it around the nose of the guilty party. The rest of us formed a circle pointing and laughing, making fun of the offender. If the bed-wetter was a boy, he was made to wear a dress. Imagine my humiliation when I saw my dress on the boy. Imagine his humiliation. If the child cried, the sheet was ripped off and his hand was slapped with a belt. The usual punishment was three swats but if you didn't cry, you would get swatted until you cried. I always sympathized with the person who was punished. In my prayers on the playground, I asked that this nasty sister would be punished. At first, my sympathy was accepted, but since I never got into any kind of trouble, my fellow classmates knew I just couldn't possibly understand what they went through. I decided to fix this by wetting my own bed.

Try as I might, though, I couldn't. I finally managed a trickle about three inches in diameter. I proudly showed it to my neighbor who was a bed wetter. I made sure it showed when I pulled my covers back. I happily went to wash up. Then Sister Delia checked our beds before we made them. My neighbor whispered down the basin line that I had wet the bed. Everyone looked at me with a mixture of pity and some with a touch of joy to see me punished since I hadn't been before. Oh, I felt like a martyr and now I would be able to experience a little of Jesus' suffering before he died on the cross. I was certainly on my way to sainthood! I said a quick prayer to make sure I had enough strength to withstand this extreme punishment. We were called to make our beds and the bed wetters were called out, but not me. What? Everyone looked at me and my witness assured all that she had seen my bed. When I got back to my bed I saw that the spot had dried and since I wasn't a regular, Sister Delia overlooked it. Since I felt a slight bit betrayed by some of the smirks, I decided I didn't want to be a martyr after all. It wasn't my fault that the nun didn't notice. We had an understanding not to tattle on each other, so I still had my place on the "Good List."

On the playground we were completely free to say anything we wished. I found I could usually talk my friends into some sort of mischief like pulling innocent tricks on each other. I was completely at ease with my friends and always looked forward to playground time. If the weather was bad, we had a big inside playroom with a wood stove on the outside of our bathtub room. This was used to dry our hair after our baths by shaking our hair by the stoves with our hands. We told each other stories and anything we remembered of our homes and about the day we would be going back to our homes. I was surprised no one could speak Athabascan with me, but it seemed all the Eskimo kids could speak their language. As a matter of fact, some of them came speaking no English. I was amused by the way they sounded. They taught me a few words like "hello" (chamai) and silly expressions or exclamations. I in turn taught them Indian and they would laugh because they thought it was a funny language and even funnier that a "white" girl spoke Indian.

Soon we had to pack all our summer clothing away to get ready for the winter. In the dorm, all our summer clothes were laid out in the playroom and our winter clothes came out, such as our winter coats, hats and mittens. I had never seen such a wonderful selection. We were each responsible for our hat, coat, and mittens and were assigned our own hook to hang them on in the dark corridor where the wood boxes were kept. We also had a little shelf for storing our personal belongings, such as our card collections.

I lived for going to school. I loved it from the first day and at the mission no one sent me home because I had baby teeth. Our teacher was Sister Mary Kathleen and no one could have been more fortunate. The first part of each day was reserved for prayer and religious instruction. On the first day of school we learned about the earth's beginning according to Genesis. I was so fascinated by this story. I proudly contributed that I already knew about God because my mom told me about Him. Sister Mary Kathleen also made us say morning and evening prayers. I had once asked her where I was before I was born and she told me I was in 'God's pocket'. That made complete sense to me. You took things out of your pocket to give to someone. So when God found a family for me, he just took me out of his pocket way up in the fluffy clouds and put me in the house where I belonged. I was so happy to share this piece of information with my fellow students and became a little angry when someone questioned this by asking the sister if this was true. Why would I mention this if it wasn't true? Whatever she said supported my idea in that God certainly knew us before we were born because he knows everything and has a plan for all his children whether we were in his pocket or not. I smugly turned around with my own smirk (since I was assigned to the front row) and felt the glares on my back from the other students. School seemed easy for me. I didn't have any problems and usually helped other classmates understand difficult concepts. The village children were also in our class. We learned about Saints and the Holy Days that we celebrated.

At Christmas, the church was decorated with the Holy Family, the shepherds and the angels. Our first school Christmas program was so exciting. I had a small bit part for the program. I was part of a train that Santa was going to put under the tree. The older students cut the tops and bottoms off cardboard boxes, decorated them like train boxcars, then glued them together. We were the toys in the train. We had to stand on a stairway in the back of the stage and when our cue was given, we just had to walk across the stage, pause in the middle, and all together say, "Merry Christmas to All," then proceed to the Christmas tree and stand under it. Well, on the stairway, the boy in back of me (the caboose) was having such a panic attack about remembering "Merry Christmas to All" that I decided to help him out. While I was making him repeat the phrase after me and mouthing the words to him, I didn't hear the cue until he nodded his head for me to look forward. Everyone had rushed off to the stage breaking the train between them and me. I was so surprised when everyone was gone; I rushed after them and in my mad dash, broke away from John, the caboose. John came running after me and everyone started laughing so hard. I noticed Sister Mary Delia giving us a mean look, which quickly made me angry. John and I said our lines nicely and clearly even though it was after the fact and we weren't connected to the rest of the train. I felt like a complete failure and now it was John's turn to reassure me. He said it was over and we didn't ever have to do it again. Even after this terrible beginning, I loved being in plays and memorizing lines, the longer the better.

I remember my stay at the mission, for the most part, as a wonderful, secure and safe experience. It was such a treat when the sisters gave us each a popcorn ball and we all marched into the show house to enjoy a good movie, whether it was about cowboys and Indians or the five Sullivan boys, while we ate our most treasured, delicious popcorn ball. Easter was always celebrated in the church. After church we had an Easter egg hunt to look for hard candy. We would make our candy last as long as possible by breaking small pieces off every day and sucking on them for as long as possible. In the summer the sisters would walk us down past the village to the meadow for a picnic. We also walked up the hill in back of the mission to a shrine of the Blessed Virgin Mary. How I loved that walk as we picked bluebells to put in vases by the huge statue. Blue was the color for Mary and any flower that was blue was picked. I still can feel the excitement of walking up that hill, smelling the comforting woodsy aroma. We all were so excited to show Sister Mary Kathleen our flowers, asking if they were good enough for the Virgin Mary. She always said yes and when we got to the shrine we humbly gave the Virgin our offerings. This felt so sacred that we automatically quieted down and whispered in respect of this huge statue. There we prayed for people all over the world, especially the Russians.

Summer also brought out the mission boat, the 'St. Theresa'. What fun it was to have our cook, Sister Ida, pack many sandwiches and Kool-Aid for our trip down the Yukon River to Paimiute to see the other sisters and the "heaven girls" cutting fish. How wonderful it was to have our picnic on the big barge and to enjoy the day. We were too young to help cut fish, but we were looking forward to being transferred to the big girls' section so we could also learn to help. It certainly looked like a lot of fun. We probably didn't know when we were well off.

The big preparation for our first communion arrived one day after what seemed like years of religious study. We memorized our catechism and all our important prayers and practiced faithfully to swallow the host without getting it stuck to the roof of our mouths. We practiced going to confession and finally the big day arrived. We were so nervous, as we had to walk up the aisle in the big church paired with a boy. The "heaven girls" helped us dress in our communion clothes. Everything we wore was white: white undergarments, white stockings, white shoes and a white veil. We already practiced walking down the aisle with our partners. My partner was a village boy named Ishman, who seemed to be very shy. When the big day arrived, we were the last couple down the aisle and I heard a woman say, "Oh look, just like married." I turned bright red and thought Ishman was going to run out the door. But the Lord was more important, so I kept going. I felt so holy and the church felt like the presence of God was everywhere and in that moment I knew what the sisters meant when they told us God was everywhere. He was certainly present on this special day. When I received my communion, I just knew I was a saint and was going to become a nun just like Sister Mary Kathleen, a pretty big decision for a 7 year-old. Of course, my friends would probably tell you they didn't think I would be a good candidate. This was our day though, and we had a wonderful feast after communion. After the feast I went to the home of my cousin Genny, who checked me out of the mission almost every Sunday for an hour. She had a nice cake at her house for Ishman and me and we felt pretty special. I was trying my best to be holy.

Now that we had our first communion we were supposed to go to confession every Saturday. I was practicing for sainthood and was so good all week that I felt I had no sins. When Sister Delia asked me why I wasn't going to confession I told her I had examined my conscience and felt I had no sins. I pretty much knew that after I received communion my heart was pure and white and not a trace of original sin was left. It was absolutely the wrong thing to say. She yelled at me saying that I was not above God and only He and He alone was sinless. I was to go to the confessional immediately. I hurried ahead of her, but try as I might I could not think of a single sin. When it was my turn I humbly walked past her to the confessional. I kneeled and started, "Bless me Father for I have sinned...." then suddenly blurted out, "I dreamt about the devil last night." The priest told me to try to have pure thoughts, but my sin was bad enough to say a penance of three Hail Marys.

I walked out of the confessional with my scarf pulled forward to let everyone know I was going to say my penance. I dragged it out by saying a dozen Hail Marys so Sister Delia wouldn't talk to me again. How dare she get mad at me when I was sincerely trying to be a saint? The following Saturday I found Sister Delia myself to announce I was going to confession. She gave me a look of approval. I went back to the confessional and asked the priest, "Remember last week when I told you I dreamt of the devil? Well, I lied to you." I closed my eyes to get a good scolding. He preached to me about the dangers of lying and I still got two Hail Marys. After that I was pretty sinful whenever I thought of Sister Delia and became a regular at the confessional.

I was so hateful while thinking of Sister Delia that I decided to do something about her. All the other kids were afraid of her and despised her also. We then all met on the playground, where I told them we were going to play "Mass" and I would be the priest. There were strong objections from the boys, but I convinced them I was going to be a boy when I grew up, so they allowed me to be the priest. I asked them if they believed God answered prayer and they all said yes. So I told them we were going to pray that God would take Sister Delia to heaven; we wanted her to die. Some of the students were afraid, but all prayed as I, the priest, had instructed.

It wasn't more than a week when one of the sisters came to us on the playground to say that Sister Delia was leaving on the plane and needed our prayers because she was ill. Everyone looked at me as though I was a murderer. For a long time, I had no playmates, but I was happy. When I didn't have friends for quite a while, I went to the priest to ask him if a person was a murderer if she wished and prayed for someone to die and that someone soon died. He told me that God could do what He wanted and prayers and wishes couldn't make one a murderer. I explained this to my friends and they forgave me. I asked for forgiveness a million times and prayed for my pitiful soul. Years later I found that Sister Delia did not die at this time. I had wasted years worrying.

I felt quite special when I was one of several students who were checked out by a relative to visit in town. My cousin Genny was so important to me while I was at the mission. Most of her nieces and nephews were close to my and my playmates' age, so I soon just picked up the name they called her, Auntie Genny. Later in life I asked her why I was so privileged to be with her on Sundays and she said she promised her cousin Papa Woodford on his deathbed that she would always look out for me and my two sisters. She said it was very important to keep her promise. I enjoyed these Sunday outings and I got to see my sister Celene at least twice during this time.

Holy Cross seemed to be divided between the mission people and the villagers. If you lived in the mission, you were referred to as a Mission Girl or a Mission Boy. Since this was my Mother's town, I got to know the people quite well on my Sunday visits, especially when I told them I was Matilda's daughter. Also, Aunt Genny took me everywhere she went, as she was always doing good deeds for everyone—bringing people fresh fish, bread, meat or anything she could share. I always enjoyed visiting others with her and we covered a lot of territory because she was a bundle of energy, always working and on the move. She and her husband Willie ran the Post Office from their home, so their house always had people there. I loved them and learned many things from them. She sewed beautiful fur garments and did beautiful beading. She was an expert in making Indian baskets and trays. Even when talking to her though, I felt there was a definite division between the downtown villagers and the uptown mission folks, as if they were two separate communities. When I was in town I would hear the people talk about the mission as if they felt the mission personnel thought they were better than the village. Living in the mission, my sense was they felt superior to the villagers. We were always challenged to make ourselves better in life. The expectations at the school were very high and laziness wasn't tolerated. We had to do everything right the first time and as perfectly as possible. While I was there it never seemed the mission kids were allowed to go to any town functions, but the villagers could go to mission functions. I always was curious on how the Holy Cross people held Indian dances as we always had those in Shageluk but

I never did see any. It was as if the responsibilities for the mission kids were so great, they weren't allowed out of their caretaker's sight for fear of repercussion from the parents who entrusted their children to the mission. The orphans seemed to be encouraged to hang around with their own mission peers. I never knew whether I should be complimented or insulted when I was called a "mission girl" by the villagers. I preferred to be complimented, of course.

I witnessed three mission weddings and thought they were the most beautiful weddings I ever attended to this day. They were full formal Mass weddings and all the mission children were in attendance. It was as if we were invited to a royal wedding with the mission as the bride's family. All three girls married boys from the town. In those days the Holy Cross people seemed to all be good practicing Catholics, as our church was always full. I didn't know the courting practices, as I was still in the baby section of the mission. The brides' perfect white dresses made them so beautiful and the handsome grooms looked so lovingly at their new brides. These weddings gave us something to talk about and made the boys run away from us if we wanted to have a pretend wedding. We never got groom volunteers unless we promised candy from our next town visit.

When I went to town with one of the sisters on medical visits, we always stopped at the local store called 'Turners'. Mr. Turner always gave me a piece of candy before we left. The sister took it and would give it to me on a special occasion. Mr. Turner's wife was from my home village and I remember Mama taking me along when she visited her in Shageluk. I thought she was so beautiful and she would always fix my hair with pretty ribbons and barrettes from her store. She would tell Mama she wished I were hers so she could dress me pretty because she only had three boys. She was so kind and I felt really sad when we heard she died. I remember visiting her grave with Aunt Genny, who was one of her best friends, and we felt very mad at the mission because they wouldn't allow her to be buried in the Catholic section of the graveyard, so they buried her outside the fence because she was Episcopalian. I thought she must be pretty lonely outside the fence. Aunt Genny must have thought so also, because we always visited her grave more than anyone else's. We always stood there so solemnly and silently and talked to her in our heads.

I was very grateful to "Turner" (as everyone called him) for my candy.

My favorite candy was an apple-shaped, red and yellow wedged lollipop. It was so huge, I could break it into many pieces to share with my friends or trade for a Christmas card. It was very delicious, with a flavor never duplicated in my lifetime.

All of our candy had to be completely gone when Lenten season came around. This was the time in our church when you had to make all kinds of sacrifices and be more Christ-like in preparation for the celebration of Easter. There was to be no candy or dessert during this time and it seems our meat was rationed. We had fish more than just on Fridays. This was fine with me because I could eat fish every day and it would not be a sacrifice. All the statues in the church were covered up during Lent and it was frightening to go to church. It was as if God disappeared from there. We weren't allowed to talk, as this was our retreat—a time to reflect on our relationship with God. We even had to double up on our prayers. In our dining hall, a priest would come to read from the Bible as we ate meagerly. It was dead silent. Even the nuns barely whispered.

Holy pictures were put up on all the walls and one day some new pictures were put up in the hallway going back to our quarters. I happened to see a new picture, which I now believe was Dante's Inferno. I was so fascinated and all of a sudden I spotted the devil. I forgot about the requirement of silence and blurted out "There's the devil!" A nun was escorting us back to our quarters. Suddenly she grabbed my hand, yanked me out of line and dragged me with her. When we got back to the room she took out the belt, motioned for me to hold out my hand and gave me three hard smacks on the palm of the hand. It stung, but I couldn't imagine why anyone would cry. I had harder lickings from my mother. But a game is a game so I put my hand over my eyes and pretended to cry. It started a never-ending discussion on the playground as to whether I really cried or not. Of course I was bragging how a little smack like that would never bring me to tears but there were others who disagreed. This was the first and last time I was ever punished. My thoughts for this nun would have me visiting the confessional for many Saturdays. When we could talk again, I had much to say about this episode as if it was fresh news.

The mission was famous for its huge gardens, cows and pigs. One day a sister came to pick out an obedient child to help in the garden. I was chosen, much to my delight. I would make her so proud of me and wanted to be chosen often to help in the garden. Together we had to weed the carrot rows. She showed me the difference between the weeds and the carrots and left me while she went to the opposite end of the row. We were to meet in the middle. Mama always told my sisters when they worked that they had to do it clean and fast. This was my first real job, so I would do it "clean and fast." I was busy working when I looked up and was so proud I was ahead of the sister. She turned her head toward me with a surprised look and came over to check on me. She talked so mean to me I felt like crying. She said I pulled out all the carrots instead of the weeds and I felt so dumb. She made me replant all the carrots with her and brought me back to the dormitory without talking to me. I felt so humiliated. Needless to say, I was never asked to help in the gardens again. My thoughts of her also kept the confessional busy on Saturdays. I never spoke to her again, but when I related my gardening experience to the kids on the playground, I was a professional weed puller.

Another highlight of mission life was when the great bishop came to confirm the kids. My very own sister Celene was among the candidates. When I first saw the bishop and after all the hustle and bustle in the dorm, cleaning it from top to bottom, I thought God himself had arrived. He looked like what I thought God would look like. Again, all the girls dressed in white and I thought my sister was the most beautiful. After he anointed her head with holy oils, I knew she was part angel and I lived for the day when it would be my turn to kiss the bishop's ring and have the Holy Ghost come to live in me. After this ceremony I had a goal to be extra good and maybe with extra grace from the Holy Ghost, I might still become a nun. Miracles can happen. At this point in my life I was a total Catholic and nothing would change my mind to any other beliefs in the world. I believed God would do anything for me since he answered most of my simple requests.

I knew it was fall when they let the cows come over to our playground. The cows were set loose in our area to fertilize the ground after the mission boys harvested the hay. We had fun looking through the fence at the cows with their enormous eyes. We tried to talk to them but they just stared at us with an occasional "moo." That made us laugh so much. It was also time to go back to school. The fathers would be back teaching us religion, but what we liked best was when they came to our dorm and told us ghost stories. We had two favorites who were almost priests but we called them Fathers.

The priest we loved most was Father Poole. When we saw him coming, we would all run toward him to be picked up first. He would pick us all up and tell us something funny to make us laugh. A few minutes later, after he herded us into the dorm, we would be scared silly listening to his ghost stories, but would still beg for more. He played with us and led us in evening prayer before bed. This gave Sister a break. It was also fun when two priests showed up with a guitar to teach us some songs. Sometimes on Sundays after mass, our own Father Superior would visit with us and we never wanted him to leave. He was such a gentle man. During the week, the brothers were always working on the mission grounds and I was always bothering them with questions while they were usually working near our building. They were very patient, much more than the sisters, but then again, they weren't with us around the clock. They always answered my questions and I was satisfied and added them to my list at night for God to bless.

I loved the mission life and never wanted to go home, so imagine my surprise when a nun came to tell me I was to go home to Mama in Shageluk. I did not understand this, because I hadn't seen her in almost four years. I felt this was to be my home forever, but the nun said she had to do what my Mom wanted. She gave me a small cardboard box and immediately I was ushered out without saying good-bye to my friends. I reluctantly went to the bluff road where the mission truck was waiting to bring me to the plane.

Chapter 25
BACK TO SHAGELUK

Waiting in the truck was Father Poole, one of my favorite priests. He was smiling as he got out of the truck to lift me up into the front seat. We only got to ride in the mission truck twice a year if we were extra good and well-behaved. Even then, we were only allowed to ride in the back seat. Here I was sitting in the front seat. I wished my friends were here to see me, but no one was around. They were all in bed.

Father was chatting happily with me, reminding me to be an obedient child to my mother. I must not forget to say my morning and evening prayers. I could tell he was going to miss me. He was the priest who sang songs to us and told us spooky stories. We listened very carefully when he taught catechism because he was so kind.

Before I knew it, we reached the beach where the old red Norseman, the mail plane, was waiting. I recognized the pilot as Tony Schultz, who sometimes visited the priests in the mission. The huge plane was on floats on the Yukon River and was facing away from the bank, so we had to board from the rear pontoons. Since Schultz was wearing his hip boots, Father Poole handed me to him to be lifted onto the plane. I was so embarrassed for being handled like a baby and was happy that my friends weren't there to see me.

I always longed to be in an airplane and to fly over the mission. Since it was evening, it was quite unusual that there were so few people on the plane, but I did recognize a teenage girl from Shageluk sitting in the front seat next to the pilot. Roxcenia smiled at me and told me she was scared to fly. Schultz set me down on the floor of the rear of the plane. Soon we were taking off and since I couldn't see anything from the floor, I knelt by the window to look out. I saw Father standing by the truck waving and I felt a terrible sadness. I didn't want to leave. Then I started to notice how small everything was getting as the plane climbed higher. I looked up at the pilot and he was busy talking to the teenage girl, who seemed to be very shy. I didn't realize how wide the Yukon was and then we were over the Innoko River. It reminded me of a ribbon winding in and out through the green and brown land.

I was looking down in total amazement when the pilot turned around and yelled at me to sit down. I was so hurt and devastated that he had yelled at me. Now I couldn't see out the window anymore and I just had to go over and over in my mind what I had just seen and I pretended it was like that all the way home. After my hurt subsided I started concentrating on how I would get even with the pilot for yelling at me. When he turned around again to talk to me, I wouldn't even look at him and pretended I didn't hear him.

Finally we landed and the pilot tried to lift me out of the plane. I yanked away from him and told him I could get out by myself. I was still feeling angry with him when suddenly a fat white woman and her very skinny husband came up to me. They told me they were my new parents and were there to pick me up. They had an Eskimo girl with them who was about my age. In the background I recognized the schoolhouse where my mother worked. I asked them if they were the schoolteachers and they said yes. I informed them they were not my parents, as I had an Indian mother, NOT white parents. They told me that my mother had given me to them and that the girl was my new sister and they were to bring me to the schoolhouse to live with them. As young as I was when I left Shageluk, I knew the schoolhouse was haunted and even as religious as I was, there was no way I was going to live in a haunted schoolhouse. I was told that Etola's ghost still wandered the school every day. So I told them

I was not going to live with them and I was going to find my mother. Just then I saw my older sister coming down the bank. I ran past her to where I remembered our old house stood. I reached the house and was amazed to find it was all boarded up. I couldn't imagine what happened. My sister finally caught up with me, panting from running, and told me we didn't live there anymore. Someone else lived there and they were away at fish camp and would be returning soon. I couldn't even imagine anyone living in our old house. I asked Celene what happened to my doll and the wheelbarrow I left behind. She told me to ask Mama. I asked her where our Mama was and she pointed to another house. I immediately recognized it as a Dutchman house, where my friend Franklin lived.

I was running and skipping through the grass, which was taller than I and couldn't see my sister Celene. I got to the house and, as was usual in the village, threw the door open without knocking and there was my mama with a baby. She looked up at me and asked why I was there. I was in shock when I saw this baby and wondered where it came from. Celene, finally catching up with me at the door, told me it was Mama's baby and this was our house now, as our mama had married Roland Dutchman. So I asked where Franklin was and they told me he had died while I was away. I did not know what to think. I felt devastated that Franklin had died, angry because my mama remarried and very jealous of this baby. After all, I was the baby in the house when I left. From now on my mama wasn't Mama to me, she was now "Mom." She asked me why I was there. I was supposed to go home with the new schoolteachers because she had given me away and hadn't they met me at the plane? Then she turned to talk to her husband in Indian, thinking that I had forgotten the language since I had been at the mission for four years and had been "whitematized," but I understood every single word. In a desperate tone, she asked him what they should do. They didn't count on me not cooperating with them and that must come from the white side of me, she explained to him. The teachers had already paid them ten dollars for me and they paid ten dollars for my ticket back and there was no way they could pay the twenty dollars back to the teachers. Also, they were very worried about what the teachers would say. She turned to me and very angrily told me to go live with the teachers, that I was not welcome in the house and she didn't want me. In Indian she added that I was worthless since I didn't know the Indian ways and that I only knew the lazy white man ways.

White people were not used to hard work. They had already spent the ten dollars and she was worried as to how they were going to pay it back.

Suddenly they saw the teachers walking past the window coming toward the house. This was even worse. I was the cause of these white people coming to the house when they were not welcome. Mom told me to go out to see what they wanted, but I wouldn't budge because I was too angry. We heard the knock at the door and someone said "Come in." The three of them all came in and my Mom was really angry. In Indian I heard her say the white people come to our houses so they can talk and make fun of how we live. That made me angry, so I glared at the white people. They looked at me and told me they had come to take me home. I just laughed and told them I belonged to my mom and no one else. I said I came home to work for my mom, as I was pretty strong now that I was almost nine years old. I felt pretty strong from all the good food at the mission and I felt educated. After all, wasn't I almost in third grade? In a thick German accent, the woman told me that my mother did give me to them and maybe I would change my mind by the next day. I could tell by her looks that she was threatening my mom about the ten dollar fee she paid for me. My mom looked a little panicked and assured her that they would talk me into moving up to the schoolhouse the next day. They left.

A short while later, the teachers returned with a bed since I didn't have one. They told my mom that maybe I would love the white man bed so much I wouldn't give it up. Maybe they could bribe me to move to the schoolhouse with the bed. They were talking to each other as though I wasn't even there! That was when I followed them out and told them not to come back because I hated them, especially her for being so fat and for talking so weirdly. It was the worst thing I could think of and it had the desired effect. They looked shocked and my mom looked shocked, as neither of them were used to such an outburst from a child who should be totally obedient.

I was also angry at the nuns and priests for not fighting to keep me at the mission. I came back to the house and started to yell at my mom. I told her she had two choices: to keep me or send me back to the mission. I felt I had only one mother and that I was old enough to work around the house. She had no other choices; keep me or send me back.

(I knew she didn't have the fare to send me back to the mission.) There was sudden chaos and everybody was yelling about me being an extra mouth to feed and that they should have left me alone. It also felt really good to be yelling, since we were to be totally obedient at the mission and were never allowed to express our feelings. Suddenly I felt that I had power with my mouth. I would never live in the schoolhouse (but secretly I wondered what it would be like, it was almost tempting), because my sisters, Celene and Agnes, told me it was very haunted. THAT was something I would not fool around with. People I could handle, but NOT ghosts.

Mom settled down, then tried to convince me to move in with my own "kind," reminding me of all the nice clothing I could have since she could not afford to buy them for me. I could also visit my Indian family during the day, but I would not relent. I was going to punish my mom by being stuck with me because she was always trying to get rid of me. I even promised that since I was educated, I would grow up to be richer than the teachers and I would give her back the twenty dollars and maybe even more. But I would certainly earn my keep by working at anything she wanted me to do. While I was busy defending my case I saw my sister breastfeeding the baby. I knew only real mothers were supposed to do that for their babies. I asked again whose baby that was and my sister said it was Mom's but she was helping out since our Mom was old (45). Celene asked me if I wanted to hold the baby and I said "No."

After all this chaos I decided to look around the house. I saw the old Big Ben clock and it was close to 10:00 p.m. Wow! At the mission we were in bed between 7 and no later than 8:00 p.m. I felt pretty good about being up so late. Then I saw the blind lady who always lived with us, sitting quietly, listening to everything that was said. I was happy to see her and ran over to her. I asked if she knew who I was. She said yes and was very happy that I had come home. I was so excited to see her. I asked her if she wanted to see the clothes I brought from the mission. In my mind she wasn't blind and was the smartest person in the world. The others in the house were gesturing to me that she couldn't see a thing. I ignored them. She said she would be happy to "see" my things. She always combed my hair before I left for the mission and now agreed to "see" how much I had grown. I told her I was standing right in front of her. She put out her hand and started to touch me all over. Her excitement and exclamations as to how much I had grown made me feel very important. She asked me what color I was wearing and explained to everybody present all the details of my clothing from the buttons to the zippers and how beautiful I was with my soft hair and my wonderful eyes, nose and mouth. I felt like a movie star! I didn't even mind that she almost poked me in the eye a couple of times. I just closed my eyes and enjoyed the attention.

I then went to get the box I brought from the mission that had all of my nice clothes. I told Lilly that I was going to open the box, describe every item of clothing to her and let her feel them. Imagine my surprise when all there was in the box were the clothes I was wearing when I went to the mission three years earlier. I was so mad at the nuns that I vowed I was not going to pray for them anymore. Lilly felt my pause and asked what was wrong. I told her that all there was in the box were my old clothes and a red sweater that I had always loved. She wanted to see them anyway. I handed her the dress and she laughed so loudly because it was so small. As she laughed and talked about how much I had grown, her laughter became contagious. Soon everyone was laughing with her. Then I showed her the red sweater. She thought it felt familiar and believed it was a sweater that a teacher had given to them and that they had mailed to me. I then remembered when a nun told me I had a package in the mail. It was this red sweater with three huge buttons on the left shoulder. I was so possessive of this sweater. When I looked at Mom, she confirmed the story and I wasn't so angry anymore.

Lilly was a very devoted Episcopalian and prayed daily. I knew all her prayers were always answered because God allowed it. She had told me that her father, in a fit of rage, had hit her on the head with a board when she was four years old, while God was busy with other matters, which caused her blindness. I knew God felt bad, so he always answered her prayers. I knew she never lied, so I whispered in her ear asking whose baby was in the house. She told me that it belonged to my sister, but that my mom was going to raise him. For some reason I felt better about this information and went to my sister asking if I could hold the baby. She handed him to me and I was amazed at how small the two month-old boy was. He was so warm and cuddly. I just knew he loved being held by me, so I fell in love with him. I even told my sister she could lay on the new bed with him and I would sleep on the floor. I guess I was forgiven for my outburst since I was now showing my considerate side. It was agreed that I would live there and my stepfather would work for the airline to pay the twenty dollars back to the teachers, a little at a time. I was to feel totally indebted. If I misbehaved I would be sent back to the mission, which was fine with me. But it was agreed that I would live here for a while so I would have many adventures to talk about when I went back.

I slept on the floor on a bearskin rug and was happy that the baby had a nice bed. The teachers came the next morning to get me and in a very snotty manner I told them that I was living with my mom, plus I was happy to inform them that the baby wet the bed. They told my mom that I had to go up to the schoolhouse every day to play with their Eskimo daughter from 1:00 to 3:00 p.m. Mom was to return the money and we were allowed to keep the bed. I refused to do this because I knew that Eskimos were the enemy. I heard stories about how the Eskimos attacked our village and captured our grandma. I was very young when I heard this, but I had not forgotten. I hadn't even forgotten my Indian language, although I wasn't as fluent, but would become so soon. Being smug about the situation didn't last very long. After the teachers left the house, Mom smacked me so hard across the face, informing me that she was the boss and I was not. I was to do everything she told me to do and to never talk back to her. I glared at her, with my face stinging, and was told to get wood for the stove and then mind the baby. Huh! This was easy to do. I was already earning my keep.

After dinner (the noontime meal), I was to walk up to the school-house to play with the teachers' daughter. I arrived at the school and since it was locked, I had to knock. Mrs. Kass finally arrived and said she was sending her daughter out to play with me. I met Nancy and we became pretty good friends. She came from Mountain Village with the "live-in" housekeeper who was an 18 year-old girl.

On bad days we could play in the schoolhouse playroom, but I was never allowed in their living quarters. But one day I convinced Nancy to let me see her bedroom while the teachers were busy. I wanted to see how white people lived. I told her she wasn't white, she was more like me. She thought I was more white than Indian because of my fair skin and my nickname being "Blue Eyes." She was good company, but I'm afraid I wasn't a good influence on her because I led her into mischief. I felt it fair that I show her my bedroom since she showed hers to me. One day when I knew everyone was away from my home, except Lilly, I brought her to see my "bedroom," which was nothing more than a bearskin rug rolled up under my mother's bed. She was so afraid I had to laugh at her.

Since I didn't have any clothes, the teachers gave me some of Nancy's old ones. I was very appreciative of the clothes I received, but since I was such a tomboy I would rather wear the blue jeans and not the dresses. The dresses hindered my movements in all my adventures, so when I found the blue jeans, I lived in them even though there were many protests from my family.

My new household consisted of a double family. My mom, Matilda, brought Lilly the blind lady, a mentally handicapped boy, my little nephew, my two sisters, Celene and Agnes, and me, for a total of six. Her husband, Roland, had four boys for a total of five. He also had three daughters who lived elsewhere. When I arrived, all the older boys were in fish camp, which was fine with me because they intimidated me. My sister Agnes was also at fish camp. Almost everyone was in fish camp at that time except for the teachers, the postmaster and my step-father, who worked in freight for Alaska Airlines.

I asked Mom what happened to my doll and my wheelbarrow. She said she had given it to one of my close friends. I couldn't wait for her to get back from fish camp. I also wondered what happened to my cat, "Pussie." She told me a boy shot it, so I couldn't wait until he came back from fish camp. Then I would seek the endless revenge I had planned in my head. With most of the village at fish camp in July, I had a whole month to get used to the house and to explore in the village.

Near the end of August and the start of school, everyone returned from fish camp. When my step-brothers arrived, they were surprised to see me. They were amused by my constant jabbering and were nice to me as long as I behaved. I was Johnny Dutchman's favorite and was allowed to tag around with him everywhere he went. The other boys were friendly to my sisters, so we all got along pretty well. At first there was a little animosity because we were on their turf and "This is not your house" was often used in little battles. We replied with, "Who cares?" The step-brothers and sisters were in the same age bracket so aside from my baby nephew, I was still the youngest child. I don't think anyone was prepared for my constant jabbering. I asked questions about everything. I wanted to know the entire history of the village and who was related to whom. I was often told, "You talk too much," and that didn't sound too complimentary

Dutchman Children (not pictured, Ida and Esther)

I learned a lot of history while visiting the cemeteries, where I memorized everyone's gravesite. I learned who was related to whom when we went to funerals or honored Memorial Day. My favorite pastime was to walk through the village to question everyone about the history of Shageluk. I reported my new information to my mom and she either confirmed the story or corrected me. When people confided some tidbit of information with me they knew I shouldn't know, they had to swear me to secrecy.

One piece of information I learned was that my father had been a teacher in Shageluk. He was born and raised in Norway. I had two white sisters, one who was named Etola, who died while my father and his wife were in Shageluk. I had heard about her before but did not know she was my sister. I wanted to ask my mom, but my sisters told me never to do so. The younger women in the village who had him for a teacher said that he was very handsome and that I looked just like him. My sisters, Celene and Agnes, said they had him for a teacher and that he was mean and that I was never to talk about him again. I was told the Larsens left when I was a year and a half old with their remaining daughter, another sister, who was almost the same age I was. They said my father had a wonderful, kind wife and my mom worked for them as a domestic worker who chopped wood for their stove, washed their laundry, and cleaned the school and their living quarters in exchange for food and clothing for her family. I still had my curiosities and fantasies, but was not allowed to discuss the matter.

A wonderful thing happened to me at this time. The family who moved into our old house arrived back from fish camp. They had a little girl close to my age (two years older). She became my very best friend and a lifelong friend. She was like a sister to me. I also loved her family and they treated me as one of their own. My family was kind to her also, so she and I were always close. I didn't want to play with Nancy anymore because I found someone who shared my same background and who knew the same people. I loved her stories about the settlement she grew up in, a village below ours that was now abandoned. I knew it was a wonderful and exciting place. I remembered visiting there when my mom took me on a boat to Holy Cross, but I didn't remember seeing her. She and I had had an interesting life thus far and enjoyed discussing our many village adventures. She told me to be obedient and that I had to play with Nancy. She wanted to hear about what Nancy and I had done later. That was fun to do because I had usually instigated some form of mischief. Then she reprimanded me for being so devious. She was one of the four people I would listen to besides my mom, my step-brother Johnny and my aunt Grace.

Chapter 26
THE FIRST HUNT

I was very spoiled by my step-brother Johnny Dutchman. He would do anything I asked him to do. In exchange, I would get things done for him with my very bold and aggressive personality. When he went to Anchorage, he would write letters to me asking me what I wanted from the "big city." Actually, I think he wanted news from home. Since I was pretty much the town crier at this point in my life, nothing escaped my eyes and ears. I kept a daily journal, which helped me to remember all the details about which he inquired. I was taught to never accept gifts from anyone without working for them, so I justified in my mind that I had always done errands for him when he was home. I delivered love letters to his girlfriends and sometimes waited hours for the reply when the girlfriends couldn't make up their minds as to what they wanted to say. I was sworn to secrecy and could not mention the clandestine love letter writing to anyone, especially not to my mother, as an unwanted marriage might be arranged with the wrong person. Most of the time I didn't charge him for this tedious job, nor for packing in wood for him on poker nights, sweeping the floor or doing his dishes.

After thinking his offer over carefully, I decided to ask Johnny for a view master and comic books. I believed he owed it to me so I could lose myself in the wonderful pictures of the Grand Canyon, the "outside Indi-ans" with their colorful regalia, the cowboys of the wild west and, of course, the cartoons. We had no books in our home and we were not allowed to touch the books on the shelves at our school because we might create clutter. I loved to read in our reading book and was highly amused by the Dick and Jane series and the Peter and Peggy series of our basal readers. I was always showing off my reading ability by reading every label on cans and products from the store. I read them over and over again until my mother said I was "making everybody's head sick."

Some of my favorite labels were Hills Bros. Coffee (what did Bros. mean?), Klim (milk spelled backward), iodized salt (no one knew what the white man word "iodized" meant) and a variety of other labels found in my stepbrother's grub box (which he used for hunting and fishing). I couldn't wait to get some comic books, because I lived and died for comic books.

I truly did receive my precious gifts from Johnny. On this particular day I was on my comfy little lumber bed covered by my soft moose skin mattress, engrossed in my comic books. I loved reading "Junior Illustrated Classics" and was soon fantasizing that I was the heroine in the Robinson Crusoe family. Once I was engrossed in a book, no one could pull me away unless it was a matter of life or death or until I had finished. While I was busy looking for the fruit trees on the island, my teenage sister Agnes walked into the house. She wanted to talk to me but I was too involved in my story. I couldn't even tell her the story because she hated school and wanted no part of it. She was totally involved in a subsistence way of life and she knew everything there was to know about it. Then she mentioned that I was old enough to start supporting myself by going with her and one of the young boys in the village on a duck hunt. Now THAT caught my attention. Only boys were invited to go on hunts to protect us against anything in the wild. Nevermind that this boy was about my age; I now had a chance to go hunting with my sister and a boy.

My sister Agnes and I had an age gap of eight years. She had to take care of me and did not like it. I was a total pest in her eyes. My older sister Celene tolerated me and my somewhat strange behavior, but not Agnes. She always told me that I asked too many questions and talked too much. She was quite pretty and had many boyfriends. Being married was the last thing on her mind. I noticed her boyfriends were writing many letters and I was so curious as to what they wrote. In one of her good moods, she shared what one of them had written (her best friend was out of town, so she had to share with someone). It seems as though this boy was really serious about her, but was more serious about his dog team. He wrote, "I really want to marry you... but right now I have too many dogs to feed." That was fine with her, because she didn't want to move to Holikachuk and she hated doing anything that had to do with house-work, i.e. cleaning, Indian crafts, cooking or sewing. She lived for outdoor work. We always had plenty of wood for the stove when she was around because she loved hitching up the dog team to go over the frozen lakes and rivers for wood. She often dragged me along in the process to check the rabbit snares. I loved standing behind her on her snowshoes as we trudged through the vast whiteness of the snow, which seemed to stretch out endlessly until we reached the woods and her snares. She also loved fishing and dip netting whenever the season was right, whether it was spring, summer, fall or winter. It was cold in those winters and Agnes would keep me out in the cold until I thought I would turn into an icicle. She hadn't hunted for big game yet and daydreamed about going one day. If I behaved myself, I would surely be invited to go along, even if I was "too small." Bear and moose hunting was the ultimate hunting privilege.

Well, today I was in training for the big duck hunt. Our mother was gone for the day and my sister said Mom would praise us to no end for putting food on the table. We were actually going to be worth something. Wouldn't I like to hear all the praise at the supper table when the adults talked about all the important feats of other people? We will hear about how important we are when we bring all the ducks home. Wouldn't I like this better than reading coffee, salt or milk labels at the supper table? Well, yes, our mother wasn't in a good mood lately, so we had to do some-thing to brighten up her life and have her be proud of her daughters since she had no sons. After this speech it didn't take much for me to toss my comic book aside and run down to help prepare our boat. We hauled our oars down the bank along with our grub sack (an empty sugar sack filled with tea, sugar, crackers and dry fish). We brought our 'chi nik' (an empty coffee can with a wire handle filled with water and hung over a fire to boil) for our tea. Also, we remembered to bring burlap sacks in which to bring our ducks home. We were set to go! We were going to row one mile downriver and head for the slough on the right bank above Lower Village. Then we had to row another mile into the slough toward the geese and duck nesting grounds. We were going to be happy if the three of us each got a duck for the evening meal. Also, we were not wasting gas because we were rowing ourselves. I couldn't wait to eat fresh duck soup. It was so delicious! The ducks are boiled with some onions, a little rice and diced potatoes. I could taste it now and was very excited to go on this extraordinary hunt—a first-time experience.

In the boat I noticed we only had one gun, but Aggie assured me we could share it. She was in a good mood and I wanted to take advantage of that because she was such a moody person, mad at the world and only happy when she was outdoors.

The weather was beautiful and it was soothing to hear the oars silently splashing in the water, creating intermittent forward thrusts that caused my body to sway in the same rhythmic motion. Soon it was my turn to row, and I was happy to do so since I didn't get to do it very often. Since the boy and I were the same size he had to take an oar on one side and I on the other because the boat was too wide for one of us. It took us a while to get synchronized, as we argued about who was out of sync. Meanwhile, the boat was moving sporadically in the water with the oars making huge splashes. We no longer had a peaceful ride. Aggie was steering in the back of the boat and after yelling at us, we finally got into rhythm. We finally reached our destination. After tying up the boat we decided to have lunch. Soon our fire was roaring and our chi 'nik was bubbling over the fire, causing it to hiss and spit. My sister threw in a handful of tea leaves and immediately the smell permeated the crisp, clean fall air. The woods smelled of grass and spruce trees mixed with the smell of the muddy river. It was funny—I didn't see any ducks, but my sister was the expert, so if she said there were ducks here I had to believe her.

After our delicious lunch we put our food supply back into the boat. NOW we were ready to hunt. But, where were the ducks? Aggie called me aside, without the boy, and started one of her Indian lectures. This was serious and she told me she would always look out for me. She would make sure I was always more Indian than white. I was in awe of her that she was entrusting me, a half-breed, to be in on one of her Indian words of wisdom. She explained that we should always work hard to bring food home and we would gain respect for being great hunters. I was to follow everything she said very carefully and since I was too young to handle a gun (I target practiced with my step-brothers since I came back from the mission), I had to hunt with my bare hands. I had to believe that it was braver to hunt with my hands. She told me we were hunting in a new way, which was a big secret. She showed me on the ground where there were clumps of dirt shaped like a head with grass protruding out of it. She explained that the ducks like hiding between these clumps of dirt. The clumps were hard to walk on but for certain she assured me that the ducks would be hiding there. "This was the way," she said, "that our grandparents hunted long ago." I was never to share this information with anyone whatsoever. I promised. The way to hunt was like this: when I saw a duck crouching between the clumps of dirt, I was to grab it by the neck, bite it firmly on the head and hold its neck tightly until it died, then throw it into the burlap bag. I was not to follow her or the boy. I should stay quite a distance away from them since this was my first hunt. I asked her if the ducks would bite me, but she said as long as I clenched my teeth firmly around their heads there would be no problem. I was a little skeptical but she said that she and the boy were going to hunt in the same way and Mom would be happy that we didn't waste any bullets.

I was a little nervous as she walked away from me to join the boy. Soon I heard them shouting and saw them running and looking at the ground. Then Agnes gleefully lifted a duck above her head to show me and with her back to me she turned and stuffed the duck into the sack. Soon the boy got one and she pointed to an area where she wanted me to look. I looked carefully in the grass and suddenly I saw a duck crouching down between the dirt clumps. I looked at his eyes and I felt so bad that he looked scared and I called to my sister to tell her that I found one. She yelled at me to do what she told me to do and reminded me of how happy Mom would be. After the encouragement, I reached down and grabbed it by the neck. It took me by complete surprise as to how strong it was as it struggled. My heart was beating wildly. I pulled it toward my mouth when it suddenly started clawing my arm. I was so scared that I squeezed it as tightly as I could and I felt the pain on my arms as it scratched and fought. I suddenly became very angry because of the pain in my arms and bit into its head like my sister demonstrated. I then felt the warm blood flowing in my mouth and didn't know whether to swallow it or spit it out. I knew one must respect food so I opted to swallow it and held onto its neck until he stopped quivering. Then with great excitement I knew I was a great hunter. I yelled to my sister. She gave me the O.K. sign and told me to stuff it in the bag and continue what I was doing. She said the duck might still have movement in the bag, but not to worry about it, just carry it to the next kill. The next duck also struggled and clawed me. My arm was aching. I decided to grab them facing away from me so they could claw in the air. Smelling the duck feathers on the head as I bit them was a little unnerving until I got used to it. I found the exact spot to bite, but pulling it out of my mouth before the blood flowed was no easy task. I also dipped the head into the water between the clumps as I choked the life out of them so there was less commotion in the bag. After getting about 21 ducks in my bag I went to show my sister. They had their bags full also, so we decided to head for home. I guess I was a sight to see with blood all over my face and arms. When we got to the boat she made me wash up in the river and told me never to tell about our secret hunt.

As it turned out my mother was extremely happy with us. She took my ducks, cleaned them and prepared them for supper. She invited all the elders as this was the custom for a "first hunt." I was glad she was treating me like a boy. I was ecstatic about the day. It was the best day of my life and all the elders were praising me since it was through my hard work that there was food on the table. I am afraid I had a big head, as I was very proud of myself. I asked my mother and my step-dad or anyone else who would listen to tell me again about what a great hunter I was.

My sister Agnes was rather nonchalantly standing in the background. I was wondering why she didn't object to all the praise I was receiving, since she was always putting my accomplishments down. She had this funny smile on her face so I decided to keep an eye on her. After the excitement died down and everyone went home, she asked Mom if she could take a walk with her friend. I watched her going down the road to her friend's house and soon they were heading down the road. I decided to follow them. They went behind the store and I knew my sister was there to smoke a cigarette. Older girls could smoke, but she didn't want to be asked about where she got them (I knew that her boyfriends supplied them). I decided to sneak in the grass and listen to their conversation. As I got closer I heard them laughing hysterically. Soon I heard her friend asking her to repeat her story and I heard Agnes saying that she told me a big story about our ancestors hunting like that and I fell for it, biting 21 duck heads to kill them while they were molting! She said that since I was a half-breed I must believe anything and that I must have been born dumb. I was so devastated and humiliated that I ran all the way home. My face was burning red. I was so ashamed that I was tricked. When I got to the house I ran to my bed and grabbed a comic book. I peered over the comic book and asked my mom if she had ever heard of anyone biting the heads off of a molting ducks. She said only someone who was pretty stupid would do that and asked me if my sister told me to do that. I didn't answer so she continued on and on about how only a stupid person would do something like that. Everyone in the house was now laughing so hard just thinking about how stupid that would be. After school the next day, as I was coming on to the porch, still angry about the hunt, I heard everyone in the house laughing about me since my sister told them about the prank she pulled on me. I was so angry that I saw red. I burst into the door and called everyone in the house some names which I thought were awful, mild by today's standards, but my tone of voice silenced everyone. I vowed to take revenge on my sister, but as her luck would have it, she was called to McGrath, Alaska, to work in a hotel. Luckily, I wouldn't have to see her anymore. For the time being, I was satisfied.

Chapter 27
SHAGELUK BIA SCHOOL

I n the fall, I attended the Shageluk Bureau of Indian Affairs School. The teacher found I was quite advanced for my age group, so I skipped a couple of grades. The mission school in Holy Cross had been very strict and we had to work very hard, so I was far ahead of the other students in my age group in Shageluk. I didn't like being in a class by myself because I liked competition. There were 32 students in grades 1-8. All of the eighth graders were waiting for their 16th birthdays so they could drop out. The boys could then go hunting and trapping and the girls would get married and stay home. My sister Agnes went to school and was in the fifth or sixth grade when she finally dropped out. She found a job as a roadhouse maid in McGrath and married there. Celene got married at the end of the first year; I was home and left with her baby boy. One of my step-brothers was in school for a short time and soon dropped out to hunt and trap. He still lived at home, as he was his father's youngest son. All the other step-brothers were out of school and on their own. Each one was living in a house that he had built. Our household was very quiet after everyone left and life wasn't great after that.

There was a lot of drinking going on at home and my mom and her husband were constantly fighting. That made Mom quite violent. The drinking would go on for days and I was afraid of her. I tried not to show my fear by being defiant, but it seems I could never do anything right and I was constantly being beaten in her drunken state and even in her sober state. I felt she hated me and soon I started hearing about my white father and that I should go live with him, but when I confronted her when she was sober, she would say it was just drunk talk. She would say that I was just as useless as he was and that he probably was in jail somewhere and that was where I would end up. I was a bastard, which I did not understand. Soon the abuse started on the boy who lived with us. I made up my mind that it was my job to take care of him, because he couldn't defend himself since he was a couple of years younger than I.

I turned into a hostile, defiant person in my household. I was at the point where I didn't care if I talked back and was disobedient. I was always criticized for everything I did. I was called "white" when I made simple mistakes, so I constantly tried to be perfect. Once I remembered my mom telling me that I must be the daughter of the devil since I was so hostile. I flippantly answered that she must be the devil itself because I was her daughter. She grabbed me by the hair and slapped me so hard I flew across the room. When my step-brother saw that, he gave me the lecture of a lifetime. I was not supposed to talk back to my mother. That episode cured me. I only thought of talking back to her. In a few cases when I felt like being mouthy when she was drunk, I made sure I was by the door ready to run out. My step-brother couldn't believe how I asked for the lickings by being so disobedient. I felt that I had to defend myself because what they were calling disobedient was just innocent questioning. I felt that what she was saying to me was wrong. I still had the goal to be the best in everything I did.

Mom was teaching me all about the Indian culture, which I learned quickly. I danced in the Kashim when she wanted me to, but I felt she was always embarrassed about the way I looked. Once she told me she wished I was beautiful like an Indian, not ugly like a white person. I reminded her that she sent me to the mission to train me to be an obedient good girl and I learned we are all creatures of God and she can't call me ugly because He made me. If she was questioning God she was a sinner. (Run for the door!) The message hit home but I was still full of resentment and hatred. She taught me to cut fish, pick berries, get wood, set snares, make

Cecilia(Lori) Woodford in front of Johnny Dutchman's House

Ralph and Cecilia Woodford and Frances Charles with Dog Team

baskets and to take care of my nephew, whom she took back when she mellowed.

At one time, Mom and I had a great time. She asked me to join her in a canoe to go berry picking. It was a wonderful day and the lake waters were calm and as smooth as glass. I had to sit back to back with her and not move at all because the canoe tipped so easily. We went across the lake listening to the loons and the fish ducks calling. It was so sunny and peaceful. We saw the gulls flying over the islands in the lake. The foothills were such a beautiful blue color. She told me stories of what she did when she was my age and how she went berry picking with her mother. We made a fire for her tea, which she had with her lunch, and she even gave me a sip. I felt pretty grown up getting a sip of her tea. We filled our birch bark baskets with berries and went home. It was the best day I ever had with my mother.

The most terrible thing that ever happened to me was when I reached age ten and suddenly turned into a "corner girl." This is when a girl starts to menstruate. I had no idea what this was and when it happened I knew I was dying. It felt like 20 degrees below zero one November day when I took a trip to the outhouse and discovered I must be dying of something strange, since all the dead animals I had seen always had a lot of bleeding before they died. I didn't want to leave the outhouse. If I was going to die, I wanted to be found dignified, not yelling and screaming or begging for my life, as this is not the Indian way. Soon Mom came looking for me, as it was getting really dark. Our monthly movie had arrived on the mail plane and was about ready to start at the schoolhouse. She knew I never missed a single movie. I knew every actor and actress and could repeat the movie dialogue for a month until the new movie came. Well, I wasn't interested in going to a movie while everyone should be holding a vigil for me before my death. I had to tell my mom.

Imagine my surprise when Mom didn't react like I was dying. She just told me I had to wear monthly rags and that all women went through this. I wasn't a woman! I wanted to be a kid and enjoy my childhood. I had heard from the villagers what ridiculous things corner girls had to do but I didn't know why they became corner girls. A corner girl cannot eat fresh meat for a year or the spirits would get angry and your whole village would suffer from starvation. You had to wear a scarf over your head to prevent your head from shaking like a berry on a bush blown by the wind when you get old. A corner girl could not ride in a boat for fear of stopping the fish run. You couldn't walk on the roads or trails where the men had just traveled from a hunt or you would bring them bad luck. All this would last a year.

I wasn't about to advertise my private life by going through all of this. I made my mom promise not to tell anyone, but she had to tell my step-dad because he was the chief of the village. He would forbid me to go to the Kashim. I lived and died for the doings in the Kashim. I was so angry because once my mom told my step-dad, he had to tell his sister, the medicine woman of the village, about this important event in my life. Mother said I had to obey the medicine woman because she saved my life at birth. I was a favorite of the medicine woman's daughter, whom I called my Auntie Grace. When I was a baby, Auntie Grace wanted to adopt me. She took me home, but she was too young to support me, so she had to bring me back to my mother. She always felt I was her baby. Perhaps she could talk her mother into anything. Grace was a forceful person in town and I talked her into getting me out of this corner girl business. It was easy. All I had to do was promise to help her in any way I could and when I grew up and was rich, she would be the first on my list. (By this time I believe I had promised the whole town that I would share my wealth when I grew up. They just laughed.)

Grace certainly did try everything she knew to get me out of the corner girl status. She began by bringing wonderful gifts to my mother, such as her delicious homemade ice cream. I helped her by caring for her children, as I was a trained babysitter. I helped her quite a bit. In repayment she went to her mother, the medicine woman, and told her that since I was half white I wasn't qualified to have the full Indian benefits of being a corner girl. One day Mom called me into the house and asked what I was up to. She had been summoned by Great Aunt Sarah, who was asking if I was obeying all the rules of a corner girl. By this time Mom was tired of me complaining about no meat, no dogsled rides and the horrid scarf which I had to wear on my head. She lectured and reprimanded me sternly about being Indian and how important it was to follow the rules. After the lecture she told me that since I was only half Indian my sentence was shortened to six months, but in those six months I had to follow the ritual. She had to practically bribe the old medicine man to shorten the sentence for an ungrateful wretch like me. I would take any abuse humbly just to get out of my predicament, but secretly I was gloating. Mother had to pay the medicine man five dollars, which I was reminded was half the household budget. I was to reimburse her when I grew up and was earning my own money.

The medicine man came and led me upstairs. He made me kneel on the floor and then started to sing softly in Indian to the spirits. He had a willow brush which he used to club all around me. Then he sang again. He did this about four times, and then suddenly blew down my neck really hard. Then he took my scarf off and flung it to the floor. Taking an exhausted breath, he said I was now free from being a corner girl. He looked at me disdainfully, as though I was not as tough as a real Indian to go through the normal rigors of my present state. I wanted to comment, but I promised my mom to keep my mouth shut.

He went downstairs to eat the big meal Mom had been preparing all day. Then I had to call some other elders and Great Aunt Sarah, the medicine woman, to come to eat on my behalf. I enjoyed my freedom and the food was excellent. I could now go outside without a scarf. The other kids would never know I had been a corner girl. Every girl wore a scarf in the winter, but now it was spring. I told all of my friends that it was just a rumor that I had been a corner girl.

I was enjoying most everything about my life at this time but suddenly I started brooding. I really didn't know what I wanted. I wanted to leave the village and yet I didn't. My sisters were gone and my favorite step-brother joined the army. Another step-brother got married and the other went to work in Anchorage. It didn't help matters that my step-father had been recently killed in a drunken tragedy. He was an excellent provider and we lived very comfortably. I used to help him with his "Chief of the Village" mail by reading his letters to him. He had a limited education and when the teachers weren't available to help him respond to his government mail, I advised him what to do and answered his mail for him. He was a true leader and everyone in the village looked up to him.

We had a spectacular funeral for him with all the people from the neighboring villages attending. When he was laid out, Great Aunt Sarah, his sister, made medicine on the family who she thought was responsible for his death. She said all the boys in that family would die at an early age. She made the medicine right in front of me. The other elder women told her to take it back, but she could not in her moment of great grief. It wasn't long afterward that all four boys met early and tragic deaths. It was a bad revenge on those handsome young boys. I will never forget this and I have never doubted Indian medicine after that—good or bad.

I loved learning and was a very good student. School occupied much of my time. I was always on the honor roll but Mom didn't seem to care. She was more concerned about my learning the Indian ways. She never checked on me at school and never came to the parent-teacher conferences. I was on my own as far as school went, but certainly she cared about religion. We had a Catholic priest come to our house once a year to hold mass. We made sure the holy area in our house was always respected. Mom would scrub the area with bleach until the boards turned white. We used a gasoline box for the altar. I thought our house was holy, but my friends told me that since so many people died in our house, it was haunted. I believed that since mass was held in our house, it was protected from spirits, but my friend and I encountered them a few times and that made a believer out of me. I really do believe in spirits.

Just when I was sure I was becoming depressed, an Episcopalian missionary, who was also a nurse, arrived at the village and became a positive influence on my life. A new church was built and I practically turned into an Episcopalian with the permission of my priest, as long as I didn't take communion. The nurse held activities for the young people. There was a boys' night, a girls' night, and choir practice. She played the organ beautifully to accompany our choir. On Saturday the young children had Bible school, followed by regular services for everyone, then Sunday school. I was fully involved in her activities and was her right-hand girl. I learned so much from her. She told me all about her home in California and about her college experience at Berkeley and Columbia University. She wanted me to go on to high school, which would really be an accomplishment as I would be the first in the village. Then she explained that I would be an excellent candidate to go on to college—another first in the village. Compared to the other three teachers I had in the last few years, she was the most intelligent person I had ever met. We were welcomed into her house. She always talked with me when I was being called white woman, half breed and a white man's bastard. I now had an obsession to find my father. I fantasized that he was rich and I would take revenge on him. During this time, my mom told everyone I was moody because I had the Bear Song put on me when I was a baby and that was why my temperament was like a bear, always grouchy. She was always apologizing for my orneriness. I was grouchy in the house, but was always friendly and helpful to everyone in the village and my classmates were my friends. Cruel things were said by people who were mad at Mom or by people who were drunk. The cruelty bothered me.

At age eleven I discovered boys. At the dances the boys from the neighboring villages were very attentive to me. Any boy who looked at me when he visited my house was informed by my mom that he would have to give her a dowry of fine skins, moose meat and many cords of wood before he could have me. I resented the teasing, but the boys assured me they would be ready to give her one hundred times the amount she wanted.

One day I decided I wanted to know what a kiss felt like, as I only faintly remember being kissed as a very young child. I saw all the beautiful women in the movies with their eyes closed as they were kissed by their leading men. I knew boys had something to do with having babies but I didn't know what. Mom told me I was not to let any boys touch me after I became a corner girl because I might have a baby. The following day a boy tapped me on the shoulder in school and asked to borrow a pencil. After I slugged him, I ran home and told my mom that I was going to have a baby because a boy touched me. She told me not to be so crazy. Then I knew kissing was not that type of touching. No one in the movies had babies after they kissed. I asked my girlfriend if she ever kissed a boy and she said no. I told her I really wanted to find out how it felt and wondered if she would mind if I practiced on her. She was so appalled and advised that I should ask one of my admirers. What a wonderful idea. I promised I would explain how it felt in detail. I wondered why those involved closed their eyes but she didn't know either.

My admirers were pretty old by my standards, as I was eleven and they were eighteen and above. My victim was going to be a fellow from a neighboring village who had an airplane and was related to my stepfather. He used that excuse to visit my mom. One night there was a movie at the schoolhouse. He flew in and was going to spend the night. On my way home from the movie, he was waiting behind the church and softly called me over to him. I asked him if he saw the couple kissing in the movie and he asked me if I had ever kissed anyone and I said no. He asked if he could teach me and of course I was very eager. He was about six feet tall, so I told him to move over to a snow bank. I could stand on it and we would be about the same height. There was a full moon, so it almost looked like daylight. I glanced at his airplane parked on the little lake and the snow glistened like a million diamonds. It was so romantic with this handsome boy getting ready to kiss me. As our faces got closer and closer, I closed my eyes feeling my heart beating wildly when suddenly I was grabbed from behind and flung into the snow bank! Oh Lord! Caught by my mom! There was some scuffling going on and a voice said, "Oh gosh, Blue Eyes. I'm sorry. I thought you were my wife." I was more worried the man would tell my mom what I was up to and that God was definitely punishing me for my behavior. I jumped up from the snow bank and ran home. The boy was trying to catch up with me after his encounter with the married man, but I had already reached my house. I never thought about kissing for at least two more years.

I spent the next summer with my older sister at a fish camp called Rapids. It was a wonderful summer. We went to a big Fourth of July dance in Anvik where I enjoyed the attention from all the handsome young men. I danced with all of them and cherished the many compliments. I thought boys were the greatest creatures on earth. They were great and kind friends who did all kinds of nice things for me. I noticed it was mostly the half breed boys who were interested in me. I knew I intimidated the boys at home with my aggressive behavior—wanting to be in charge of everything, even being the leading men from the movies we would re-enact. They didn't like me because I insisted on being Roy Rogers, Gene Autry and Tarzan. Now these new boys were more important than Roy Rogers and I was interested in making money to pay for the stamps required to answer all the letters from these cool boys. I didn't mind scrubbing the whole school for a week to earn a dollar. Just think of all the three-cent stamps I could buy!

Too soon I finished the eighth grade. Since I was only fourteen, I could not quit school, as state law required that I had to be sixteen. I had been elevated two grades in school, but one of the teachers moved me back because I was too young to quit. I had met all the requirements to pass the eighth grade, so for the next two years I was a teacher's aide, helping the first graders in reading and spelling.

Cecilia Woodfoord and Louise Dementi, 1955

Cecilia (Lori) and Ray Hamilton, 1955

My eighth grade advancement was an exciting event for me, as I reached my goal of finishing grade school. It was in the spring of 1956 and I was the first student from the village to accomplish this at the Shageluk BIA School. No one from my family, not even Mom, attended the short ceremony, as they did not consider this a major accomplishment. Students in those days just quit school and started to live in the subsistence lifestyle. The Territory of Alaska required that I go to school until I was sixteen years old. I wasn't that old yet, so arrangements were made for me to attend the Mt. Edgecumbe Native Boarding School in Sitka, Alaska. This was great news for me, as I was getting very restless living in the village. I wanted to experience the great outside rather than just read about it.

One of the missionaries gave me a necklace she had gotten on a trip to Old Mexico and the teacher gave me an outfit that was proper to wear for an advancement ceremony. I was very impressed receiving these presents, as I had never received such lavish gifts before. I had mixed feelings on this occasion. I didn't know if I was quite ready to leave my family even though many negative incidents had occurred. But receiving my certificate signed by the Superintendent of the BIA schools gave me a good feeling, even though I felt I was more of a teacher's aide for the little ones than a student and I felt quite unprepared for high school. I was really worried I might not make it to my next goal to be the first one from Shageluk to graduate from high school.

Cecilia (Lori) Woodford, 1955

Chapter 28
THE MCGRATH ROADHOUSE

S ince this was a big step in my life, my brother-in-law, whom I dearly loved, sent for me to come to McGrath, Alaska, where he had just purchased the McGrath Roadhouse. He would give me a job so I could earn money for clothes and other incidentals I might need on my education adventure. My mother was very happy that I could start working to support myself, so off I flew on the old Norseman on my way to a very different part of Alaska. I arrived in McGrath and was in awe of the beautiful setting on the Kuskokwim River. The people were so friendly. I was more comfortable with the native families than with the CAA employees, as I still was uncomfortable around the white people. The CAA was the Civil Aeronautics Administration before it became The Federal Aviation Agency (FAA). I didn't realize such a large community existed in Alaska. The big airfield had flights twice daily from Anchorage on Alaska Airlines and Wien Consolidated Airlines.

In McGrath there were several small airplane companies that serviced the interior of Alaska. It was the biggest town I had ever seen and I fell in love with it. I met the local teenagers who were also going to boarding school in Sitka. They were going to the Sheldon Jackson School rather than Mt. Edgecumbe. Here I had my first experience with teen music (a group called "The Platters" was popular at the time) and I was fascinated.

My brother-in-law sat me down and explained just what he expected of me. I was to live with him in the roadhouse since my sister Agnes and her children were back at the village helping Mom with summer fishing. I was the only help he had and I had to do the work my sister would normally do. Our day started at 6:00 a.m. and usually ended at 8:00 p.m. I was to be paid $25.00 a week with room, board and meals provided. I had what I thought was a beautiful room all to myself. It even had a lock on the door. Actually it was just a bed, a dresser and a closet, but it was better than anything I'd ever had in my life.

My brother-in-law was from Switzerland and spoke seven languages. At first I had problems understanding him, but he was patient with me. He was from the old world where the work ethics were of a high standard and, as he was a professional chef, everything had to be perfect. If perfection was what he wanted, then perfection was what he was going to get. Every morning my breakfast was waiting at the counter. Imagine having your breakfast prepared by a professional chef. I had the best menus you could think of and learned about a vast variety of different foods which I never knew existed. I knew nothing about cooking and seeing all this food was amazing. I only knew about boiled fish and meat for most of my life. Now I became acquainted with chicken, turkey, hamburger, salads and desserts. At the mission we didn't have food like this. There we had fish prepared many ways. I do remember the delicious split pea soup. I pretended I knew all about these foods, but inside I was tickled to death to see so many types of things that were edible.

My brother-in-law was also a master cake decorator and the cakes he put out in a short time were beautiful. I once sat down to learn to make the decorative roses for his cakes but after my first attempt creating perfect little cabbages, I decided to forget it because he wouldn't let me tint the frosting green to create gardens of cabbages on the cakes.

I was amazed at the taste of everything. Hamburger was so bland compared to moose meat, I almost hated it. It reminded me of a sawdust-y type of bland blob in my mouth. Bananas tasted like the smell of fingernail polish, although they were very good. I loved the smell of turkey baking in the oven and the taste was something I have not replicated to this day. I should have learned how to prepare food by watching my brother-in-law, but I was too young and full of other adventures to be a student of cooking.

After breakfast at 6:00 a.m., I had to set the dining room table for breakfast, as we had 18 permanent boarders at the roadhouse. They ate three meals a day family style. During breakfast I had to wait on everyone to make sure they had enough coffee or whatever else they needed. They were all men based in McGrath who had various jobs. Some worked for the air force at nearby Tatalina Air Force Base. They were all very friendly and protective, as they soon realized how naive I was. After breakfast I washed dishes and rinsed them in boiling water, thinking I was cool wearing rubber gloves. In the meantime, my brother-in-law was getting ready for lunch and manning the counter where people dropped in for coffee and donuts or breakfast. I then changed the beds for overnight guests, made the boarders' beds, changed the towels and scrubbed bathrooms. After that I had to vacuum (very exciting to run a motorized broom) every room, the hallway, stairway, the hotel lobby, then dust. When that was done, I helped make 132 sandwiches for the local airline with which we had a food contract. With that out of the way I set the tables for lunch. I then waited on the men and enjoyed listening to them talk about their morning.

After lunch I washed dishes and manned the counter, selling coffee and donuts while my brother-in-law napped for an hour. If someone wanted a hamburger, I had to wake him up. Once he was done napping, he started dinner preparations. I helped with the salads or peeled potatoes. I happily watched him make all kinds of desserts and donuts. I fetched the ingredients as he needed them. Our local laundress came by in the afternoon to pick up the big bags of towels and sheets. Then it was time to set the table again to serve our boarders a three-course meal at 5:00 p.m. At 6:00 p.m. the dining room was opened to the public. I waited tables again and the roadhouse was always full because of the fine reputation for excellent meals. After the evening meal, the lobby was full of people from the last flight and our counter was open for coffee and dessert. I washed dinner dishes at this time, then started winding down for the night. After the plane's departure (we were situated right next to the runway), I cleaned and mopped the floors. Finally I was free for the evening!

I sometimes went to the movies with other teenagers or danced at a local teenage hangout called "Cokey's." There I met some handsome and mannerly boys my age. Cokey's had an area that was reserved for movies, but was changed into a dance hall with a door separating us from the bar. The door was made of glass so we could see the adults and they could see us. The adults would buy us coke from the bar and I thought this was a life worth living. Since it never got dark at night during the summer, we had some very long days. Several of my girlfriends brought me to their homes. I thought they all lived pretty modernly. They had real furniture and beds, even refrigerators and electricity. I became known to my friends as Blue Eyes from Shageluk. Along with several episodes of puppy love, this was my routine for the summer. It went by quickly and soon I would be on my way to boarding school. Shortly before I left, my mother and sister came back from down river. I had made a lot of tips, which I put in a mayonnaise jar. I also deposited my paycheck into it. My brother-in-law and I counted the money and found I had made over $700.00! I was going to give my first month's pay to my mother as was the custom, but soon found that she and my sister beat me to the jar. I guess it didn't take long to use the money up as they timbered the bar all night. It took me a few years to forgive them.

Cecilia Woodford with Infamous
Haircut, 1956

Chapter 29
BOARDING SCHOOL

My brother-in-law decided to take his family and my mom and move to Anchorage. He had a buyer for the McGrath Roadhouse, so we all went to Anchorage to see me off to boarding school at Mt. Edgecumbe. It was my first trip on a Constellation with four engines and that to me was a huge plane. I enjoyed the ride over the majestic Alaskan mountains. They were no comparison to our hills back at the village. Those hills seemed so enormous but not after going over the Chugach Range. Landing at the Anchorage International Airport was quite an experience. I entered the terminal building and could not get it through my head that it was possible to go into a building on the ground, go down a flight of stairs, walk out the door and STILL be on the ground. Everyone was impatient with me, as I wanted to stay there until I figured out the mystery. I went up the stairs several times to check it out for myself until my brother-in-law told me it was built on the side of a hill.

Anchorage was a town where I experienced many firsts. For the first time in my life I saw cars. I thought they looked like houses on wheels. I touched my brother-in-law's car, a 1950 Mercury, and had a good laugh before I got into it for a ride. I had only read about cars, so seeing them now was quite an experience. We passed by department stores, actual

Lori with her mother, Matilda

movie theaters, drive-ins and the Piggly Wiggly grocery store. I repeated the name "Piggly Wiggly" often in my head and had a good laugh. When my sister turned on the television to watch a movie, I couldn't figure out where the projectionist was. Then I was shown the T.V. tower, which was not far away, and they explained that a signal came to the square box when it was plugged into electricity and the movie showed up on the screen. It was a simple explanation, but good enough for me.

If all the other new experiences weren't baffling enough, the telephone was the worst. My sister asked me to babysit while they went grocery shopping. On the way out she pointed to a black phone and told me to answer it if it rang. She said it was just like the radio at the village school-house that the teachers used to communicate with to the pilots. Well, it did ring and I knew exactly what to do, as I had seen the teachers using the radios often. Agnes forgot to give me her call letters so I was going to use Shageluk's G-5-0 and if that didn't work I would use the letters for McGrath, K-4-6. So I answered, "This is G-5-0, Shageluk, do you read? Over." There was a pause, then a voice that sounded miles away. So I repeated, "This is G-5-0, your transmitter is coming in weak. Over." About this time my sister came back and grabbed the phone. She was laughing so hard she couldn' speak. After apologizing to her friend, she hung up. She told me I looked pretty stupid yelling in an upside-down phone. After some instruction on using the phone, I was glad no one from home could see this eighth grade graduate making a fool of herself.

After shopping the next day at the Salvation Army Store for my school clothes ($2.00), my mom handed me five dollars for spending money for the year at school. I was to return in the spring and continue working somewhere. We drove to the airport, where there was a contact person who handed me a name tag. She said there would be others at the airport in Juneau with name tags and I was to follow them. I said good-bye to everyone and boarded the plane. All of a sudden, I felt so alone and scared and didn't think it was a good idea to get an education. Then I remembered I had friends in McGrath who were going to school in Sitka, so I might find them. I arrived in Juneau after what seemed an all-day flight and found some students with name tags. I was a little shy, so I did not speak to them, just looked at them and watched what they did. We left on Ellis Coastal Airlines to go to Sitka. I sat with an older boy with a name tag. I asked him if he was going to boarding school and he said yes. He told me he was 20 years old and was going to be in the same class I was. He had not started school until a few years previously (in the Wrangell Institute) and wanted to finish his education. He was a very nice and polite person and would be my friend for the year at Mt. Edgecumbe. He laughed at me when we landed in Sitka on the water and suddenly went right up a ramp into the hangar. I couldn't believe how magic it was that a plane on floats could travel on land.

The rest of the students gathered together waiting for our ride. They looked at me as though I had no sense in my head. They were returning students, so of course I looked quite inexperienced. The aide didn't show up so someone called a cab. Upon its arrival we all piled in. The driver asked if we had money and I was the only one who gladly showed him my five-dollar bill. At the end of the ride to the ferry dock he collected three dollars from me and I was left with two dollars for the year. I felt I was taken unfair advantage of; when everyone started laughing, I was near tears and I wished to go right back home to my mother. The boy could see I was upset and tried to comfort me. In his broken English he said he would walk me to the girls' dorm, as he had been here before.

I felt a little better but after he dropped me off I didn't know where to go, so I just wandered the hallways until a matron found me and asked who I was. As she read my name tag I was crossed off her list and asked where my suitcase was. Someone took it in Anchorage and I had not seen it since. She brought me to her office and, after a few calls, we discovered it was lost. I then went to a room with her where I was to pick out a nightgown—another first, as up to now I always slept in my clothes. Then we went to a room, which I was to share with seven girls who were going to arrive in the next several days. I could choose which bunk bed I wanted and whether I wanted the top or the bottom. We each had our own dresser and clothes closet, but I had nothing to put in them. Next we went to the laundry room, where I was to wash my clothes every evening after I put my nightgown on and ironed the clothes in preparation for the next day. This was to be done daily until my luggage arrived. After explaining all of this to me, she left.

Again I felt a loneliness that was like no other I had experienced before in my life. I was so homesick. I was so sorry I was acting smart at the village and in McGrath, saying I was going to high school. They could have this high school. I would rather be with my mom and my friends. McGrath wasn't so bad either, as it was just a plane ride away. I could climb on the plane and be home in a couple hours, but not here. Here I was about 900 miles away from home, which seemed like an eternity. I sat on the bed, wishing I could stop being so depressed. Then the matron reappeared to show me where the bathroom was so I could wash up for dinner. I followed her to the end of the hallway and there was a huge bathroom with many showers and sinks. I again had to choose the sink I wanted and after I washed she walked me to the dining hall. She showed me how to get my tray and food and to choose a spot where I wanted to sit. I sat by myself and soon the boy I was with on the airplane came to sit by me. I was so happy to see him! I asked him if he ever got homesick and he said he did when he was sent from his home in the Aleutians to relocate in Southeast Alaska at Wrangell during the war. After his parents died, he was very lonely. He vowed to do everything right from then on because his parents told him to.

After dinner he showed me around campus and promised to see me at breakfast. I felt better until I got to my room. I went to take a shower, then to the laundry to wash and iron my clothes, then went back to my room. I cried all night. The next morning my eyes were swollen, but I took another shower, put my clean clothes on and walked to the dining room. My friend was there with about five of his buddies. They all sat with me. They were mostly Eskimo boys and we all confessed how home-sick we were. I was feeling right at home with them, as most of them were from way up north and we had a lot in common. We each could speak our own language and laughed at each other when we said the same word in Indian and Eskimo. It was extremely funny.

Soon my new group of friends was showing me around campus again and suggested that we go dance at a place called "Ship Service." There was a jukebox where we could play three songs for a quarter. I felt pretty smug telling them I knew all about a jukebox from McGrath and was familiar with Elvis Presley's songs "Don't be Cruel" and "Hound Dog." At Ship Service, they treated me with a Coke and snacks, which was lucky because I didn't have the money. We had fun and I was never homesick again.

Finally the rest of the students showed up and I was anxious for school to start. I had a good bunch of roommates from different areas of Alaska: Metlakatla, Clark's Point, Fort Yukon and St. George Island. I even ran into some upper classmen from my neighboring village of Anvik. After orientation we registered, received our class schedule and started our daily routine. I was signed up for math, science, physical education, band, two hours of home economics, history and English.

It wasn't long before many cliques were forming, including my own. We all, girls and boys, had our little group of friends and were faithful and loyal to each other. One day, a girl from another clique came over to me in the dining room and asked me where I bought my clothes. She told everyone at her table that I bought my clothing at Sally's Department Store. They all laughed like a pack of crazed wolverines and then she told her buddies that I wore the same clothes every day (my luggage was lost for six weeks). I just laughed with them, not knowing they were making fun of me. I did think she was pretty stupid because I told her I shopped at the Salvation Army, NOT Sally's Department Store. Then she asked me sarcastically, "Do you ever change shoes?" I didn't feel I needed to, since the Salvation Army had this nice pair that should last me a couple of years if I didn't grow. I asked her where she bought her clothes and she informed me that they came brand new from Sears and Roebuck. I was impressed. I only dreamed of ordering clothes from a catalog, but there were other things in my life more important than clothes. I loved the weekly dances and movies and I was involved in the Catholic Church. I loved my life! Who cared about clothes as long as you kept them clean? I no longer had to haul water to heat on the stove and use a washboard to wash my clothes. I just put them in a machine and pushed a button. To iron, I no longer had to wait for it to heat up on the stove, I just plugged it in. I found I loved to iron and did a good job on my dark green slim skirt and my white blouse. I ironed my skirt until it was shiny.

When we got back to our room, my roommates told me they were sorry the girl was making fun of me. After they explained what she had done, I was totally embarrassed. I didn't want to see the rich girl and her friends so they could laugh at me again. My friends said she picked on me because I was very attractive and they were just jealous. I was always embarrassed about my clothes after that. My luggage finally arrived and a bottle of Evening in Paris perfume that I had gotten as a gift from the teacher for my eighth grade advancement had spilled all over the clothes. My roommates were excited to see my clothes but I didn't want to show them because the perfume had stained and run the color on most of them. They helped me wash and iron them but I hated the sight of them. My close friend was my size and began to loan her clothes to me. She had a summer job working in a cannery and was able to order nice clothes from a catalog, so now I was well dressed too. We told everyone that we just ordered the same clothes from the catalog. She was so good to me and helped me with everything. We were going to grow up, visit each other's village, get married and be neighbors.

When I left Shageluk there was an epidemic of mumps and measles. I was about the only one who did not get ill. I remember the nurse writing on my health records, which I was to bring to Mt. Edgecumbe, that I was in robust health, whatever that meant. After I left McGrath for Anchorage I heard that the measles and mumps invaded that community. Soon the epidemic invaded Anchorage, but I was left unscathed.

Well, there was a big dance being planned for the weekend and I couldn't wait. My roommates were trying on all their beautiful dresses and told me I could borrow any one I wanted. The boys were all asking us out to the dance but we had decided to go stag so we could dance with all of them. They were all so cute! By this time I was setting pins at the local bowling alley to earn extra money. When the medical staff from the hospital bowled I earned two dollars a game. That was big bucks and I could take the ferry to Sitka to see a movie with my friends, buy junk food and buy my very own new dress.

The day before the big dance, the matron came to check our rooms, as she normally did, to see if our beds were made properly and our closets were neat and tidy. If they were not, she would strip our beds and dump our dressers so we would have to re-do everything. By this time I was a tease and a chatter-box, even during inspection. She looked over at me and asked if I was okay since I wasn't doing much talking. She was one of my favorites and I told her it was the day before the dance and I was just thinking about it. She came and put her hand on my forehead and said she thought I should go to the sick bay. It was like a mini hospital. I told her I felt fine and the doctor would also say I was fine. The doctor was presently busy, so I had to go to Sick Bay until he could see me. I couldn't believe it! I was fine! Once a person was sent to Sick Bay you couldn't see anyone until you were discharged back to your room. I thought I would be obedient, spend the day and night there and be completely well by Friday. I couldn't afford to be there, as I was chosen to be a cheerleader and the boys assured me they would cast their votes for me to be the freshman queen. I had already been to one cheerleading practice and it was so much fun. Everything was so exciting!

Friday morning came and I was bouncing all over the bed waiting for the matron. She arrived and I told her I had done everything she wanted me to do. The doctor had to see me first and I reminded her of the dance. She said she would try to speak to him personally, but when the afternoon wasted away and he didn't come, I knew I would miss the dance. I was so depressed. To cheer myself up I wrote a note to my roommate asking her to tell the boys I was in Sick Bay. I also wanted all the girls to come by my window, as I was on ground floor, to show me their pretty dresses. I sneaked to the door leading to the hallway and found a girl going back to class who would deliver the note to my roommate.

That evening my friends knocked at the window. I slipped my bathrobe on and ran to the window and opened it. I was talking and laughing through the open window with my behind sticking up in the air when I felt a playful slap on my backside. The matron closed the window telling the others not to talk to sick kids as we might catch pneumonia.

I didn't think it was possible to catch pneumonia in Southeast Alaska. To me it was so warm compared to the sixty below zero temperatures and heavy snow at my village. No matter how much I pleaded with her, she would not discharge me. She reminded me there would be other dances. I wanted to go to the bathroom down the hall to see if I could find someone who would tell me who was dancing with whom. She told me to get right back to bed and maybe the doctor would come by soon. I did not feel sick. I wasn't coughing nor did I have a runny nose, so I knew she just didn't want me to have fun. When I reached the bathroom there were a couple of girls fixing their hair and I started questioning them. Soon another girl came in and told me to get back to the sick bay, as the matron was looking for me. I ran into a stall and pretended I was using the bathroom. Then I heard her calling me. I looked into the bowl and saw a drop of blood then another one. I told her I had a nosebleed. I was to get some tissue and go back to bed immediately. As my head touched the pillow I started choking. She came running with a towel when I called to her and the blood was flowing down my throat, all over my nightgown and the towel. She sat me up and told me to hold my head over the garbage can full of soaked tissue. The blood was coming out my throat and my nose and I could hardly breathe. The next thing I heard was an ambulance. They placed me on my side on the stretcher with wads of towels all around me. They were soon soaked with blood. My eyes were swollen and I couldn't speak. I was being taken through the front door and I wanted to tell the matron that I did not want to be seen in my nightgown, but I couldn't speak. The stairway was lined with students, even the boys, gaping at me in my nightgown. How embarrassing!

The next thing I knew I was in the emergency room. A doctor was looking down at me with a huge needle in hand. He was smiling and warned that the shot would hurt but I would be okay. Then the needle was inserted into my nose and I felt the most excruciating pain that seared across my eyes and through my head. That is all I remembered. I was told they had to cauterize the vessels in my nose to stop the bleeding. When I woke up I was in a darkened room and a nurse was rubbing my naked body with ice. I tried to reach for the sheets to cover my nakedness when she said, "Oh, you are finally awake. Don't move. You have a temperature of 105.6 and we are trying to get it down." I started shivering violently and she covered me with a sheet while she went to get the doctor. I tried to find some clothes, as I didn't want to the doctor to see me without them. Then I looked in the mirror. I was covered with measles and my eyes were just slits. The doctor came and after the examination told me I was a sick little girl. I asked him if the dance was over and he told me it was Monday and I was placed on the critical list. It was quite an ordeal. I was there for several weeks with the ten day measles, pneumonia and whooping cough all at the same time. When it was time for me to eat solid foods (I was tired of milkshakes and Jell-O), they asked me what I wanted and they would get it for me. All I wanted was my mom's dryfish, but they couldn't get any. Then all of a sudden I craved yams right out of the can. They did bring the yams. I was on complete bed rest and had to stay in the dark. I asked to see the priest for last rites but was assured I didn't need him. I was allowed to read or do homework but my steady coughing allowed me to get nothing done. Other patients were telling me to shut up because I was coughing so much. I would have gladly shut up if I could.

Meanwhile, down at the dorm, if someone was placed on the critical list, it was assumed he or she would die in a few days. So my roommates were mourning my passing even though all my belongings were still in the room. I was a healthy 120 pounds when I arrived and now I was barely 100 pounds. I was discharged one sunny day and was told to walk back to the dorm. Halfway down the hall I felt faint. There was no one around so I just stood there until it passed and then continued to the dorm. I was excited! It was almost supper time and I would get to see everybody. I walked into my room and you should have seen the expressions on my roommates' faces. They acted as if they had seen a ghost and I was wondering why they weren't happy to see me. One of them was combing her hair and dropped the comb as she backed up to the rest of the girls. They were huddled together on one of the bottom bunk beds. I asked what was wrong. They had heard I was on the critical list and assumed I died. They knew I was a ghost. The matron came in and assured them that I didn't die. I got hugs from each and every one of them. I was so happy to be back.

The following day I checked our daily bulletin for messages. My name was on the list to see the doctor immediately. I went to the clinic and he said I had to have my troublesome tonsils removed the next day. The good thing was that some of my friends were going to have tonsillectomies also and would be my roommates. As luck would have it, my three-day stay ended up to be nine days, as I had bleeding complications then also. Finally, I was well! Now I had to catch up on my homework. That wasn't difficult, as I was eager to be in school. Finally I could read again.

During the holidays I wrote a letter to my step-brother Johnny and received a nice card back that said "To a very sweet girl." I had to laugh, as I didn't think I was very sweet. He told me he was working for the Alaska Railroad at Healy Fork, Alaska, and was going to Anchorage for the weekend. He was going to buy something special for me for Christmas. I wrote him a letter and told him about my hospital stay. Maybe I would be somewhat of a celebrity at home when everyone found out I almost died and people would talk about me. I had not heard from anyone at home, even though I wrote many letters.

In January during mail call one afternoon, the matron gave me the last letter I had written to Johnny. It had deceased written all over it. I didn't want to sound dumb but I asked the matron who was sorting the mail what it meant if a letter came back to you like that. She replied that whomever I wrote to had died. I laughed and told her she was wrong because this was a young healthy person, not an old one. She said she was serious. I wrote to my sister in Anchorage asking how our step-brother was. I received a letter back from her and was devastated. She sent a newspaper clipping of his horrible accident. It seemed as though he was going to make a phone call to Anchorage to let them know he was coming for a week. As he stepped on a steel plate at the base of the telephone and picked up the receiver, he was electrocuted immediately. A truck working for the Anchorage Sand and Gravel Co. evidently hit a power line, which fell across the phone lines. I was told about the traditional funeral but I didn't want to hear about it. The only person I felt who genuinely cared about me was gone. I couldn't share anything with him anymore, not about high school or life in general. A part of me went with him.

Chapter 30
TO ANCHORAGE

I enjoyed the boarding school experience. It wasn't too different from my earlier years at Holy Cross. We had to live by the rules, which was easy for me. We even had to go on the ferry to Sitka alphabetically. With the last name of Woodford, I was not on the first ferry. That didn't bother me at all. Rules added structure to my life. I was told there were over 600 students who had to take turns going to the big town of Sitka by ferry so they could shop, go to movies, etc. There was a list, though, of students who were outstanding in behavior and if your name appeared on that list you could go to town every weekend, as there were several ferries coming and going each day. Many students just chose to stay at the dorm to visit with each other, walk around the campus or, if you were an upperclassman, you could walk around the island. I made the outstanding behavior list all but once.

I was feeling particularly blue after I heard about my step-brother's death and went for a walk when I accidentally walked out of the campus boundary lines. I was sitting on a rock staring out at the ocean when a car came speeding up to me. It was the superintendent's car. He rolled down the window and ordered me to get in. He never asked my name and started preaching to me about not following the rules and stepping out of the boundary lines. He escorted me to the head matron's office. I was restricted for a week and assigned to extra work duty.

Saturday mornings we all had to clean our rooms and change our beds. This was the first time I had seen a floor polisher. Our floors were so shiny we could almost see our reflections. I was so excited about this neat invention. I asked the girl using it if I could give it a try, as it didn't look so hard. She showed me how to turn it on and the next thing I knew I was being controlled by a floor polisher. I was flying after the thing, couldn't turn it off and everyone was dying of laughter. I was practically sailing into the air after the thing. After a very hard workout, someone pulled the plug and I never wanted to try the polisher again. After a while I knew I would master it and finally I could buff any floor needing attention. We also had to wash down our windows and sills. Once we were done and passed inspection, we were free for the weekend. If you were on the misbehavior list, you were assigned extra work duties on Saturday.

Because I had wandered off to the ocean, I was assigned to scrubbing the main stairs all the way up to the third floor. I felt my punishment was severe for what I had done and grumpily assembled my cleaning supplies. I guess part of the punishment was humiliation, because everyone running up and down the stairs had a smart remark and rubbed in how bad I must have been. A few asked why I was there and some tried to make me feel better by telling me they had that detail themselves at one time. I had to continually wipe up the areas where the students smudged. The stairs were steel with a cut design. I tried to scrub the indents until there wasn't a trace of dirt. Needless to say, it took up half my day and I never had to do extra Saturday duty again.

I was aware that the higher you climbed on the education ladder, the more privileges you were allowed. I decided it would be fun to return the next year as a sophomore with more privileges and transfer to the second floor. While I was scrubbing the stairs, I peeked on each floor and noticed they seemed to have more than the freshman dorm in the way of furniture and less beds to a ward. On the senior floor, I was invited to one of the rooms. There I entertained my friends with village antidotes, mimicked various matrons and spoke in Athabascan to them. I was impressed by the privacy and the material possessions they had and couldn't wait to get to reach that level.

I decided I couldn't wait to move up to the second floor. I overheard one of the matrons talking with another, complaining about two girls who could not get along in the freshman dorm. If one were moved to the second floor, it could indeed be a solution. I decided to pick on one of my roommates. She didn't seem to mind, so in frustration I told her that she should turn me in to the matron. I pleaded my case, saying the only solution should be to remove me to the sophomore dorm because we were so incompatible. After moving to the second floor I invited the very girl I had problems with up to the second floor, much to the chagrin of the sophomores. Now they had to tolerate two freshmen on their floor. The problem girl and I were close friends for the rest of my stay at Mt. Edgecumbe.

Feeling guilty, I decided to report to the matron and confess what I had purposely done to move to the second floor. I would choose to scrub the stairs for the next few months until it was time to go home. I would have that silver metal shining so brightly it would hurt your eyes to look at it. I marched down the stairs to the first floor and just as I was almost to the office, I heard the superintendent's voice. He was talking to the matron. I didn't mean to listen, but he said to her, "Our goal here with these students is to make sure the girls can clean houses and cook. That is why they have two hours of home ec. The boys take two hours of shop so that they will know how to build houses for the girls. Other than that we have done our job when we send them back to the villages. I doubt they can handle any education higher than high school. They are incapable of that." I was devastated by what I had just heard. I ran back to my room and flung myself on the bed, which I normally did when I had some deep thinking to do. So, all they thought was that we were dumb natives, huh? Well, I'd show them.

That night I wrote my mother a letter and told her that I was homesick and the only thing that would cheer me up would be a letter from her. It didn't have to be long, but the school wanted our parents to sign both their first and last names on it; it was just one of their strange rules. I waited impatiently every day until I finally heard from her. Mom's letter was short and to the point. I was not to ever think of quitting school! She did sign her first and last name on it.

I went to find my favorite matron and told her I wanted to share my mom's letter with her. I was so proud of my mom finishing the second grade and what wonderful handwriting she had and could really write her first and last name. I compared her handwriting with mine and told her to notice how older people write versus young people. I made sure she examined Mom's signature carefully. When that was over I went to my room and started to practice my mom's handwriting.

After I thought I was pretty good, I wrote a letter to the superintendent, telling him I wanted my daughter to go to Anchorage, Alaska, and when they made out the spring airline ticket to send me home, my destination would be Anchorage, not Shageluk. I thanked them for taking care of me and explained they would be saving money on the fare when I was just going to Anchorage instead of going all the way to Shageluk. I told him my sister really needed me for the summer. When that was done, I addressed the letter and put it in an envelope. I was now ironing in Sitka on weekends to earn extra money, as the doctors told me not to set pins until I got stronger after my illness. I then wrote to my older stepbrother, included five dollars and told him to mail the enclosed letter from Shageluk. For five dollars he didn't question me and mailed the letter. I also wrote to my mom and told her I had a job in Anchorage and that was where the school wanted me to go. I also told her I would be visiting off and on with my sister. I told her I would be going to school in the fall and would maybe visit her the next year. She had no reason not to believe me.

One day I was paged on the intercom to come to the office. The only time you were paged was if it was really important. My roommates all looked at me and wondered what the matter was. I just shrugged my shoulders. When I got to the office, I was told to sit down and then I saw the letter I wrote on the desk. My heart was pounding so hard I thought the two matrons could hear it. They said the superintendent received a letter from my mom and I was to go to Anchorage. They were working on student tickets at the time and mine would be changed. They told me I was a great student and they were looking forward to seeing me in the fall. They wished me good luck and I didn't have to say anything, which was fine, as I was so scared I was speechless. Mission accomplished!

The big day arrived and with many tearful hugs, all the students went their own ways. I arrived in Anchorage, Alaska, feeling free and liberated.

I didn't bother writing to my sister and brother-in-law, but in Indian way they would ask no questions and would welcome me. I had no doubt in my mind. After I deboarded the plane, I called a taxi to go to my sister's. The driver was an older man and asked me what I was doing in Anchorage. To impress him, I told him I came to Anchorage to find a job. He asked me if I ever dispatched and I told him proudly there was nothing I couldn't do. He said he was looking for a dispatcher, as his had just quit. I had no clue what a dispatcher did. He asked me if I was interested and of course I was interested, whatever it was, and it shouldn't be so hard to learn. I told him since I never had a job before I felt there was nothing I couldn't learn. With that we reached my sister's house, he shook my hand and told me he would pick me up at 6:00 a.m. to start training. I would work until 6:00 p.m. That was fine with me. I proudly announced to my sister that I was sent to work in Anchorage from my school. She was impressed. I was eager and ready at 6:00 a.m. I was to be paid a percentage of what the four drivers brought in and my boss said it sometimes was seventy dollars a week. Wow! I could send my mom some money. If one did this twice, I imagined I would be twice as rich when I grew up. I needed all the luck I could get.

When my boss picked me up I had every question on earth. The company was called the Gray Top Cab Company. I was talking so much I didn't realize the small shack he drove up to was my place of employment. It was directly across from where the present REI (a large sporting goods store) is located on Northern Lights Blvd. I happily skipped into the office and told my boss I was ready to dispatch. He told me all I had to do was answer the phone when it rang, write down what they said and call the cab drivers on the radio. What was so hard about that? He showed me the radio, the coffee pot, which I was supposed to keep full, and my desk and chair. I was impressed by all the cars racing by and noticed a palm reading shack directly across the street. The palm reader was sitting outside on a bench wearing a blue gown with yellow stars on it. I couldn't wait to write to my friends about this. Just then the phone rang and I answered it. I could not understand a thing they said no matter how many times I asked them to repeat what they said. This went on for about an hour and finally my boss called on the radio and asked if there were any calls and I said, "No." Soon he drove up and came storming in the open door. About that time the phone rang and I answered it and was asking, "What? What?" He looked at me and snatched the phone away, saying I had the phone upside down. He looked at me with a very serious glare, and then hung up the phone. He went to the radio, relayed the message to one of his drivers, and then came over to me. He asked me why I didn't speak to the customers and I told him I couldn't hear them and he told me it would help if I closed the door and answered the phone right side up. I remembered this happening at my sister's house a year earlier but I had forgotten what I was really doing wrong. I just remember her laughing at me. Then he walked me through the next call and the radio relay. I finally got it. He acted so mad but I could tell he really wasn't. He was a kind, gruff man and I really learned to like him. I learned my job and kept his office clean. I told him I wanted to go see the palm reader and he told me he better not catch any of his employees walking over there. He was sure he could tell my future for free. When he drove me home at night, he always gave me some advice on how to be good.

One day as I was flipping through a magazine, a very handsome boy in a Navy uniform walked in, smiling at me. He asked where my boss was and I said he wouldn't be back for a while. He said he would wait and started to ask questions and was teasing me. He was very complimentary and I immediately liked him. He asked if I wanted to go to the movies with him and at that time the boss drove up. He walked in and was surprised to see the boy. He asked me if I introduced myself and I said, "No," so he introduced me to his son, who was on leave for a few days. The boy said he asked me to the movies. Somehow we were talking about ages and the boy asked me how old I was. I said I just turned fifteen and my boss almost choked on his coffee and shouted, "What?" I repeated fifteen and he said it was against the law for me to be working there; I had to be sixteen. He told his son there was no way he was going to take me to the movies, as I was "jail-bait" and to go home where he would meet him later. So much for my first Anchorage date! He explained he thought I was a very good worker but he had to let me go. He would help to find a job I could do and he was very sorry. I was too. I liked him and all the other cab drivers. They all took good care of me.

I went home and told my sister the job ended but I would be working again soon. Meanwhile I would help with her children. A few days later, my boss Curly called to say he found a live-in babysitting job. A couple who were nightclub entertainers and had a television show needed help.

Unfortunately they worked around the clock. No problem, I could do the job for twenty-five dollars a week. I moved in with them and their two month-old son. It was an easy job and the baby was very good. They asked me what grade I was in and I said I would be a sophomore. They sent me to register for school.

Anchorage High School had over two thousand students, so we were going to be split into shifts, from 6:00 a.m. to noon and from 1:00 p.m. to 6:00 p.m. I went to the early shift. This worked out perfectly, as the entertainers came home at five-thirty in the morning and the mother stayed up until I came home shortly after noon. Then I took care of the baby and did my homework. I loved school, but it was ten times harder than Mt. Edgecumbe. I had to study hard and look up many things the other students took for granted. I started in September and in October, my boss told me her mother was going to visit for three weeks. She had to give my room to her and wondered if I could stay with my sister for a while. That was fine as I could walk to school from my sister's house.

Meanwhile a friend from McGrath, Carol Demientieff, decided to move in with me, as I had written some fantastic letters about how well I was doing. I had the run of the house and my own room. I encouraged her to move to Anchorage. The day before I was to move back to my sister's, Carol showed up in a cab at my front door. I was so shocked I didn't know what to say. Of course I couldn't let her stand there with her suitcase. I invited her in and showed her the baby. I had to confess I didn't have the run of the house and was moving out the next day. I didn't have permission to invite her. Just then a car drove up. I stuck her in a closet and told her not to move until I came to get her. Carol was in the closet several hours before the couple left for the nightclub. She was so mad and had been holding back a cough the entire time. I apologized and called the entertainers at the nightclub to see if she could spend the night and they agreed. The next day they drove us to my sister's house.

Carol registered at school, where she was a junior. We did well for a while, but soon my sister and I got into a big fight and she threw us out at 5:00 one morning As we walked with our suitcases, I told her to admire the beautiful stars and to listen to our footsteps making all the neat sounds in the crisp cold snow. She was not impressed, blaming my big mouth for getting us kicked out. I wasn't going to let this little episode get in my way. I suggested we stop at my old cab boss's house and he would tell us what to do. For some reason I thought Anchorage was just like the village, if you needed a place to stay you just showed up at someone's door. Besides, his house was on the way to school. I could not stop admiring the beautiful night sky with the stars so bright when I suddenly discovered we were looking at Sputnik, the Russian satellite, orbiting the earth. I was jumping up and down pointing to the sky, but Carol would not cheer up and was freezing to death. I couldn't wait to tell my history teacher I saw Sputnik.... still no excitement. She felt a little better when my old boss answered the door. He was surprised, told us to come in, but we could not stay there because his family was returning from a vacation. He offered to take care of our suitcases. I told him I had a fight with my sister and why I could not go back to my babysitting job for at least two weeks. He drove us to school. Carol was so upset and was jabbering about never being homeless before and I made it sound like she could just move in with me and now what were we going to do? I laughed and said my old boss would think of something.

I asked one of my teachers what she would do in a situation like this and she said she would talk to one of the staff counselors. Why didn't I think of that? We would have our problem solved before the end of the day. I finally met with the counselor in his office which was a bad, very bad mistake. He explained my dilemma to the principal. They looked in my records and found that Mt. Edgecumbe was trying to find me. They had written to my mom to see if I was coming back since I was such a good student. Mom told them they were last in charge of me and they should know where I was. Mom thought I was just going to work in Anchorage for the summer. She had no clue that I planned to go to Anchorage High School. The next thing I knew I was told that I was a ward of the state! Then Carol was called into the office and everyone was standing around wondering what to do with two homeless teenagers. They called the welfare department, but they had no homes. As luck would have it, the phone rang. The secretary answered and had a big smile on her face. A well-known doctor's wife was on the phone asking if they knew of any teenager who might need a home. The secretary mentioned that there were two teenagers who needed a home. The doctor's wife said she had a friend who had emergency housing for us until she could sort out the details.

Chapter 31
ANCHORAGE HIGH SCHOOL

really felt I should be on my own, so I asked the counselors if they knew of a live in babysitting job or I could iron to pay for my own apartment. They said I was too young to think of that; Carol and I would be going to emergency housing. Instead of being grateful, I was miffed! I certainly could take care of myself. Now I would have to answer to welfare or be bossed around by some strange family.

A woman named Mrs. McClasky arrived at the school and told us she was going to provide housing for us until our case was settled. She was pleasant enough, but she was so blonde and blue-eyed it was intimidating. I immediately felt we were inferior. Once in the car, I noticed Carol was quite comfortable. She sat in the front seat with her and they chatted all the way to her house. The woman looked at me in her rear view mirror and was probably put off by the sullen look on my face and my attitude problem. I answered her questions in a smart-alecky tone. Carol gave me a look to tell me to cool off, which only made me angrier.

When we arrived at her house, she took us to the basement to show us our temporary room with two beds. She had a very nice house. She set down a few rules, and then said she had to fix dinner. After she left I was still complaining about everything imaginable and how I could have easily made it on my own. I took out a cigarette and started smoking. Carol was a little uneasy but there was an ashtray in the room. She reminded me that Mrs. McClasky could keep only one of us for the school year and she hoped it was her. I hoped it was her, too.

We were called to dinner after we washed up. Mr. McClasky had come home from work. He was also friendly and was happy to see his wife and two babies. Carol did most of the talking and I could tell she really liked this family. They seemed to like her too. After dinner, we helped clean the kitchen, then played with the little boys. Mrs. McClasky spoke to us privately again about her expectations and told us another woman was going to come to choose one of us to live with her—a doctor's wife. I wondered what kind of woman this was. Oh well, I had my questions answered a few days later.

We settled down in our room and were getting used to this family when a woman drove up, knocked on the door and walked in! She was extremely loud and I could tell she was going to be extremely bossy! Oh no! I decided I wasn't interested in that family, as the present ones were mild mannered and easygoing. We were in our bedroom when we were summoned upstairs. We were introduced and suddenly I felt we were on the slave block, being checked, examined and interrogated. I answered each question with stinging resentment. She then said, "If you don't mind, I want the younger one." Oh no! I didn't want to go with her—she sounded so mean and firm, reminding me of some of the nuns in the mission. She told me to get my suitcase; we were going to her house and I was going to move in that day. Carol helped me pack my few belongings in the suitcase, I lit another cigarette (so did everyone else) and walked out the door with her. We arrived at her house and I was still sullen, answering her questions sarcastically. I felt she thought she was better than I because she was white. When she opened the door, we were blasted by three lively children all talking to her at once. After formal introduction she announced that I was going to be living with them. They were a little curious and asked my name. I answered "Cecilia." The two year old repeated "Soya?" Close enough.

I was shown my room (Imagine! My own bedroom!) upstairs, which was across the hall from the children's room. I felt so rich! At home, richness was having an upstairs in your house. Here I not only had that, but two beds, so my friends could come to stay overnight. That evening Dr. Perry Mead arrived home. At that time he was Alaska's only neurosurgeon. I found him to be friendly. He told me I was their third foster child. I couldn't tell if it irritated him or if he was okay with the situation. I mumbled most of the answers to his questions. After all, he was a doctor and I was taught to respect his position.

Three days later I was lying on my bed when suddenly I heard someone hollering. I quickly ran downstairs and found my foster parent, Wanda Mead, glaring at me. She told me to sit on the couch so we could have a little "chat." Then she yelled at me for my bad and ungrateful attitude. I couldn't believe how she struck a fear in me that only my mother could. She reminded me of all the things they were doing to make me feel welcome and were only rewarded with my sarcastic attitude. I certainly toned down in a hurry and agreed to comply with her rules. First of all, cigarette smoking would be allowed in the living room and in the car. I had to remember I was a lady and should not look cheap by walking around with a cigarette hanging out of my mouth. I could smoke her cigarettes as long as I asked permission. Secondly, I would not be rude and if I was to be treated like part of the family, I had to act like part of the family; with a smile on my face. She made a believer out of me. I was never sarcastic again. Even though I was afraid of her, I felt pretty special because she had chosen me and I thought she was the smartest woman I had ever known. I didn't need to be afraid of her. As long as I was doing the right thing, there was no problem.

My life fell quickly into a routine of schedules and activities. Since I lived in a different part of town, I had to ride on a bus with a set of students who were different from the ones I had known. The Mead home was in quite an influential part of Anchorage, known as Turnagain by the Sea. I had to walk about two blocks to catch the bus. I remember waiting for the bus across from the main entrance to the subdivision which had a sign that said "Turnagain by the Sea." I admired the sailboat that was part of the sign. It always seemed to be stolen during wild weekends, then found and put up again and disappeared again for as long as I lived there. My school schedule didn't change and I had to catch the bus at about 5:30 every morning. I met new friends and enjoyed going to school.

My new foster parents didn't sign up for the welfare checks that were due them as they had welcomed me into their home as part of the family. The social worker told them they were entitled to the $98 a month since I was a ward of the state. They were adamant in not taking it. As a part of the family I had to do my share of work around the house to earn my allowance, which was generous for that period of time. In fact it was just as much as the payment the social services were going to give them for housing me. I had to babysit the younger children, who were then two, four and six years old. I was also encouraged to earn extra money by babysitting in the neighborhood for 50 cents an hour. If I cleaned the house and did the dishes, I could easily earn another two dollars. My foster mother taught me HOW to clean the house. I already knew how to iron clothes but she had an ironing machine, maybe called an Iron Rite, that I also learned to use. I didn't know how much work went into polishing furniture. We first had to wash the furniture with a light detergent, rinse it and then polish it. This was ALL the furniture in the house from the dining room to the living room and all four bedrooms. Our Saturdays were bustling with activity, scrubbing the house from top to bottom. My daily job was to prepare salad for dinner and wash the dishes.

Pam Mead, Lori Woodford and Perry Mead III, 1957

I became close to my little foster brother and sisters. They were a lively group of children and kept me on my toes whenever I had to babysit. They had a Boxer dog, a purebred, which I hadn't known existed before, who joined in with the active children. The house was never quiet. On weekends we all went skiing at the local ski club in which we were all active. I loved skiing and learned quickly even though I had never skied before. I worked at the concession stand so I could have free passes for the day. I enjoyed meeting many different people who became my friends. Living in a Caucasian household was certainly quite different from living in a village, with so many things to remember, such as how to act during different occasions, how to introduce someone properly, manners at the table, being a good role model for the children, when to talk and when to listen. I believe everything I know today was learned during my teenage years. I met all of their friends and learned good study habits. I never lacked for the latest clothes, as my foster mother made most of my clothing. When she didn't have time to sew, we went shopping at the finest stores and charged my new clothing to their account. I look back and am very grateful for all the things this family did for me.

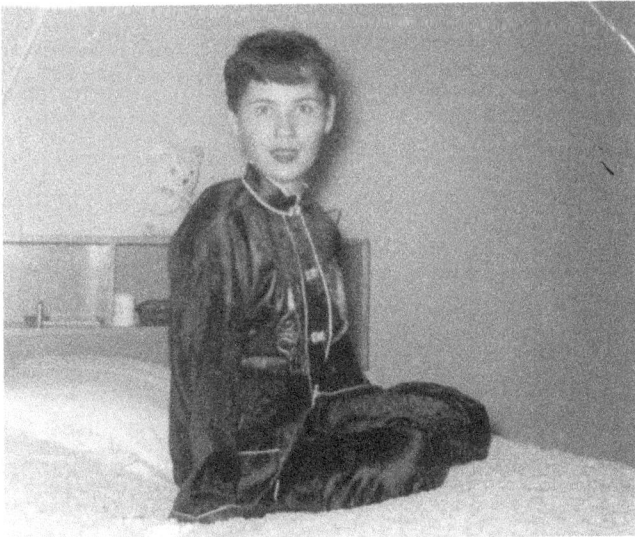

Lori at Mead Family Home

I remember I missed my cousin so much that my foster mother made arrangements with one of her friends to take her into her home. My

Lori with Mead Family Daughter

cousin soon came from the village and I had a very good year. My foster mother trusted my judgment regarding my cousin's character and no one regretted her coming. Of course, growing up in the village with my cousin, confiding everything in one another, was no different than living in Anchorage. She was still bored to death with my fascination with boys. I insisted that one day Prince Charming would come to rescue me and we would be rich and happy forever. The trouble was, there were so many cute boys going to Anchorage High School, it was tough to pick just one. She was tired of hearing about all my latest conquests at school. At home, however, there were rules regarding boys. Any boy who wanted to date me had to make three visits with my foster parents to answer their questions. If they didn't return to complete this requirement, I was informed I would be better off without them because it meant they didn't respect me. So any boy who wanted to date me had to put up with the inquisition and to my credit, there wasn't a boy who didn't pass. (I don't think my bribing had anything to do with it, such as paying for their school lunch, helping with homework, dancing at the school dances or promising a long goodnight kiss.) Let's face it: I thought boys were the most wonderful creations in the world. They did anything I asked of them. I had a date to every prom and dance there was. I simply was having the time of my life. I loved this part of the white life, especially the dances. I would swoon to the music and dance close to a handsome boy who would whisper in my ear or sing the song to me so romantically, as if the words were meant just for me. I loved learning the new fast dances, such as the jitterbug. I dreamed of going back to Shageluk to teach all my friends the new dances and to have them listen to the wonderful fifties music. I planned that everyone in the village had to join the modern times. I loved the dances but I could also be put on "restriction" pretty fast if I disobeyed the rules. I had to be home at a certain time and not one minute later. After a few times of being late by only minutes, I was never late again.

Lori and Gary, one of her many boyfriends

Lori with Friends in Anchorage

The following summer I was allowed to go home to visit my mom and family at the village, but my trip was delayed. I promised my foster mother I would help with babysitting for a few weeks. She was getting company, a friend from Seattle and she wanted me to entertain her teenage son, a boy from the great outside city of Seattle? That wasn't a bad assignment! I could impress my girlfriends with stories about "a boy from Seattle" in the fall when we discussed what we did on summer vacation. It was getting boring, since all my friends had left for summer vacation and I still had a few weeks before returning to my village. I could even dazzle my friends up north with "the boy from Seattle."

The big day came and the Seattle guests arrived. I couldn't wait to meet this boy, but when the mother came she said he was with his aunt and would be coming over the following day. I rather forgot about him when my foster mother left me in charge of the kids and the house, saying she was entertaining her friend for the day. I was reminded to be polite to this boy, as he was from a prominent Seattle family. After I did my chores, the breakfast dishes, dressed the kids to play outside and vacuumed, I sat on the settee by the living room window. I noticed a new boy walking up the street. He was tall and thin with red hair. He reminded me of someone you would see in a Disney movie. Soon he was coming up the driveway and I thought this had to be "the boy from Seattle," so I opened the door, smiled at him and said, "Hi, I'm Lori, you must be Rusty." He just stared at me. I invited him in and informed him I was here to keep him company and to answer any questions he had about Alaska. Of course I wanted to know ALL about Seattle, but the goofy kid kept talking about cars! I didn't know anything about cars, but I pretended to know about them. I just kept smiling and agreeing with him. I finally got around to asking him how old he was and he was one year younger than I. How embarrassing! He was a mere child. Oh well, I guess I could babysit him with the rest of the kids (so much for the big summer romance). Rusty became a good friend and came to the house every day. He was good company and kept me from getting bored.

One morning I got up early and heard Rusty's mother talking to my foster mother. I heard them mention that Rusty really liked me. Then his mother mentioned how horrible it would be if something came of this and she had to tell her friends there was an Indian in the family. That's all I needed to hear. I was on a mission. I was also hurt since I admired her and thought her to be a friend, but not anymore! I called my cousin and told her about overhearing this horrible conversation. Now I had a mission to make this boy fall in love with me. She told me not to be crazy but I was determined to be crazy and I needed her help. I don't remember what I promised but she agreed to go on a walk with us. I was going to seduce this boy. After I told her my plan she thought I was even crazier than she thought. I would do anything for revenge against prejudice. Anchorage at that time was full of prejudices against Alaskan Natives. They even had signs that said "No Natives Allowed" displayed in various establishments. Restaurants were serving natives in the back of the room. I don't know if I was lucky or not, but I did not look native and wasn't treated so badly until I told someone I was native. Then I was an outcast. Even the theatres had a special section for natives in the back. Lucky for me, that is where I preferred to sit.

Anyway, I informed my foster mother that I would show Rusty the property, the land they owned and had planned to build on in the future. It was nice and woodsy and overlooked beautiful Cook Inlet with a perfect view of Mt. Susitna. My cousin was going with us and Rusty would enjoy the hike. When we got to the property, I shared my plan with my cousin. She was to stand on the road and let me know if any cars were coming to the area. Possibly his mother or my foster mother would come looking for us saying we needed to go someplace. I was taking this boy into the woods and after I was done with him he would be madly in love with me.

Rusty and I went into the woods, where I was showing him what kinds of plants grew in Alaska. Then I discovered a stump. Since he was about six feet tall and I was only five foot two, I was going to stand on the stump to see what it was like to be as tall as he was. I jumped on the stump and asked him to come over so I could see if we were the same height. I was soon looking at him eye to eye. Then I put my hand on his shoulder and asked him if I could feel the haircut on the back of his neck. He just stared and couldn't speak. Then I asked him in the most seductive voice I could muster if he had a girlfriend in Seattle. He nervously shook his head no as I continued stroking the back of his neck. Then I asked him if he wanted a girlfriend from Alaska and he just stared at me. There I was, just turned sixteen and he would turn fifteen in a month. How degrading! But a mission is a mission. I asked him if he had ever kissed a girl and he nervously said, "No." I started playing with his cheek and asked if he wanted to learn. I moved closer to his face and told him to close his eyes when suddenly a shot rang out and a bullet whizzed by our heads. I just knew his mother had caught me and if it wasn't his mother, then God was punishing me for being sinful. My cousin came running and said a bullet had just passed her head and we all hit the ground. I asked if there were any cars and she said, "No," so we crawled on our bellies to the direction of the shot. When we got to the edge of the embankment, we saw a couple of ten year-old boys on the beach far below who were target practicing in our direction. We yelled at them but the wind was blowing so hard they couldn't hear us. That ended my great seduction of the fifteen year-old "boy from Seattle." These were fun and innocent times.

I didn't regret my time in this household and I did graduate from Anchorage High School on May 18, 1960. I reached my goal of being the first from my village to have a high school diploma. I went on to marry my high school beau and together we survived the earthquake of 1964 (March 27, Good Friday). I had been at my foster parents' house ten minutes before the quake hit and later learned that they weren't so lucky. Two of their five children did not survive the earthquake, one of the largest in history. Tragedy struck again when one of the three surviving children died in a car crash. It seemed so senseless to me from both the Christian and Indian viewpoints as to why those beautiful and active children had such short lives when their parents helped so many unfortunate girls experience a home and a sense of belonging and their father saved so many lives as a doctor. The only thing they asked of me was to help other needy children of the world, which I hoped I did when I myself had eleven foster children.

Lorl's Graduation Picture, Anchorage High School

Lori's Wedding Day

Chapter 32
CATCHING UP

The phone lines between North Dakota and Alaska were busy in the fall of 1993. I was working the evening shift as a registered nurse at St. Luke's Hospital in Fargo, North Dakota. I was often able to get home by midnight, which was only nine o'clock in the evening in Alaska, and I couldn't wait to give Lori a call several times a week to discuss the last fifty years.

Lori graduated from college in 1969 from Alaska Pacific University with a Bachelor of Arts degree in education, K-8. She was a product of the Bureau of Indian Affairs schools in her formative years and wanted to be a better teacher than the ones she had had. Her goal was to challenge her students to the highest and not talk down to them as though they were incapable of learning—a goal which she accomplished.

We then discussed the events leading to Dad's death. He went back to Norway after Bud was married in December of 1965, five months after my wedding. By summer Mom could no longer work at the Graver Hotel because she had quite a severe case of rheumatoid arthritis, which had started to develop in the fall of the prior year. She received a call from the school in St. John, North Dakota, a small, predominantly Native

American community located north of the Turtle Mountain Indian Reservation. Mom contacted Dad in Norway via telegram, explaining that he was offered the superintendent of schools position in St. John. Dad accepted the position and because school would be starting soon, he had to fly back to the states. He was afraid of flying, so at the airport in Bergen, Norway, he took out a large flight insurance policy before boarding the plane.

Mom and Dad quickly moved to St. John and spent the last two years of his working life there. He retired in 1969, and then built a small house in Mandan, N.D., not far from where Yvonne and her family were living. While living in Mandan, Dad's diabetes began to take its toll. He started to lose his sight and complained often of numbness in his lower extremities. Mother tried her best to take care of him even though she was very crippled from arthritis. Her knees were bent and locked in nearly a 45-degree angle and she ached from head to toe. She waited on Dad at all times in spite of her affliction. When she suggested hip and knee replacement surgery, Dad forbade her to do so. He did not allow her to be under a doctor's care because he felt that doctors did not know what they were doing. (She had one hip and both knees replaced after he died.)

In the fall of 1980, Dad's kidneys began to fail. He refused dialysis and when Mom could no longer care for him he was hospitalized in Bismarck, N.D. Toward the end of Dad's illness, I took the bus from Fargo to Bismarck to say good-bye. Dad had become so confused because the build-up of toxins in his blood had affected his mental acuity. He was blind and the doctors had removed the black gangrenous tissue from his toes. The nurses had him sitting up in a chair near the desk where there was a telephone. He was on the phone, which he thought was the Shageluk School radio. He was summoning any pilot in the area to please come to get Etola. She was gravely ill and needed help immediately. He attempted to get help for her for over an hour. He didn't know me as I watched him frantically radioing for help. Finally the nurses came to put him to bed. I went out to the lounge until I was called back to his room.

When I went back to his room, he recognized my voice. With Yvonne's help in holding a flashlight, Dad tried to "see" me. He thought he could see my dark eyebrows but nothing else. Needless to say, I was sad. I told him I had to catch the bus back to Fargo to take care of my two young children. I covered him up with a fuzzy brown blanket that I had given him for Christmas. He told me that he was scared and I said, "You will be fine, Dad, and remember that I love you." He said, for the first time in my memory, "I know you do, and I love you too, Elaine." That very sentence will always be with me. It was somewhat like an apology and at last he seemed so very human.

I boarded the bus for the trip back to Fargo. During the six-hour ride home in the darkness of the night, I thought of how life would have been so different for Dad and for all of us had Etola lived. I will never forget how he was still trying to save her in the last hours of his life. I couldn't sleep the entire night. At home early in the morning the phone rang. It was Bud calling to say, "Well, it's all over. Dad had a massive stroke in the middle of the night."

We buried him on January 5th in the cemetery on the prairie, next to where a marker had been placed in memory of Etola, on Mom's family farm 10 miles southwest of Mandan. A military honor guard was present, as Dad had been in the Army. Mother cried when taps were played and she was given a United States flag in Dad's honor. They had been married through happiness and tragedy for 51 years.

Lori was sad to hear about Dad's death, but admitted that she had always wanted to find him and confront him, verbally and physically, with the fact that he denied her existence. He left her in the village where she was beaten, sold, abandoned, slapped around and starved when there wasn't enough food to go around. She was also ridiculed for being "white." She thought maybe Dad was rich, living in luxury somewhere, and wondered why he was so irresponsible in not helping her. Certainly had Etola lived, Dad would not have been able to deny Lori. Etola had held her just as she had held and cared for baby sister, Yvonne. Etola told everyone in the village in the Athabascan language that she had two baby sisters because both babies were white, blonde and looked so much alike. More than likely she would have heard from the people in the village that Dad was Lori's father. In the minds of the Athabascan people, there was no shame in having a baby with a man other than one's husband, but having a white man's baby was unacceptable. Had Etola lived, she would have questioned Mom about who Lori's father was, but she died three months short of her thirteenth birthday and the secret was kept for fifty years.

Lori felt it was quite strange that Dad was present at every birth in the village, but would not assist Matilda when she was giving birth. He visited her a few days later, saying the baby looked "real Indian" and that "Woodford was part Russian" and that the villagers were a bunch of "gossips." Perhaps Mom never wanted us to go back to Alaska because she didn't want to chance our hearing the truth of what she suspected or even knew —that Yvonne, Bud and I have a half-sister in Alaska. I felt it was strange that Mom had taken a picture of almost everyone in Shageluk and even though Matilda worked for them, there was not one picture of her or Woodford or Lori in our Alaskan photo album.

I was sorry that Dad did not acknowledge Lori. He was supposedly in control of himself and his family at all times. He convinced everyone around him that he could do no wrong and if something went wrong, it was always someone else's fault. No one ever crossed Herman Larsen.

When Dad went back to Hydaburg in southeast Alaska in the fall of 1962, he put a picture of himself and an ad in a state-wide distributed magazine asking if any of his former students or friends would please write to him. Now that he was in Alaska it would be nice to get in touch and maybe arrange to meet after so many years had passed. A lady from Shageluk, Grace John, noticed the ad and replied immediately. She wrote, "Dear Mr. Larsen, Here is a picture of your daughter Lori and her mother Matilda. They can be reached at....." Dad never wrote back, of course, and although he kept every letter ever written to him, we have not been able to find that letter in his belongings. Grace told Lori about the letter she had written to Dad. Lori was hopeful that she would get a letter back, as she was in Anchorage at the time. Dad left Hydaburg without a forwarding address in the middle of the school year, supposedly because the leaky roof and the mice were ruining his belongings.

In another conversation, Lori asked if I had read about the earthquake that took place in Alaska on Good Friday, March 27th, 1964. I managed to get a copy of the July 1964 issue of National Geographic magazine to read about her foster family's involvement in the earthquake as written in an article by Mrs. Lowell Thomas, Jr. called "Night of Terror." Lori was married and living in another part of Anchorage at the time. She decided to jump into her Volkswagen with her three and a half year-old son, Robbie, and drive to Dr. Perry and Wanda Mead's house so Robbie could play with their children. When she got there, the garage door was open, which was unusual, as they never left the door open. No one answered the door, so she got back in the car and went home.

Later she found that Wanda had left the children to make a quick run to the grocery store. When the mother was gone, the children often did things they weren't supposed to do. They had taken the dog into the house and were playing in the basement. The two older children Perry, 12, and Pam, 10, had been arguing, so Pam left the house to go see her friend who had a horse. She planned to be back before her mother returned. When the earthquake hit shortly after 5:30 p.m., Lori was in the driveway of her own home, Mrs. Mead was in the grocery store where all the food was crashing off the shelves, and Dr. Mead left his office and across the street, right before his eyes, a brand new six-story hotel that was to be dedicated on Easter Sunday fell to the ground in a heap.

Dr. Mead jumped into his land rover and drove home. The car was shaking and swerving. He parked as close as he could without falling into the large crevices in the road. During the earthquake, twelve year-old Perry had taken his younger brothers and sister out of the house. He placed Penny, eight, and Paul, four, on top of their station wagon. When he went back for two year-old Merrill, the ground opened up and he fell into a deep shaking crevice. Little Merrill slid down the seventy-foot cliff with the Mead house. Pam was safe at her friend's house. When Dr. Mead got to the top of the cliff, he saw two teenage boys bringing Penny and Paul up the cliff. They had rescued his children, who were sitting on top of the station wagon floating in Cook Inlet. All he saw of his house was the roof floating in the bay. Perry and Merrill were never found. Everyone in the neighborhood survived the earthquake except for these two children. Lori had taken care of all of the Mead children for most of their young lives and this event was devastating.

At one time in Dr. Mead's later years, Lori went to see him. They were visiting when she recognized the picture frames containing photos of his children on the shelf of his closet. They had been hanging on the wall in his office. She asked him about them and he said he could not take them down nor hang them up. It hurt too much to look at them.

At the beginning of December 1993, I had to tell Lori that my mother was hospitalized and we were all hoping for the best. Lori told me that her mother, Matilda Woodford Dutchman, passed away on October 30, 1983, at the age of 77. She had been living with Lori and one day told her she had to go home to die. She knew it was soon her time to go and flew back to Shageluk. She was persistent. It wasn't long before she got pneumonia and was flown to Bethel, where she died. She was buried after a traditional Indian funeral.

Yvonne flew home from Kipnuk, Alaska. She and Bud and I all went to the Bismarck Hospital to see Mom. She looked quite fine but had some pain in her abdomen. The doctors could not find her aortic aneurysm. Bud and I went home after a few days and Yvonne stayed with Mom. The aneurysm burst and Mom was taken for emergency surgery. She lay in a coma for a few days, then passed away. Her funeral was very difficult for all of us. She was such a loving person and we, in turn, loved her so much. Bud wrote in her funeral brochure, "We were poor, but Mom did not allow us to develop a poverty mentality. We were encouraged in music, art, literature and education. Among her three children there are two art teachers (Bud and Elaine), a linguist and Bible translator (Bud), a German teacher (Elaine), a school counselor (Yvonne), a special education teacher (Yvonne), a registered nurse (Elaine) and a community development coordinator (Bud)." She was buried in the cemetery on December 14, 1993, on her family farm next to Dad's grave and Etola's marker. It was the saddest day of my life.

Chapter 33
BACK TO ALASKA
1994

A t the beginning of the year we were told at the hospital that our geriatric floor was closing down and most of us had to find employment elsewhere. That was fine with me. I had been a nurse for only ten years, but was getting burned out. I called my husband, Loren, who was working as a real estate developer in Vancouver, Washington, at the time, to tell him the latest news. He told me to simply resign from my job at the end of the month because we needed to make plans to go to Metlakatla, Alaska, to meet Lori. I was thrilled and nervous. I called Lori immediately to ask when we could come to meet her. She suggested it was best to come during Easter vacation.

February and almost all of March seemed to last forever. Finally we were on our way to Seattle, Washington, where we turned north to drive through beautiful British Columbia. We were to catch the ferry at Prince Rupert, B.C., to meet in Ketchikan, Alaska, on March 30th, 1994. The scenery was breathtaking but, quite frankly, my thoughts were elsewhere.

I was thinking about Dad and what a fragile and tragic life he lived. He probably couldn't live his life to the fullest because he was suffering from intense grief over the loss of Etola. Why was he calling for help for her in the last hours of his life? He certainly could not have known what he was doing when his mind was so clouded from kidney failure. It may have been a desperate attempt to care for some unfinished business in the depths of his mind. All through my life he went through the motions of living, barely able to care for himself, much less for Mom and the three of us children. It was as though he was running from himself when he was employed for only one year at a time in so many of the small communities in North Dakota, Minnesota, Washington and Alaska. Mom found comfort in Yvonne, Bud and me. She did little else but take care of us and provide for us. Dad, on the other hand, was so nervous around us. The only thing he could think of doing was to holler and remind us that we would never be as good as Etola, no matter how well we did.

He often accused Mom of killing Etola because she fed her a few small fish when she was so ill. His orders were that she could not have any food, just water. Mom replied meekly by saying, "Herman, I did not kill her." She said no more and we could see how hurt she was by this accusation. Dad certainly drove a big wedge between himself and Mom and when she wasn't as loving toward him as he felt she should be—he then accused her of having an affair. I don't remember Mom having any close friends when we were growing up. We, her children, were her best friends. All she did was work and come home to us. Oh, how I wanted to tell Dad to go away forever so we didn't have to suffer any more. I was tired of his accusations, sadness and anger and I did not understand him at all.

It was certainly strange that he accepted a job in St. John, North Dakota, and took Mom back into his life when we children were grown and gone. Maybe it was better for him when he couldn't count his own children standing in front of him. Now we were all "gone." They did quite well together for the last years of his life. He still had a temper, but Mom went on as though this was normal. I mulled everything over and over in my mind as Loren and I traveled, and I wanted to share these thoughts with Lori after I met her.

In the evening of March 29, 1994, Loren and I stayed in a beautiful old hotel in Prince Rupert, overlooking the harbor. We went down to the restaurant and ordered a most delicious meal. The waitress, a very attractive woman perhaps in her late fifties, came to our table to see if we needed anything and noticed that I had barely touched my food. I told her we were going to meet my newfound sister and a bit more of the story and that I was nervous. She was so kind and gentle, telling me to relax because life has its twists and turns which only God can control. I should be happy, feeling like I was going to Alaska to find gold. She was so wonderful and made so much sense. I told her she must have been an angel. She said, "In fact, my name is Florange, which in French means 'flower angel'." She was appropriately named.

We boarded the ferry, named the 'Taku', early the next morning. Loren drove our car onto the lowest deck then went to the upper passenger deck to find a seat. It would be about six hours before we would get to Ketchikan. My mind was too unsettled to stay seated, so I walked endlessly on the upper deck, consuming the beauty of the ocean, the mountains and the clean air. I was so anxious to get to our destination and the time passed more quickly than I had anticipated. Soon we were in Ketchikan. Loren went down to get the car and I was to meet him near the ferry terminal. We arrived a bit earlier than Lori's ferry was expected, so we decided to jump into the car to take a short tour of Ketchikan. We drove only a few yards when Loren spotted a beautiful Indian girl holding a sign with "Loren and Elaine" written on it in big letters. I rolled down the window and she explained that she was Lori's niece, Amy Modig, sister Celene's daughter. Lori had called her to say that her ferry was going to be two hours late, so Amy and her husband Doug would show us around.

Elaine at the Rail of the Taku

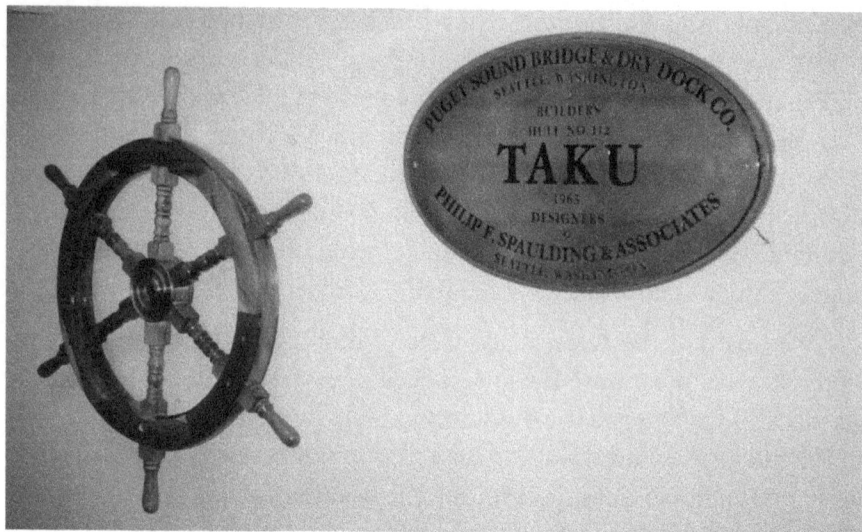

Taku Sign

Loren told Doug to take the driver's seat because he knew where he was going. Amy and their little daughter, Sasha sat in front with him. I was behind Doug in the back seat. I mention this because he had black hair almost down to his waist that fell over his seat and I managed to feel the thickest, most beautiful hair I had ever seen in my life. I hoped he didn't mind. We went for a bite to eat and, again, I didn't have an appetite. I wanted only one thing: to meet my sister. After lunch we toured Totem Pole Park, and then went to the Longhouse. Doug gave us a thorough history throughout our tour, most of which I can't remember. They were such gracious people to take the time to show us around. Soon it was time to go back to meet the ferry, which had just arrived from Metlakatla.

I made a mental note that it was March 30, 1994, and how I wished I had been only five years old rather than 48. I felt too old to be meeting a sister for the first time. Amy was laughing at me because I was so anxious and nervous that I could no longer hang on to my camera or my purse so I handed them to Loren. Then she said, "Here she is in that big Suburban coming our way." All of a sudden the Suburban stopped and Lori was out the door. I ran to her and finally we stood face to face, hugging and crying in the rain at the ferry terminal in Ketchikan.

Amy, Sasha and Doug

Sasha by a Totem Pole

Sasha in front of a Longhouse

Meeting for the First Time

Looking Better, Later in the Day